RESURGENT IN THE MIDST OF CRISIS

Sacred Liturgy, the Traditional Latin Mass, and Renewal in the Church

Peter Kwasniewski

RESURGENT IN
THE MIDST OF CRISIS

*Sacred Liturgy, the Traditional Latin Mass,
and Renewal in the Church*

✛

Foreword by
Jonathan Robinson, Cong. Orat.

 Angelico Press

For information, address:
Angelico Press
4709 Briar Knoll Dr.
Kettering, OH 45429
angelicopress.com

978-1-62138-087-0 pb
978-1-62138-088-7 ebook

Cover photograph: Solemn Mass in St. David's Church,
Pantasaph, near Flint, North Wales, during the St. Catherine's
Trust Summer School and LMS Latin Course, 2014, courtesy
of the Latin Mass Society of England and Wales.
Cover design: Michael Schrauzer

CONTENTS

To
His Holiness, Pope Emeritus Benedict XVI
and
The Very Reverend Cassian Folsom, O.S.B.
for teaching us the spirit of the liturgy
by word and example

The Holy Spirit has made the liturgy the center of his working in men's souls.

Dom Prosper Guéranger

If anyone should attentively consider the progress and the decline, and the reformations of life which have often occurred in the Church, he will find that neglect or abuse of this Sacrament has been the cause of decline; and, on the other hand, that faithful worship and devout frequentation of this Sacrament have wonderfully contributed to progress and reform. . . . Whenever the divine mysteries are neglected or undevoutly performed, no hope of any good need be entertained.

St. John Fisher

Watch ye, stand fast in the faith, do manfully, and be strengthened.

1 Corinthians 16:13

Foreword

by Jonathan Robinson, Cong. Orat.

S t. Benedict in his *Rule* lays it down that nothing is to be put before the Work of God: "nihil operi Dei praeponatur" (Chapter 43), that is to say, nothing is to assume greater importance for the monk than the Liturgy. Yet there is a widespread conviction that the Liturgy is really only of interest to specialists with a rarefied concern for matters which have no importance for the living of Christianity at the level of ordinary parish life. Alright for Monks, maybe, who might be thought to be unrelated to and uncaring about the anguish and concerns of our contemporaries, but not for ordinary Christians living in the 21st century. Perhaps, it might be admitted, the meetings of the parish liturgical committee are a bit more important than those of the committee on floral arrangement. But the rooted belief that *nothing* should be thought of as more important than the Liturgy now seems like the stale relic of a dead past—a dead past, which often carries with it suspicions of an unpleasant aestheticism.

Dr. Peter Kwasniewski has done a real service in publishing, in this readily accessible format of a book, his series of articles on the sacred Liturgy. A great merit of his work is his arguments to show the truth of St. Benedict's teaching that nothing is of greater importance than the Liturgy—not just for the monk, but for all the rest of us. Dr. Kwasniewski maintains that since the Second Vatican Council, the Roman Catholic Church "has experienced an unprecedented crisis in her very identity, extending even to her hitherto impregnable sacred doctrine and spirituality, her apostolic and missionary activity." The most important source of this crisis, he goes on to argue, is the corruption of the sacred Liturgy. This crisis in the liturgical worship of the contemporary Church, then, has consequences for every aspect of the Church's life. If this is the case, then Liturgy must be of central concern for anyone who cares about how authentic Catholicism is to be lived in our day.

Many of the discussions in this book will be welcome confirmations of what a lot of us think, and some of us have written about. An index of its ambition and scope can be gleaned from glancing at the topics that frame the central portion of the book. The opening chapter on "Solemnity" strikes a note that is often overlooked in liturgical writing. This is the effect on children of the way Mass is said. The author notes, correctly, that for decades liturgists have advocated special children's Masses, and since people tend to heed experts, many parishes have instituted such stripped-down Masses. He then argues that the new rite cannot nourish children's souls as effectively as the old rite is capable of doing. "Conceptualize, if you will, the difference between a child seeing a traditional Solemn High Mass and a child seeing a typical Sunday parish Mass. Anyone with a reliable knowledge of child psychology would be able to see which one of these liturgies, when coupled with catechesis, will have the greater and deeper long-term effect":

> The ultimate "children's Mass"—and I mean for everyone, from the wee lad to the ancient, who seeks to live the vocation of a *spiritual* childhood, not for those who remain (or would have others remain) locked at a childish stage of human development—is a Tridentine Mass with all the stops pulled, thundering orthodoxy and whispering mystery to all present. If you want a church full of Catholics who know their faith, love their faith, and practice their faith, give them a liturgy that is demanding, profound, and rigorous.

I think that Dr. Kwasniewski has made a very important contribution to the liturgical debates in emphasizing the effect of Liturgy on children—on real children, not creations of a liturgist's wishful thinking. Moreover, he intends to address as well the child in man. Dr. Kwasniewski writes, and I think it is true, "the human psyche *needs* a certain opacity, an unsoundable depth, a source of resistance and difficulty, a foreign grandeur that stands in sharp contrast to the familiar shadows of ordinary life."

From little children in his initial section, Dr. Kwasniewski's project mounts towards the unfurling of the grand canvas of his last chapter, entitled, "A Threefold Amnesia: Sacred Liturgy, Social Teaching, and Saint Thomas." Here, the author urges that what is desperately needed now, for the good of the Church, is "the sacred liturgy in all its sacredness, the Church's social doctrine in all its breath and boldness, and the teaching of the Angelic Doctor in all its expansiveness and depth." This is a tall order. At present, Dr. Kwasniewski's prescribed approaches to the cult, code, and creed of the Church survive, it seems, only as *disjecta membra*. He gestures towards the reintegration of Christendom, and doubtless he will have more to say about it in years to come.

In justice one should note that although Dr. Kwasniewski affords no doubt that his heart and mind are solicited ultimately by the beauty of Tradition, a line of pragmatic conservatism also runs through his text. He certainly sees the *usus antiquior* as the ultimate cure for what ails the Church, yet his book has broader designs and is patient of a more gradualist approach, as he enjoins us not to "exclude entirely the modern Roman rite when celebrated in a manner that is solemn, dignified, beautiful, and reverent." In this way we can understand the commendatory references throughout this book for what one might call the "Oratorian option" or a Reform-of-the-Reform *ars celebrandi:* "in Latin, *ad orientem*, with Gregorian chant, incense, and suitable vestments." As Dr. Kwasniewski notes, such an "Oratorian option" is found not only at the Oratories in Vienna, London, Oxford, Birmingham, and Toronto but also at, to take other vibrant examples, Stift Heiligenkreuz and the Sacred Music Colloquium of the Church Music Association of America. A Novus Ordo Mass, even one said in English, need not be an insuperable obstacle to a proper liturgical act. This, at least, has been the experience of the Oratorians. The *spirit* of these celebrations is traditional, but the form is not completely so.

Regardless of differences of approach or emphasis, all Catholics who dearly love the Sacred Liturgy and wish to see the Work of God accorded its primacy can be grateful to Dr. Kwasniewski for having penned another potent and enthusiastic document in aid of the movement to recover and understand that *liturgical spirit* which is the Church's true patrimony.

Preface

T HE CHAPTERS OF THIS BOOK engage fundamental issues concerning the sacred liturgy, with a particular focus on the permanent and preeminent value of the traditional Latin Mass (also known as the *usus antiquior* or Extraordinary Form of the Roman Rite), the presence of which is growing apace, especially in the English-speaking world. I also frequently take up themes familiar in "reform of the reform" discourse. Now, more than ever, there is a need for theological and philosophical reflection on the revival of the *usus antiquior* and on how this older form can enrich the newer form as well as expose certain of its weaknesses that stand in need of correction. The combined apologia and critique offered in these pages is my contribution to the "new liturgical movement" inspired by Pope Benedict XVI and to the great ecclesial renewal he has set in motion.

Since the Second Vatican Council, the Roman Catholic Church has experienced an unprecedented crisis in her very identity, extending even to her hitherto impregnable sacred doctrine and spirituality, her apostolic and missionary activity. As Pope Benedict XVI acknowledged, this crisis stems in large part from the corruption of the sacred liturgy, afflicted by wave after wave of novel theology and experimentation. The result has been confusion, dismay, and devastation. During the same half-century, a growing number of Catholics have come to see in the traditional liturgy of the Church one of her very greatest treasures: a witness to the orthodox faith, a rock for the spiritual life, an ever-flowing fountain of authentic and nourishing devotion, a living expression of the Catholic spirit. These believers joined the small number of those who, during and immediately after the Council, knew that the way for the Church to reach modern man was not to reconfigure herself and all her resources to a shadowy and shifting modernity, but rather to work zealously at reshaping man by the ageless teaching of Christ and the time-honored, time-seasoned means given to her by Divine Providence.

With Pope Benedict XVI we observed the fiftieth anniversary of the opening of the Second Vatican Council—a Council in which he vigorously took part. Although initially sympathetic to the liberal party, he later lamented the way the Council's teaching had been manipulated and distorted by the antinomian spirit of a "virtual" or "media" Council. He rightly demanded, as would any Catholic, that the Council be read in a "hermeneutic of continuity" with everything that had come before or had been clarified since. In keeping with the inherently protective nature of the papal office, Pope Benedict sought to rectify something, or many things, that had gone desperately wrong in the past five decades.

One way of understanding what has happened over this half-century is to think about the delicate balance between *ad intra* and *ad extra* concerns, which are two sides of the same coin. The Church has, one might say, her own interior life—a liturgical, sacramental, spiritual, intellectual life, defined by the confluence of sacred scripture, sacred tradition, and the Magisterium—and this life must be tended, nurtured, guarded, deepened, so that it remains healthy and vigorous in itself. Simultaneously, the Church has a permanent "missionary mandate," a calling to go outwards into the world of unbelief, to preach to it, convert it, sanctify it, confront its errors and wrestle with its problems. The noble intention of Saint John XXIII, a very traditional Pope in many ways, was to bring the treasures of the Church's inner life to bear on modernity and the modern world. It was to this end that he convened both the Roman Synod and the better-known Second Vatican Council. He wanted the Catholic Church to send forth God's light and truth, to intensify an apostolic activity that, under Venerable Pius XII, was already flourishing.

What actually transpired in the years of the Council and immediately afterwards is well known. The Church went through a period of *ad intra* amnesia and lost herself in *ad extra* intoxication. It was forgotten that if one's own house, one's own soul, is not in order, one has nothing worthwhile to share with the world; that preaching the Good News to unbelievers is effective only to the extent that there is something transcendently good awaiting them when they arrive at church. Instead of recalling the people of God to a sane repentance and inaugurating massive repair work *ad intra*, however, Pope Paul VI and countless churchmen pushed an ill-conceived *ad extra* agenda further and further, with greater and greater incoherence as the result. The promulgation of a radically new form of liturgy sealed this modernizing trajectory and stifled, for a time, the cultivation of institutional memory and identity; indeed, the retention of a strong connection with the past came to be regarded by many clergy and laity as a dangerous thing, an obstacle to relevance, effectiveness, humility, poverty.

In short, the history of the Church from the Council to the present is a history of unremitting *ad extra* efforts without sufficiently deep interior resources, or worse, accompanied by the distortion or suppression of those resources. As many have pointed out, it has often seemed in the past half-century or so as if the institutional Church cared more for atheists, modernists, and every type of non-Catholic than for her own faithful children who want to believe what has always been believed and want to live as holy men and women have always strived to live, "in the world but not of it." One thinks of the words of Saint Paul: "So then, as we have opportunity, let us do good to all men, and *especially* to those who are of the household of faith" (Gal 6:10); and again, "If any one does not provide for his relatives, and *especially* for his own family, he has disowned the faith and is worse than an unbeliever" (1 Tim 5:8).

The Church is the family of God, and the pastors serve *in loco parentis*—so why are they absent? Are they truly taking care of their children, and of their children's *primary* needs? Ecumenism, interreligious dialogue, efforts for social justice, even evangelization efforts are worthless if the faithful themselves are not first being well clothed, nourished, and taught—clothed by sacraments frequently and worthily received, nourished by a sacred liturgy offered with beauty and reverence, taught sound doctrine in catechesis, preaching, and schools.

Hence, after forty years of wandering in the desert, the pontificate of Benedict XVI seemed, and truly proved, a watershed moment, a breath of fresh air. It was time to attend to the state of our soul, to put our own house in order, to renew our liturgy from its deepest sources, and to learn once again what exactly *is* the Good News we are supposed to be sharing with our neighbor. The pontificate of Joseph Ratzinger began to undo, in a systematic way, the amnesia and the intoxication. Over and above the countless fruits it has yielded among Catholics throughout the world, *Summorum Pontificum* stands forever as a symbol of the effort to bring about meaningful change by recalling the faithful to a tradition, spirituality, and way of life that are *not* in flux, as its symbolic date—the seventh day of the seventh month of the seventh year of the new millennium—plainly announced.

While Pope Benedict's was a short pontificate, the teaching, example, and legislation of those eight years will, as the new century moves on, prove to be either the mustard-seed of an authentic renewal or the prophetic condemnation of a failed one. In any case, it is our privilege, through no merits of our own, to embrace with gratitude and zeal the traditional Catholic identity, the fragrant living memory of God's gifts, that Joseph Ratzinger/Benedict XVI has done so much to protect and promote, and to let these seeds bear fruit in our own lives. There is no more any one of us can do, and yet this is enough. For God can take the few loaves and fishes we have and multiply them endlessly.

When one thinks of the greatness of the task Pope Benedict entrusted to us—the task of renewal from the very sources of our faith, in continuity with tradition—and when we contemplate how much work and suffering faces us as we strive to put into practice the profound teaching on the sacred liturgy Our Lord has given us through this great pope, we might be tempted to grow weary of the fight and fall away from it, especially at a time when so many in the Church seem to be running away from the dawning light back into the stygian darkness of the seventies. Let us take heart, however, from the many noble men and women, clergy, religious, and laity, who have fought the good fight, from the time of the Council even to our day; and let us also take heart from the unchanging spirituality that sustains the Benedictine monastic ideal that so inspired His Holiness. As expressed by the Right Reverend Dom Paul Delatte, O.S.B.:

"Patience hath a perfect work," and its work is to maintain in us, despite all, the order of reason and faith. Let us take our courage in both hands; let us grasp this blessed patience so tightly and so strongly that nothing in the world shall be able to separate us from it: *patientiam amplectatur.* This is not the time for groaning, for self-justification, for dispute. We should not have been saved if Our Lord had declined to suffer. It is the time for bending our shoulders and carrying the cross, for carrying all that God wills and so long as He wishes, without growing weary or lagging on the road. . . . There is no spiritual future for any but those who can thus hold their ground. When we promise ourselves to stand firm and to wait till the storm is past, then we develop great powers of resistance.[1]

---

1. Dom Paul Delatte, O.S.B., *The Rule of St. Benedict: A Commentary,* trans. Dom Justin McCann, O.S.B. (London: Burns, Oates, and Washbourne, 1921), 116.

Acknowledgments

WHILE TEXT AND NOTES have been modified, sometimes extensively, for their use in this book, the material that constitutes Chapters 1–12 and 14 first appeared in *The Latin Mass: The Journal of Catholic Culture and Tradition*, as follows: "Solemnity: The Crux of the Matter," in 17.1 (Winter 2008): 8–12 and 17.2 (Spring 2008): 6–11; "The Word of God and the Wordiness of Man," in 17.4 (Fall 2008): 12–19; "The Symbolism of Silence and Emptiness," in 15.5 (Advent/Christmas 2006): 6–11; "Contemplation of Unchanging Truth," in 17.5 (Advent/Christmas 2008): 14–19; "The Liturgy Forms Christ in Us: 'He Must Increase, I Must Decrease,'" in 15.2 (Spring 2006): 12–15; "Offspring of Arius in the Holy of Holies," in 15.4 (Fall 2006): 26–33; "The Five Wounds and the Church of the Future," in 21.2 (Summer 2012): 12–19; "A Rite Histrionic and Disoriented," in 16.1 (Winter 2007): 34–39; "The Loss of Liturgical Riches in the Sanctoral Cycle," in 16.4 (Fall 2007): 30–35; "Loss of Graces: Private Masses vs. Concelebration," in 19.1 (Winter 2010): 6–9; "The Liturgical Reform's Long-Term Effects on Christian Ecumenism," in 15.3 (Summer 2006): 32–36; "Latin, the Ideal Liturgical Language of the West," in 20.2 (Spring 2011): 6–9; "Sacred Liturgy, Social Teaching, and Saint Thomas," in 16.5 (Advent/Christmas 2007): 6–11. In their original form, Chapters 2, 5, 8, and 11 were published pseudonymously. Chapter 13 was published under the title "Education and Liturgy: Thoughts on the Fortieth Anniversary of the Closing of Vatican II" in *The Downside Review* 124 (April 2006): 135–48. I thank the editors of those periodicals for granting permission to republish material that first appeared in their pages. The afterword was first published as two articles, one at New Liturgical Movement and the other at One Peter Five.

Unless otherwise noted, translations from St. Thomas and other authors are my own. For the *Summa theologiae*, I drew freely upon the classic translation of the Fathers of the English Dominican

Province, now in the public domain. Quotations of Scripture are usually drawn from the Revised Standard Version.

Over the years, many friends have been willing to read my drafts and make suggestions that have led to countless improvements in both content and style. I would like to thank them by name: Rev. Thomas Bolin, O.S.B., Rev. Robert Fromageot, F.S.S.P., Jeremy Holmes, Thaddeus Kozinski, Ronald Lawson, and Rev. John Saward. Having acknowledged their help, let me hasten to add that the opinions expressed in these pages are not necessarily theirs, and any remaining infelicities or errors are certainly mine. I submit all of my opinions and judgments to the authority of the Holy Roman Church, in obedience to which, and in submission to whose Sovereign Pontiff, I desire to live and to die.

I thank also my wife, Clarissa, and my children, Julian and Rose, for their patience and good humor with a man who tends rather to confirm than to refute the stereotype of the absent-minded professor.

Lastly, I wish to thank in a special way two shepherds who have taught me how to follow our Lord on the royal road of sacred liturgy and holy tradition: Pope Emeritus Benedict XVI, and the Very Reverend Cassian Folsom, O.S.B., Prior of the Monastero di San Benedetto in Norcia, Italy. Of the former I scarcely need speak, as his teaching and example are well known throughout the world and, moreover, stand behind all my thinking and writing on the liturgy. Of Fr. Cassian, let it suffice to say that before I met him and became associated with his community, I knew of the beauty and holiness of the liturgy more by reputation—as from a distance; but through him and his fellow monks, my eyes were opened wide to the unfathomable depths of the liturgy as an ever-present, inexhaustible font of life. To Pope Benedict and Fr. Cassian, I gratefully dedicate this book.

1

Solemnity:
The Crux of the Matter

I

S ISTER THOMAS AUGUSTINE BECKER identifies what she con-
siders to be a prolific source of current liturgical tensions in
the Church:

> It seems to me that most of the disagreements about the liturgy
> since the implementation of the reform initiated by the Second
> Vatican Council concern solemnity in one way or another....
> Whether the arguments assert too much, not enough, or a wholly
> new understanding of the shape that solemnity in the liturgy
> should take, the question of a certain solemnity in the liturgy has
> been at the heart of almost all of the controversy.[1]

Now, one might wonder if there could ever be "too much" solemnity.
One might also wonder if, in the past few decades, the parish committees that have autocratically determined the worship life of
parishioners have given much thought, or any thought, to the notion
of solemnity. Still, the speaker was stating an important truth. The
difference between good liturgy and bad liturgy, as far as the mind of
the Church is concerned, often does come down to a difference
between worship that is solemn, formal, and devout, and worship
that is slipshod and superficial, with a decidedly casual air. So, I
began to wonder: Why is the contemporary liturgy, as celebrated in

---

1. Sr. Thomas Augustine Becker, "The Role of *Solemnitas* in the Liturgy According to Saint Thomas Aquinas," in *Rediscovering Aquinas and the Sacraments*, ed.
Matthew Levering and Michael Dauphinais (Chicago: Liturgy Training Publications, 2009), 114–35, at 133–34.

churches across the world, generally so lacking in anything that could merit the description "solemn"?

At first, I asked myself if this might be a fault endemic to the Ordinary Form of the Roman Rite of the Mass, that which follows the Missal of Paul VI. But my happy memories of Oratorian liturgies in which the same missal was employed with splendor and *gravitas* compelled me to acknowledge that the problem was not— at least not simply and altogether—a problem with that missal as such, flawed though it is in many respects. For, on the one hand, it is *possible* to bring the celebration of the modern Roman Rite into manifest *visible* continuity with the preceding usage, as the aforementioned Oratorians are wont to do, but on the other hand, there are many ways in which the missal of Paul VI neither encourages nor demands solemnity whereas the traditional missal does this, indeed methodically. Among the reasons why some priests today are *un*willing to learn the old Mass must surely be that it is too particular and demanding in its regulations of speech, posture, gesture.

As I reflected on the matter, the pervasive lack of solemnity seemed to be more a problem with the people and their shepherds. It was caused by what parents call a "bad attitude." This attitude might be characterized as an embarrassment or (may the good Lord help us) boredom about the very idea of solemnity, about treating *anything* with utmost reverence—the kind of reverence that issues in angelic music or silent contemplation. The result is, alas, more than a mere "lack" of solemnity: it is negligence or contempt of the solemnity demanded by the Eucharistic mystery. Even though it *might* be done properly, the Ordinary Form of the Roman Rite is but rarely done in a spirit of *comprehensive* solemnity, whereas solemnity, or at a minimum, sacred dignity, is the very atmosphere in which the Extraordinary Form lives and moves and has its being. A Solemn High Mass illustrates this truth with particular forcefulness, although a sung High Mass or *Missa cantata* is not far behind, and a fervent monk's private Mass can be a life-altering experience for anyone privileged to attend it. Supported by the rich liturgical culture of thirteenth-century Europe, St. Thomas Aquinas could calmly state: "Because *the whole mystery of our salvation* is comprised in this sacrament [of the Eucharist], it is therefore performed with greater solemnity than the other sacraments."[2] Implied is that *all* sacraments were (and should be) celebrated solemnly.

The death of solemnity—as witnessed by the uninspiring music used at vernacular Masses, the way priests and servers are dressed and their relaxed bearing, the placement of a clunky table to function as a turned-around altar, the distracting sign of peace, and other such things—points to a loss of faith, a loss of confidence, a loss of responsibility and spiritual authority. The priest is no longer confident of his role as teacher, ruler, sanctifier *sub et cum Christo.* Such a crisis of confidence reflects the more general loss of faith in the ministerial priest's sublime vocation of standing in Christ's place, representing the Eternal High Priest.[3] Loss of solemnity is directly traceable to loss of faith in the Real Presence, in the sacrificial nature of the Mass, and in the spiritual authority of the sacerdotal office. It is thus connected with a passive or active advocacy of the vice of insouciance toward divine things that makes them cease to appear divine in our eyes, even though they remain divine in themselves. Weakened is the earnestness, undermined the solemnity that comes naturally to a confident priesthood humbly serving the holy mysteries of God.[4]

The Fear of Ritual

One of many errors that poisoned the liturgical reform was a dis-

2. St. Thomas Aquinas, *Summa theologiae* (hereafter *ST*), III, q. 83, a. 4, emphasis mine.

3. All of these comments could be applied also to the death of homiletics in our age. Few are the priests who can preach as the Fathers or the medievals did—few would even care to aspire to the heights and depths of a St. Gregory, a St. Augustine, a St. Bernard, or a St. Bonaventure! We often hear stories, platitudes, generic advice, but little in the way of sustained and robust exegesis of Scripture, little in the way of provocative challenges against popular culture, little in the way of urging asceticism for penance and reparation. The clergy have by and large grown soft and their message is softness. The need for clergy who can effectively preach the Word in season and out of season, stirring up the people to conversion of heart, is as great now as it was at the time of St. Dominic and the Albigensian crisis.

4. It is important to realize that there are cultural and political reasons for the loss of solemnity that do not exactly correspond to the Novus Ordo's own weaknesses. We might well have witnessed a similar decay of the solemnity of the Tridentine Mass had it never been supplanted by the Novus Ordo (e.g., attempts at

dain for *ritual,* stemming from the view that ritual keeps people away, prevents the priest from "getting in touch" with the people. The new missal has been "deritualized," or at least allows and even encourages the priest to deritualize the Mass by injecting the liturgy with extemporaneous remarks, by moving about in a casual manner, and by inviting into the sanctuary numerous unvested laity, which is totally contrary to the spirit of ritual or divine *cultus.* In Thomas Day's *Why Catholics Can't Sing,* there is a hilarious (and appallingly true) description of the schizophrenic liturgies generated by the current rubrics together with poor training and clueless custom: a clearly ritual ceremony performed by people who act as though the ceremony were not a ritual. The priest, wearing ritual vestments, processes down the aisle to the tune of a hymn. He arrives at the altar. He adjusts his microphone. He looks out to the congregation. He smiles, and then descends into utter banality: "Good morning, everyone!" Back to ritual: "In the name of the Father…" Back to chatter: "Today, we remember that we are trying our best but are still failing, and so we go to the Lord for mercy." Back to ritual: "Lord, have mercy." Back and forth it goes, until he dismisses the congregation with "Have a nice day, everybody!"

For a long time it struck me as bizarre that so few should sense the utter discontinuity between ritual and quotidian modes of address and bearing, but as I better sized up the mess of modernity, I came to see more clearly how markedly anti-ritualistic and anti-religious our age has become. Anything outside the comfort zone of everyday speech about business or pleasure is alien, dangerous, and threatening, and people avoid that region of dissimilitude as much as possible. Catholic liturgy, which is all about the sacred, the numinous, the mysterious, is diametrically opposed to the mentality of the Western "marketplace of ideas"; it goes against the grain of the ubiquitous modern lifestyle of indulgent materialism. Any tradi-

---

"inculturated" Latin Masses, which were already happening before the Council). Perhaps the Tridentine Mass has retained the power to stand firm against these cultural-political forces *in part* because its distinctive solemnity, which would have been a most inviting target for secularization, was officially marginalized and is now attractively, and needfully, countercultural.

tional liturgy, whereby eyes and souls are focused on that which is above and beyond, is a serious threat to the triumph of egoism that the government, the school systems, and the private sector are all mightily struggling to bring about in every town and home. Never before have I appreciated so much the slogan: "Save the liturgy, save the world."[5]

We should be clear about this: there has been a war in modern times against *martyrial meaning,* that is, absolute truth worth dying for, worth giving up everything for. One of the main objectives of the nihilist Jean-Paul Sartre was to convince his readers that there was no "truth" to serve, worship, and die for, or put differently, that the only reason to live was to serve the "truth" of oneself. The war against ultimate, transcendent meaningfulness has also been at work in the horizontalization and secularization of the liturgy. In many instances, liturgical celebrations are no longer intensely focused on God and taken up with spiritual realities—angels and saints, grace, sin, heaven, hell. Adherence to spiritual truth is a martyrdom for the carnal ego: if one truly believes in the transcendent truths of faith, one must crucify the "flesh," which in this case means fallen man's tendency to cheapen, neglect, forget, or treat lightly the dogmas and rituals of the faith. Every phrase of the traditional Mass is worth dying for, because every phrase brings to us (and brings us to) Christ the Lord. The moment one looks upon it as a merely human construct to be tinkered with, to be socially engineered, one has abandoned the martyrial stance toward tradition and truth that has marked all the saints of our holy Church.

---

5. This is not to say that there could not be a preoccupation with ritualism that would diminish the joy, zeal, and charity characteristic of a healthy Christian spiritual life. Lovers of tradition may also suffer from the compromise of compartmentalization, whereby what happens in church has little or nothing to say to their consumerist lifestyle and neoconservative ideology. However, my purpose here is not to diagnose lapses or distortions of traditionalism, but on the contrary, to point out that its fundamental instinct is sound—the desire to worship God with the very best that our deep and rich tradition has given us. Relativism is not the final word; certain customs, rituals, sacred songs, and so forth *are* objectively more beautiful and more fitting for divine worship than others.

Can you for a moment imagine St. Augustine, St. Thomas Aquinas, St. Francis de Sales, or St. Pio of Pietrelcina tinkering with the text of the Mass, or sitting down to a committee meeting that has on its agenda the creation of new Eucharistic prayers? (As the saying goes: "God so loved the world that he did not send a committee.") The saints accepted with grateful hearts what was handed down to them and used it to sanctify their lives. They were ready to explain and defend the prayers and practices of their ancestors, even if it meant enduring torture and death at the hands of infidels or heretics.

I sometimes wonder about the Consilium entrusted by Paul VI with the revision of the Mass, or the original ICEL team that gave us a travesty instead of a translation. What were their *spiritual credentials*—not their academic qualifications, their pseudo-scientific blustering, their convenient curial connections, but, I repeat, their spiritual credentials—to undertake tasks as delicate, demanding, and dreadfully earnest as those of "reforming" and then "translating" the liturgy of the Catholic Church? Was this a question anyone thought of or bothered to ask? I am aware, of course, that over the centuries there have been commissions appointed by Popes with a view to evaluating, researching, restoring, or augmenting aspects of the liturgy. My point is not to say that there is never a place for such consultations. Rather, it is a question of the minimum qualification required of someone who dares to sit on such a commission. I think it will be impossible to refute the claim that the minimum qualification is the most profound respect and reverence for tradition, such that one would almost rather cut off one's hand than tamper with what has been handed down. As the *Notitiae* or official notices along with documents like Bugnini's memoirs reveal, however, this spirit of veneration was shockingly absent from the Consilium, the body of theologians entrusted with revising the liturgical books of the Roman Rite. The most disgraceful example, to my mind, is the reply published in *Notitiae* responding to a query about why the old offertory prayers were removed. The Consilium said, in short: The offertory prayers are redundant and unnecessary, as they merely (and, it is implied, superfluously, even erroneously) anticipate the sacrificial action that is to occur later. With one smug reply, centuries of worship and theology are swept aside, as if nobody had ever understood the offertory before the enlightened gurus of the Consilium came along to explain it.

All his life Jean-Paul Sartre warred against the belief that something can be so good, so true, so worthy, that one should embrace and defend it with utter seriousness and self-sacrifice. Yet if there is any accurate description of what the ancient liturgy does with respect to the divine mysteries, it is precisely this: it embraces and defends them with utter earnestness, solemnity, and self-surrender.

Music and Vessels Worthy of the House of God

Consider two case studies: Gregorian chant and beautiful vessels.

Gregorian chant was thrown out of the churches not because it was in Latin (for the melodies could have been adapted for English texts[6]) but that it is not "happy" music, it is not "rousing" like folk or popular music. Plainchant is not for happy cats but for God-thirsting monastic souls—the kind of monastic soul that is demanded of every Christian according to his mode of life. Chant presupposes a fundamental *seriousness* of soul, and fosters this condition more and more until it becomes what the mystics call "sober inebriation," *sobria inebrietas*. A person steeped in chant actually comes to perceive the world around him differently—with the eyes of faith, with a contemplative readiness, penetration, and serenity. Chant is a powerful agent of spiritual change and maturity: it suffuses the soul with an earnest *spiritual* longing for God, a longing embodied and expressed in every curving melody, reflecting the nameless nuances, the subtle currents, of the human soul.[7] How mature the anonymous composers must have been, how strong and soaring were their aspirations toward God, compressed into these wonderfully diverse and gracious melodies!

---

6. As Fr. Samuel F. Weber, O.S.B., and Adam Bartlett are doing with considerable success these days.

7. For further reflections along these lines, see the wonderful little book *Reflections on the Spirituality of Gregorian Chant* by Dom Jacques Hourlier, trans. Dom Gregory Casprini and Robert Edmonson (Orleans, MA: Paraclete Press, 1995), as well as two classics: Richard R. Terry's *Catholic Church Music* (1907) and Marie Pierik's *The Spirit of Gregorian Chant* (1939), both republished by The Church Music Association of America.

One morning when singing the chants for the Common of Doctors I was especially filled with a sense of awe at their beauty, their sweetness, their melancholy edge, as if to express in music what the *Salve Regina* captures in words: the blending of love, trust, joy, with longing, sorrow, tears. Yes, this is music that can, over time, make those who sing it or hear it grow mature in their faith, which means: grow into contemplatives who know how to suffer and how to rejoice *in the Lord*. With quite different means, Byzantine chant accomplishes the same goal. In stark contrast, contemporary liturgical music, with its second-rate sentimental lyrics, schmaltzy melodies, superficial emotions, and strident accompaniments, is not only incapable of producing spiritual maturity, but *harms* the Christian soul by muddying clarity of intellect, diminishing the sense of beauty, drawing the will into the grip of feelings, and creating dispositions contrary to the love of solitude and silence.[8] In short, it could neither engender nor sustain a monastic community dedicated to a fervent life of meditation and contemplation. That alone is reason enough to "banish it from the sanctuary of the temple," as the Popes poetically say.[9] If it is not healthy for people who dedicate their lives to God, it is not healthy for any of us, since we are all supposed to be a priestly people.

This was brought home to me powerfully one morning by a bizarre experience at the chapel of the campus in Austria where I was then teaching. In the baroquified Gothic church there was an upper chapel built atop a lower chapel, in such a way that occasionally two liturgies or services would be taking place simultaneously.

8. For a detailed treatment of the problems mentioned here, see my article "Contemporary Music in Church?," *Homiletic & Pastoral Review* 107.1 (October 2006): 8–15, available at www.catholicculture.org/culture/library/view.cfm?recnum =7192.

9. For documented summaries of what the Magisterium has taught about sacred music, see my articles "Cantate Domino Canticum Novum: Aspects of the Church's Liturgical Magisterium," *The Catholic Faith* 6.2 (March-April 2000): 14–23 and "John Paul II on Sacred Music," *Sacred Music* vol. 133, n. 2 (Summer 2006): 4–22. These are available at www.catholicculture.org/library/view.cfm?recnum=4440 and www.musicasacra.com/publications/sacredmusic/pdf/sm133-2.pdf. Magisterial interventions of Benedict XVI have only underlined the conclusions drawn in these articles.

On that day, a group of us were worshiping in the upstairs chapel at a Tridentine Mass, singing the ancient melodies of Gregorian chant, when suddenly from the downstairs chapel there began to emanate the cacophonous caterwauling of youngsters singing dismal ditties from the past few decades. It was a vivid study in contrasts: a traditional manner of worship that is noble, restrained, full of awe, focused on mystery, lovingly conveyed in lilting Latin lines, and a modern way of worship, hyperactive, monotonous and raucous, without measure, beauty, dignity.

As for sacred vessels, I will never forget a homily by a Swiss priest, preaching on the gift of gold brought by one of the Magi, in which he remarked: "If we do not give the very best we have to God, we do not really believe in God at all. If we have gold, which is precious and costly and beautiful, we must use it for his glorification; if we make sacred vessels out of wood or glass or clay, we are in effect saying that we do not think of him as all-excelling, beyond everything we can give, so that we *must* give him the best we can possibly manage to give, even (or especially) when it pinches our pockets. We have cut God down to our size and placed him in a tidy budget, just as we would do when stocking our kitchen at home; we believe in him weakly, or maybe not at all."

This homily was memorable not only because I had never heard a priest say anything like it—expounding venerable traditions of the Catholic Church is not, it would seem, to be counted among the more common homiletic strategies nowadays—but also because it helped me to understand why Christians have always tried to give God the very best. This kind of perseverance produced the sublime art and architecture of the Middle Ages, next to which their modern equivalents look, on the whole, shallow and rude. It is impossible to exaggerate the importance, for the entire ethos of the liturgy, of the sacred vessels appearing worthy (as much as it is possible for us to make them so) of the mysteries they are honored to contain. The elevation of the consecrated Victim at Mass is the pinnacle of the many-versed hymn that mankind and all of creation raises to God; that is the time when the supernatural inward reality of the gifts ought to be most evidently symbolized in the external beauty of the chalice and other vessels on the altar, and indeed in the beauty of the sanctuary and the entire church. Of the holy Curé of Ars, St. John Vianney, who wore tattered clothes, slept on the floor, and subsisted on potatoes, we read:

> When it was a question of the objects destined for divine worship, he could not find anything beautiful enough.... His joy was unspeakable when he received from the Vicomte d'Ars a magnificent canopy, superb chasubles, banners, a large monstrance in silver gilt, a tabernacle of gilded copper, some beautiful candlesticks, and six reliquaries.[10]

Jesus was born in a humble stable and placed in a manger, true. But the wise men did not bring him straw, dirt, and dung: they brought him costly royal gifts of gold, frankincense, and myrrh. The way in which our Lord was born revealed *his* humility, which disdains earthly pomp; the way in which the three kings adored him revealed *their* humility, which looked for the best they could offer, knowing in their wisdom that it was far beneath what he deserved. It is not for us to behave as if *we* were Jesus come into the world and thus to create churches that look like barns or stables or caves to receive us. It is rather our business to join the magi and the shepherds in heeding the divine call that beckons us beyond our limits. Responding in faith, we must give our utmost to the Word-made-flesh. The same thing can be said of sacred music. Modern man is no different in essence from man of any age, and therefore has no valid excuse for producing eyesores and earaches. Such unworthy stuff is not what most of our contemporaries would want, had they any chance to choose; it is certainly not what any of them need.

Though our Lord first appeared on earth in a humble manger, hidden and poor, the sacred liturgy is not time-travel to Bethlehem circa 4 BC. The Mass is a living image or efficacious likeness of the perfect worship offered by Jesus Christ as Head of the Church—the sinless Lamb slain on Calvary, now reigning in the heavenly Jerusalem—and so it makes present in our midst the glorified Savior whose *second* coming will not be in quiet poverty but in earth-shat-

---

10. Abbé H. Convert, *Eucharistic Meditations: Extracts from the Writings and Instructions of St. John Vianney,* trans. Sister Mary Benvenuta, O.P. (Wheathampstead, UK: Anthony Clarke Books, 1964), 100.

tering splendor. For this reason the instinct of our faith has always been to maximize the beauty of the liturgy and its diverse furnishings and surroundings, yearning for what is to come rather than indulging in backward glances. From that point of view, the liturgists who clamor for a return to evangelical or apostolic "simplicity" are the ones guilty of nostalgia, not the faithful who desire the traditional Roman rite. *They* want to go back, *we* want to press forward. It is the difference between archaeology and eschatology. The irony, in fact, is greater: one of the most ancient liturgical customs of all, and one that survived all ages and cultures until it met its match in the hubris of the modern West, is that of facing eastwards when we pray to Christ, the true light that enlightens every man (cf. Jn 1:9). In having the priest turn his back to the Sun of Justice and "face the people" in a closed circle, as if *he* were the coming light, advocates of the new liturgical style disdained universal symbolism and banished one of the few customs we can be *certain* the church of the early centuries practiced. Once again, those who defend Tradition find that they are more capable than their adversaries of preserving what the latter claim to value most—in this instance, antiquity.

II

Your primary service to this world must therefore be your prayer and the celebration of the divine Office. The interior disposition of each priest, and of each consecrated person, must be that of "putting nothing before the divine Office." The beauty of this inner attitude will find expression in the beauty of the liturgy, so that wherever we join in singing, praising, exalting and worshipping God, a little bit of heaven will become present on earth. Truly it would not be presumptuous to say that, in a liturgy completely centred on God, we can see, in its rituals and chant, an image of eternity. Otherwise, how could our forefathers, hundreds of years ago, have built a sacred edifice as solemn as this? Here the architecture itself draws all our senses upwards, toward "what eye has not seen, nor ear heard, nor the heart of man imagined: what God has prepared for those who love him" (1 Cor 2:9). In all our efforts on behalf of the liturgy, the determining factor must always be our looking to God. We stand before God—he speaks to us and we speak to him.[11]

Casual Spirituality

One may put the problem we are diagnosing in this way. As St. Leo the Great says, he who abandons the desire of making progress risks the danger of falling back.[12] St. Bernard of Clairvaux echoes him: To stand still in the way of God is to fall backwards.[13] We are all in danger of slacking off, kicking back, getting cavalier. There are no vacations in the spiritual life, but we would like to think there might be, and the temptation is strong to take one anyhow. And that means to negate God, who is a refiner's fire and a burning coal, ever near and ready to transform us if only we surrender ourselves to him. This being so, one cannot underestimate the danger of the spiritual informality so easily fed by the typical parish enactment of the Ordinary Form of the Roman Rite.[14] It is an informality epitomized in the casual entrance of laymen and women into the sanctuary for lectoring or distributing communion; the faint half-elevation of the Eucharist, not to mention many other signs of shallow or absent faith in the Real Presence;[15] the overall chummy feel-

---

11. Pope Benedict XVI, Address at the Abbey of Heiligenkreuz, September 9, 2007.

12. St. Leo, *Tractatus septem et nonaginta* 40.1.

13. St. Bernard, *Letter to the Abbot Garinus*, Letter 254, nn. 4–6.

14. I hasten to add that adherents to the *usus antiquior* face analogous spiritual dangers, all the more dangerous owing to their subtlety, their pristine outer garments. We too can become smug in our "possession" of the treasure of Tradition; we can develop a law-abiding Phariseeism that looks down upon our fellow Catholics who are not yet in a position to appreciate what *we* appreciate. We must fight against such pride and vanity without, of course, abandoning any of the gifts the Lord Jesus Christ has given to his Church.

15. A beautiful custom is the Sanctus procession with candles and the use of incense at the elevation of the Eucharist. I have seen this done in the context of the Ordinary Form, and it already catapults the celebration into a new sphere of solemnity. The very fact, however, that candles and incense at the elevations (or, for that matter, at the Gospel) are extremely rare in parishes shows how far we have fallen from any sense of the sacred—any awareness that the Gospel is the awesome word of God before which to tremble, that the Eucharist is the incarnate Word of God before which to kneel in the most profound humility, abnegation, and adoration.

ing, the "sign of peace," the lack of silence before *or* after Mass; the verbal top-heaviness that makes of God a small and tame object ready to be conjured and controlled, ready for a relationship on equal terms at best. God is made "one of us" in quite the wrong way. The Christ of today's parish is a man, yes—but only a man. As has been observed more than once, the redaction of the new Missal seems to reflect an almost Arian attitude.[16]

Contrast all this with the reverence paid to the Gospel or the sanctuary in the old rite, the magnificent prayers of the Offertory, the elaborate incensations, the Athanasian-style Preface of the Holy Trinity chanted in a solemn manner, the Roman Canon with its many signs of the cross and its reverent elevations of host and chalice—not to mention all the preparations the priest and people make: the Asperges, the prayers at the foot of the altar, the Lavabo accompanied by a psalm. Through such ceremonial actions man acknowledges the supremacy of God and his transcendent mystery, *begs* to be allowed to worship him, *begs* to be worthy to offer and to partake of the sacrifice that the Son, in his human nature, offers to the Blessed Trinity. The traditional liturgy reflects not only correct theology but correct anthropology. The anthropology embodied in the old rite, with its panoply of supporting customs and laws, is ecstatic, vertical, and submissive to God, as is *dignum et iustum*; that which is embodied in the new rite, due to its inculturation in the contemporary West, is rationalist, immanentist, horizontal, and dominative, submitting the sacred to a humanistic canon of "community." The ancient Roman Rite, stately and hieratic, gives praise and homage to the Crucified Lord, thrusting the Infinite Paradox directly into the eyes and ears of the faithful who have the eyes to see it, the ears to hear it. Does the Ordinary Form do this equally well?

Many of the prayers and rituals of the Novus Ordo are poorly proportioned to the sacrifice taking place; they are disjunct from it. The *form* and *content* of the liturgy are at odds, so that what I *believe* is taking place—my faith having been formed by the teaching of both Trent and Vatican II about the Holy Sacrifice of the Mass—is poorly manifested by the form, which functions with a fraction of

---

16. For evidence, see chapter 6, "Offspring of Arius."

the clarity and depth of the ancient rite's manifestation of the same mysteries. In the ancient rite the form and content are unified, "symbiotic," so to speak. The ancient liturgy, with its poignant symbols and innumerable subtleties, is a prolonged courtship of the soul, enticing and drawing it onwards, leading it along a path to the mystical marriage, the wedding feast of heaven.

I once had the privilege of listening to a Ukrainian bishop of the Byzantine Rite speak about the kind of maturity required of a man and a woman if they hoped to become "successful" spouses. He said that it was the ability to sacrifice out of love, and that no marriage could fail if both spouses had this virtue. He then noted, as an aside, that the Divine Liturgy should not be seen as something to be gotten over with quickly and efficiently, but rather as the very locus where love of God and love of neighbor is awakened and fostered—and not through a superficial attempt at being chummy, but by the solemnity and meaningfulness of the ritual itself, which impresses on the soul the lesson of charity that Christ came to teach, both by word and by example. This bishop was convinced that the crisis of marriage, the result of a lack of spiritual maturity, moral seriousness, and strength of commitment, was reflected in the crisis of liturgy itself, the result of a similar lack. He was likewise convinced that married love and family life could become strong again only if spouses threw themselves vigorously into formal liturgical worship. When people are drawn deeply into the mysteries of the faith in a worthy liturgy, routine antagonisms begin to fall away, because the worshipers are being led to a reality more fundamental than their own being and life.

Unless You Become Like Little Children

The vocational crisis of the postconciliar Church is linked, immediately or mediately, to the dismantling and banalization of the liturgy—this becomes clearer all the time. Why is it that the traditional religious orders and societies of apostolic life are blossoming and booming? The longing of the human heart for transcendent meaning and purpose in life, for a taste of perfection and holiness, has by and large not been met by the Ordinary Form of the Roman Rite. The problem with the new form of Mass can be stated quite simply: it has neither the mystical silence of the old Low Mass nor the political, dramatic beauty of the Solemn High Mass. It is neither glorious in its outward expression as triumphal celebration nor glorious in its inward dimension as contemplative prayer. So it has neither the external splendor nor the inner profundity of the old rite. In its effort to be everything for everyone, it ends up being nothing for anybody. In trying to reach out to the anonymous "modern man," it ends up creating a vacuum; and grace abhors a vacuum no less than nature does.

For decades, liturgists have advocated special "children's Masses," and, since people tend to heed experts regardless of how little common sense the experts may have, many parishes have instituted such stripped-down Masses.[17] The sad reality is that the standard Novus Ordo is *already* a sort of children's Mass, what with its simplistic prayers, workbook structure, and vapid transparency. Indeed—and here is another bitter irony—the new rite cannot nourish children's souls as effectively as the old rite is capable of doing. Conceptualize, if you will, the difference between a child seeing a traditional Solemn High Mass and a child seeing a typical Sunday parish Mass. Anyone with reliable knowledge of child psychology would be able to see which one of these liturgies, when coupled with catechesis, will have the greater and deeper long-term effect.

My son, now a young adult, had been present at some Tridentine Masses as an infant, but there was a period when we were not able to find a sung liturgy to attend. Around his seventh birthday, we had the good fortune to attend a *Missa Cantata* after a gap of well over a year. When we got home, he took out a piece of paper, unprompted by anyone, and drew a sketch of what he saw happening at the altar (see illustration). Notice how the key moment of the

17. Articles of mine on the liturgical reform have been criticized as self-contradictory because I am said to be an expert calling into question whether liturgical experts should be trusted. But I am by no means an "expert" in the sense of one who is so enamored of a narrow academic discipline that he loses all ability to see the big picture—the tradition and its theology. I am proud to be an amateur aspiring to follow in the footsteps of Benedict XVI, who is also not a "liturgist" or "liturgical expert" in the reductive sense. In fact, this is why his opinions on the liturgy are routinely rejected by the self-styled experts of the establishment.

celebration is immediately grasped—the offering of our Lord's sacrifice—and how the inherent sacredness of the event is conveyed (the server bending slightly to ring the bells, the tall chalice, the exaggerated candlesticks). My son has never drawn a picture of a Novus Ordo Mass, even of a very reverent one; perhaps it had never moved him or struck him to the extent that this Tridentine Mass did. I can hear the liturgical experts saying: "He did not understand that Mass, for he could not translate (or even *hear*) each Latin word." I tell you this, ye experts sorely wanting in common sense: he saw and wordlessly grasped the very essence of the Mass—an awesome, mysterious, hushed and holy act of worship centered around the Body and Blood of Christ. Pray, tell me what a 7-year-old child picks up and comes away with at a typical parish liturgy in English? Or better, don't tell me! I will tell you instead what my daughter, four years old at the time, said after witnessing a parish liturgy at which a full-grown woman functioned as the head altar server: "Mama, mama, there *are* women priests!" Opportunity for patient catechesis and mild resentment. A liturgy like that is bankrupt

before it even starts; by the time it sputters out, we will have witnessed a parody of Catholic Tradition. Only the miraculous presence of Christ prevents it from being a hollow parody.

The ultimate "children's Mass"—and I mean for everyone, from the wee lad to the ancient, who seeks to live the vocation of *spiritual* childhood, not for those who remain (or who would have others remain) locked at a childish stage of human development—is a Tridentine Mass with all the stops pulled, thundering orthodoxy and whispering mystery to all present. If you want a church full of Catholics who know their faith, love their faith, and practice their faith, give them a liturgy that is demanding, profound, and rigorous. They will rise to the challenge. Why was it that the reformers of the liturgy did not see, and why is it that their docile votaries of today still do not see, that the human psyche *needs* a certain opacity, an unsoundable depth, a source of resistance and difficulty, a foreign grandeur that stands in sharp contrast to the familiar shallows of daily life? Man needs this in order to know who he is and why he is here. Without it, he will be confirmed in the nihilistic assessment that everyday life is a trap out of which he can never escape. Liturgy should most definitely *not* be easily accessible and straightforward. That is the way a clean business transaction is—and our dealings with Almighty God cannot be so transparent and conversational. "I am He Who Is, and you are she who is not," said the Lord to St. Catherine of Siena. Liturgy ought to convey to us, or at least have the *power* to convey to us, an overwhelming sense of the "allness" of God and the "nothingness" of man, as they are united in the unfathomable mystery of Jesus Christ, true God and true man, the incomprehensible intersection of All and Nothing, a wedding that makes All minister to Nothing so that out of Nothing may be created eternal friendship with All. "How can this be, since I do not know man?"—I do not know man's potential to embrace God, and even after the Spirit's overshadowing I remain mystified, for none of it makes "sense" in human terms, and yet it makes vastly more sense than anything man has ever come up with. That is the consoling conundrum that traditional liturgy dances around to the point of reassured exhaustion. Think of the Byzantine Rite with its wavelike repetitions of "Lord, have mercy" and "Grant it, O Lord"; think of the traditional Roman Rite with its choreographed positionings, pregnant silences, and dramatic gestures.

So let us put to rest once and for all the absurd statement that "People can't understand what's going on at a Mass in Latin, but everyone understands what's going on at a Mass in English." In reality, the most unwashed, unlettered medieval peasant knew better what was happening in the lofty sanctuary of his local church—the peasant who knew, in part from the stained glass windows whose beauty and intricacy still cause us to marvel, that God died for me, the Blood of Jesus washes away my sins, and all this is wondrously present in the Mass—than does many a modern parishioner sitting in his whitewashed church of angular artifacts, who does not clearly confess the Real Presence of our Lord in the Eucharist, who confuses sentimentality with charity and sing-alongs with prayer. The kind of understanding that really matters at Mass is attainable by every faithful soul who sets foot in a *real* church with a *sacred* liturgy: it is an intuition of the mystery of the Word-made-flesh, made food for us; the once-and-for-all sacrifice of Calvary, present in our midst. Any other "understanding," no matter how actively participative, is an illusion of the real, a distortion of the form, a distraction from what matters. Having the Mass in one's native language is no guarantee that a person will understand the *mystery* of the Mass. On the contrary, if the vesture of the ceremony is too familiar, the participant too easily thinks he has mastered what it's all about. The familiar becomes the routine, the routine becomes the ignored. Our own language is a comfort zone that insulates us from the shock of the Gospel, the scandal of the Cross, the lure of the unknown. I would rather have a huge dose of foreignness, of music that is not current, words that are strange, language that is archaic, hieratic gestures that are grandly incongruous to a democratic society. A person thrown into this situation knows at least that he is dealing with something utterly different and possibly far deeper than his day-to-day occupations.

Verbum caro factum est *versus Verbiage*

If one wishes "the people" to participate actively in the liturgy— where *participatio actuosa* is understood as the *Church* understands it: heightened awareness of and receptivity to religious language and symbolism, with appropriate responses, audible and inaudible, verbal and non-verbal—then one will try to respect elementary facts of human psychology. A slowly processing line of beautifully vested ministers gracefully approaching the altar, to the accompaniment of the mighty sound of the pipe organ or the heavenly melody of chant, engages the senses and the soul to deeper, more lasting effect than an ill-clad priest sauntering out of the sacristy and beginning Mass in rapid-fire vernacular punctuated with personal touches. If the liturgy cannot immediately *show* something meaningful to a wide-eyed child, then it has failed. The bowing priest reciting the Confiteor, the acolyte swinging a censer, the subdeacon, deacon, and priest aligned hierarchically during solemn Mass, the awesome stillness of the Roman Canon—all of these things speak directly to the heart, to the heart even of a little child who has managed to sit still and watch, as I have seen countless little children do, even at lengthy solemn liturgies. The Novus Ordo liturgy has little to say to such souls because it *only* says, it does not *do*, bow, breathe, keep silent, keep watch, swing the censer, hear the melodies, watch the interplay of ministers as they reverently discharge their sundry tasks. The meaning, the *power* of the spoken word decreases in proportion to its increase in prominence. At the limit case, we have a liturgy in which an awful lot is *said* but hardly anything solemn or sacred registers on either eye or ear.

One Sunday my wife and I attended a *Latin* Novus Ordo liturgy at the Karlskirche in Vienna, and the entire liturgy was nothing but words, words, words. The priest stepped out of the sacristy and began talking. The talking went on. The readings went on, the homily went on, the offertory and canon went on, always words, rarely song, never *symbol*. And after the final prayer, the priest stepped back into the sacristy. That was all. Phenomenologically, it was no more than a prayer service. Any child who was there—a child in years or a child in heart—would have found scant nourishment for human nature, even if he received the greatest spiritual nourishment possible from the most holy Eucharist. This is the problem: how long can a situation last in which the very purpose and content of the liturgy, its infinitely precious gift of the Body and Blood of the Lord Jesus, is at cross-purposes with its hollow, banal form, the trackless waste, the desert where no man dwells? Judged by the standards of sacred significance, the new liturgy, overrun with verbiage and muzak, is frequently a lifeless desert.

In an interview, the exceptionally clear-spoken Cardinal Ranjith (at the time, working in the Congregation for Divine Worship) had this to say:

> For years the liturgy has endured too many abuses and many bishops ignored them. Pope John Paul II had made a sorrowful appeal in *Ecclesia Dei Adflicta* which was nothing if not a call to order to the Church to be more serious in the liturgy.... In the face of such a situation, the Holy Father [Benedict XVI] could not be silent: as we see in the letter written to bishops about the Motu Proprio and also in his many discourses, he felt a profound sense of pastoral responsibility. This document, therefore, beyond being an attempt to find unity with the Society of St. Pius X, is also a sign, a powerful call to arms, by the universal shepherd, to a sense of seriousness [*serietà*].[18]

This "sense of seriousness" is precisely what ritual or ceremonial solemnity serves to promote by creating and fostering the right attitude in worshipers—the awareness that we are, or will soon be, kneeling before the King of Kings and Lord of Lords, the Crucified and Risen Savior hidden under the veil of the Holy Eucharist, and that this privileged position of ours demands from us the utmost humility, adoration, and hunger for holiness. Only when these virtues (and others akin to them) characterize, *visibly and audibly,* every aspect of our public worship will we have liturgy that is authentically *sacred,* true to its own immutable nature, and therefore spiritually healthy for all who partake of it.

When I look at what St. John of the Cross, St. Teresa of Avila, and St. Thérèse of Lisieux have to say about their experience of the sacred liturgy within their overall longing for contemplative union with the Holy Trinity, I ask myself: Would they have recognized the "full, final, Sacrifice / on which all figures fix't their eyes" (Crashaw)

---

18. Parts of the interview are available at wdtprs.com/blog/2007/11/archbp-ranjith-interview-in-losservatore-romano-on-liturgy/.

in the impoverished get-togethers of today's parishes? Or granting that they would have discerned the bare reality of the divinely-guaranteed sacrifice in spite of the distractions with which it was overwhelmed, what would their reaction have been? It could only be one of utmost dismay, confusion, sorrow, even horror and righteous indignation. Let us not be mistaken: the saints know best what liturgy is about, caught up as they are in the liturgy of heaven, enraptured by reality fully unveiled. They are much more aware than we are of the offensiveness and harmfulness of an earthly liturgy that so poorly reflects and even routinely contradicts its heavenly exemplar. If we are supposed to put on the mind of Christ, we are also supposed to put on the mind of the saints who best imitated Him.[19] This means: we must stop compromising when it comes to the worship of Almighty God; we must carefully avoid, or banish from our churches, all mediocrity, banality, worldliness, and modernism. Nay, more: the rational creature, whether angelic or human, *owes* God rightful, reverent worship; we have an obligation, more fundamental and more urgent than any other obligation of justice, to praise, bless, adore, and give thanks to the Most Holy Trinity, our first beginning and last end, in the manner he has revealed to be fitting to his glory and honor.[20] This is precisely the worship offered by Jesus Christ, supreme and eternal High Priest and Head of the Mystical Body, in union with his members in the Catholic Church, according to the legitimate rites of prayer he has inspired by the working of his Holy Spirit over the centuries.[21]

The mission of restoring the traditional Mass (and, for those who are called to the work, the parallel task of "reforming the reform") is truly daunting. In the face of continued grim resistance from cer-

---

19. See 1 Cor 2:16, 4:16, 11:1; 1 Thess 1:6; Heb 6:12.

20. See Raymond Leo Cardinal Burke, "Sacred Liturgy and Asceticism: Respect for the *Ius Divinum*," *Antiphon* 17 (2013): 3–30; idem, "*Ius Divinum* and the Sacred Liturgy," in *Benedict XVI and the Roman Missal*, ed. Janet E. Rutherford and James O'Brien (Dublin, IE: Four Courts, 2013).

21. Taking it as a given that there are many legitimate rites in the Catholic Church, a truth for which the Magisterium affords plenty of evidence, I consider it more important to emphasize that the organic development of the liturgy is a reality intended and conducted by the Holy Spirit and not a sad tale of accretions and

tain bishops and priests who shepherd (if such be the right word) a poorly-formed and malobservant laity, we might at times be tempted to despair, or at least to feel discouraged. At times like this, when our movement is marked with new hopefulness and energy yet still hampered by opposition and faced with enormous obstacles, we must often remind ourselves that success will come, and can only come, from him who is all-powerful. "Jesus looked at them and said: 'With men it is impossible, but not with God; for all things are possible with God'" (Mk 10:27). Whatever be our liturgical lot in life, whatever be the fortunes of our fight, we know that Christ our King, in his Passion, Resurrection, and Ascension, has already overcome the world and is waiting for us to join him in his victory. "I have said this to you, that *in me* you may have peace. In the world you have tribulation; but be of good cheer, I have overcome the world" (Jn 16:33). This world of incessant strife is our proving ground, where our Lord tests our fidelity to the cause of Truth (cf. Jn 18:37). The good fight having been fought, the stains of our sins having been purged, we are borne off to a temple not made with human hands, a throne that cannot be overthrown, an altar that can never be altered—to the ineffable beauty of Christ and the God of infinite consolation and glory, to Whom be "blessing and glory and wisdom and thanksgiving and honor and power and might . . . for ever and ever! Amen" (Rev 7:12).

---

aberrations that must be purged by liturgical scholars in shining armor. It will suffice to quote the authoritative teaching of Pope Pius XII, who, speaking of "some persons who are bent on the restoration of all the ancient rites and ceremonies indiscriminately," says: "The liturgy of the early ages is most certainly worthy of all veneration. But ancient usage must not be esteemed more suitable and proper, either in its own right or in its significance for later times and new situations, on the simple ground that it carries the savor and aroma of antiquity. The more recent liturgical rites likewise deserve reverence and respect. They, too, owe their inspiration to the Holy Spirit, who assists the Church in every age even to the consummation of the world. They are equally the resources used by the majestic Spouse of Jesus Christ to promote and procure the sanctity of man" (Encyclical Letter *Mediator Dei*, §61).

2

The Word of God
and the Wordiness of Man

O NE DAY the thought occurred to me: extemporaneous speeches during the vernacular parish Mass are the liturgical equivalent of suburban sprawl.

Most of us have experienced instances of sermon sprawl. I would like to mention two examples that are worth mentioning precisely because the priests were, in every other respect, faithful and devout, true believers in the Real Presence (it would be too easy to cite examples of heterodox priests; my point will be that there is something wrong with a rite of Mass if it can subtly influence *any* celebrant to become a talker rather than a transmitter). In one case, before the Our Father, the priest said, not "At the Savior's command and formed by divine teaching, we dare to say" or the like, but: "Brought together as God's family by our Savior, Jesus Christ, we listen to him and learn his prayer, in which we ask to do God's will and pray for the grace to forgive those who have sinned against us and against our loved ones, even as we humbly ask the Lord to forgive the times when we have failed him." In another case, this time before the *Domine, non sum dignus*, a different priest ad libbed: "Behold, this is Jesus our brother, the good shepherd, the gentle lamb who takes away the sins of the world, whose blood redeems us, and into whose body, the Church, we are all called as brothers and sisters. We are happy and blest to be sharing in this banquet, but since at times we have failed him, we now pray: Lord, I am not worthy...."

Having heard this kind of meandering extrapolation of Mass texts all my life (I was born in the year of our Lord 1971, when artistic taste had perhaps reached a nadir beneath which metaphysical laws would not permit it to go), I continually wonder that the pope and the bishops have not come to their senses and *banned* all such improvisation long before now. As an adult in blissful attendance at the Divine Liturgy of St. John Chrysostom and other Byzantine liturgical services, I could not help but notice that there was *never* a text that was not *exactly* specified; everything the priest or the people had to say or sing was clearly and definitively *given*. The same is true of the traditional Latin Rite, and of *any* historic rite of the Catholic Church or of the Orthodox communities. It is a pure and simple *novelty*, in the strict sense of the term, to encourage or even to allow spontaneity in the sacred liturgy. As Joseph Ratzinger has pointedly written: "The greatness of the liturgy depends . . . on its unspontaneity (*Unbeliebigkeit*)."[1] While local churches in the early centuries, if historians are correct in their guesswork, may have witnessed a certain amount of improvisation, it was a relatively short time before the liturgical texts were beautifully determined in the various rites by the appropriate authorities of the Church and were considered to be formulated just as they should be. In worship no less than in doctrine, the Holy Spirit leads the Church into the fullness of truth; liturgical stability, ministerial sobriety, and ritual solemnity are manifestly part of this learning process—a process of humbly growing smaller in "creativity," so that our Lord, the Word of Truth made flesh, may become greater in his dominating, life-giving Presence. Bishops and priests are in no way authors or improvisers but only recipients and transmitters of the gift. However personally capable they might be of poetically embellishing the Mass, they are servants of an inheritance, and usually no more.[2] There is no room—or need—for verbal improvisation once the forms are providentially approved and set down.

---

1. *The Spirit of the Liturgy*, trans. John Saward (San Francisco: Ignatius Press, 2000), 166.

2. I say "usually" because there are always the inspired theologians, like St. Romanus the Melodist or St. Thomas Aquinas, who contribute to the text of the liturgy by a special divine charism. This is a far cry from a committee like the Consilium.

Word versus Wordiness

As it is celebrated today in most churches, the reformed Roman liturgy involves far too much *recitation* of appointed texts, far too little *singing* of the same texts, and far too little of song's fairest companion, silence. In the Divine Liturgy of St. John Chrysostom, a vast quantity of liturgical text, considerably more than in the Tridentine liturgy, is employed during the service—yet it all goes by smoothly and with an impression of great fervor because, on the one hand, the congregation and the cantors are *singing* much of it, and on the other hand, the priests and deacons are quietly reciting *other* prayers at the altar. Everyone knows or can easily come to know what these "private" prayers are, so no impression is given of an uncrossable divide between clergy and faithful. The overall effect is one of waves of prayer originating from many sources, rising together like incense to the glory of the Most High God. The Solemn High Mass in the Extraordinary Form of the Roman Rite is quite similar. At a Solemn High Mass, many liturgical texts are chanted aloud (antiphons, Kyrie and Gloria, Epistle, Gospel, and so forth), while the priest and other ministers have their own prayers to recite quietly. It is more sober and restrained than its Byzantine counterpart, but their kinship is readily seen in the poetry of gestures, the polyphony and density of prayers, the beauty of vesture and chant, the overall atmosphere of divine mystery.

The traditional Mass exhibits the paradox of a liturgy with more text but less verbosity than its modern counterpart. By the books it has *more prayers,* there is more verbal substance to it, and yet, without a doubt, the overall impression is one of *less wordiness,* less "textiness," than is felt to be the case with the Novus Ordo. The explanation of this paradox is easy enough. First, as is the case with *all* traditional liturgies, regardless of rite, there are many prayers in the *usus antiquior* that the priest recites silently or semi-silently while other things are happening or being sung. By contrast, the Novus Ordo, with the rationalism so characteristic of its novelties, stipulates that nearly everything must be spoken out loud, and what is worse, proclaimed to all the world—which can make the whole thing seem like a pious harangue, especially in a church with artificial amplification or a chatty celebrant or both.

Second, the prayers of the classical Roman Rite are much more stable, predictable, poetic, and profound, which means that priest as well as people get quite used to them yet find them inexhaustibly rich in content. They get better with repetition. Who would disagree that one of the most lovable qualities of a traditional liturgy is that you get to know it extremely well? You know what is coming, and you know that you *need* it; your well-thumbed hand missal becomes your companion; you gently, gratefully enter into the spirit of the liturgy as it beckons you to share it secrets once again. In this regard the traditional Mass is like a serenely shining light into which one enters, soaking it up, yielding to it. In the Novus Ordo, however, the landscape, the weather, the signposts, are constantly changing as one actualizes this or that set of options; spontaneous comments are coming here and there, poorly composed prayers of the faithful have to be read out, and so on; there is all too little that *abides* from day to day. Worst of all, you might as well give up hope of meditation.

Language Thick and Thin

It is true that the low Mass is a form of the *usus antiquior* in which there is considerable recitation of text, and this is surely not the ideal; the Solemn High Mass is the norm, and if all were as it should be in the Western Church, many more Masses would be sung, even as the Divine Liturgy in the Eastern Church has always been sung. Nevertheless, there is a decisive difference between the recitation of the low Mass and that of the new Mass. The difference lies in the very richness and fixedness of the ancient texts themselves, which become second nature to the worshiper. The very *nature of the word* in the old Mass is different because of the way it is presented, handled, spoken, because of the enveloping silence, the whispering, the alternation between public and private, outward and inward, the rhythmic utterance of psalms. In all these ways, words impregnate silence and give birth to meditation; the Mass puts its roots deep into one's soul like a plant pushing into soil. Here the "problem" of words is transcended by the liturgical form itself, enabling the event, with its words and its silence, its fixed and its changing parts, to become the blessing of a loving response to Jesus's offer of friendship, the incomprehensible mercy of God consummated on the

Cross. A low Mass is silent in its speech and speaks in its silence. It speaks of Lover and Beloved, Bridegroom and Bride—a divine romance, as St. John of the Cross calls it, wherein either ardent whispers or full-throated song is far more appropriate than plain everyday speech.

The reformed Roman liturgy, in its very design as well as by the now customary manner of its celebration, devalues silence and overvalues sound—in particular, talk, the word of men, not the more elusive Word of God. In a total inversion of the very essence of the liturgy, at many Masses the "Liturgy of the Word" far exceeds in proportion and dignity the Liturgy of the Eucharist. Sometimes the homily will go on and on, while the canon of the Mass, the part sacrosanct above all, lasts a few moments, with Eucharistic Prayer II a popular choice to keep Mass at a convenient length. Many priests are simply not aware of the gross incongruity of the imbalance of the parts. For lasting change, we will need a new generation of priests who learn from the traditional liturgy what is most important and what stands at the periphery: "*He* must increase, but *I* must decrease" (Jn 3:30).

As religious ritual, the Novus Ordo is surprisingly exiguous. The preparation at the beginning of Mass is negligible, the note of penance so faint a pin's drop would drown it out; the period from the start of Mass to the first reading sorely lacks any *lingered-over* recognition of who God is, who we are, and what is about to take place. From the greeting onwards, the atmosphere of prayer is thin, the mood horizontal, the mode talkative. Take, in contrast, a line near the start of the Tridentine Mass, said while making the sign of the cross: "Our help is in the name of the Lord, who made heaven and earth." In addition to being a blatant affirmation that God is the maker of the cosmos, a statement like this really says something about the soul, its helplessness, its *need* for God. Where does that need, that longing, that beseeching of the Blessed Trinity, come out in the Novus Ordo? Its liturgical language is practically bereft of the density, content, and seriousness that ought to be there. Even the use of biblical language or phraseology throughout the liturgy was edited out, only to be increased in a rationalistic way in a massive lectionary that no one can be expected to remember or relate to.

Absorbing Worship

I once attended a liturgy in Europe that was being celebrated by a priest whose German I could not understand very well, since the pronunciation was so different from what I had learned in school. I knew more or less *what* he was talking about, but the details were lost on me. Still, it proved an interesting learning experience. As a kind of passive sounding board, I was forcefully struck by how verbal, monotonous, and homogeneous the Novus Ordo can be. The entire thing, from start to finish, was an almost uninterrupted flow of verbiage. To complete the picture, however, I was also blessed to be able to attend many Tridentine Masses in Europe, and the experience was exactly the opposite: the prayers—sublime sanity and simplicity!—were ever the same, regardless of the priest's native language; there was a sense of homecoming, warm welcome, consolation; Mass was, and *felt* like, the ritual reenactment of the sacrifice of Calvary at which I, a lowly sinner, could assist with all the attentiveness of my soul, in the company of Holy Mary, St. John, and the whole company of angels and saints.

Although the ecclesiastical hierarchy continues to pretend that there is not and never was a postconciliar crisis specifically connected with the reformed Missal, longsuffering Catholics on the ground are well aware that there has been a crisis of massive proportions. The tremendous drop in Mass attendance was not accidental or caused only by external factors; to a greater extent than the Church's pastors have yet had the courage to admit, it was precipitated by the utterly banal communion prayer service which seemed to have replaced the Holy Sacrifice, a factor which worked on many of the wavering faithful in the 1970s and pushed them from Mass-going entirely.

Then we must consider the more tragic case of deeply devout Catholics who loved the old Mass and were crushed, dazed, shocked, scandalized, and embittered by the sudden changes, which ripped from their hearts the practice of religion that was dearest to them and dared to set up in its place an ersatz ritual, a circus of exhibitionism. I have conversed with many of these estranged Catholics over the years, people who will never be able to forget what was done *by priests and bishops* to Catholic life and culture, to the

Mass, to the Faith. The liturgical reform has left in its trail countless graves of wounded and broken spirits whose sufferings, whether loss of faith or heroic preservation of faith, will only be known to us in the world to come, at the Last Judgment, when all that is hidden will be laid bare.

A steep decline in Mass attendance was a normal and predictable reaction, sociologically speaking, to a rapidly and radically revised liturgy, in gross discontinuity with the preceding tradition—the irony being that this new sleek ceremony was designed to "speak more directly" to modern man, in contrast to the distracting complexity and aestheticism of a hieratic, symbolic Latin liturgy, which, according to the experts, "few understood." Never has the fallacy of "naturalness" been more fully exposed. The prayers and ceremonies of the traditional Mass are, in the best and fullest sense of the word, a *natural* response to the transcendent mystery of the Incarnation— that is why this Mass is such a perfect vehicle for the supernatural grace that presupposes nature even as it surpasses it. The liturgy developed organically out of revelation and the graced human response to it, which is why, given due exposure and effort, *everyone* can understand the ancient rite, but no one can fathom it. The Novus Ordo, on the other hand, is an aesthetic-intellectual construct: its aesthetics are as shapelessly ugly as most churches built during the postconciliar period, and its "accessible content," precisely on account of its verbosity and cerebrality (two things that almost always go together), is boring and superficial. Everyone can understand it—and see through it. Is this *really* all there is to the "mystery of faith" at the heart of the universe?

Hence, at the mainstream Novus Ordo, there is often little or no feeling of *absorbing worship*, in both senses of the phrase: an awareness that the liturgy itself has the wherewithal to absorb your heart and mind, and an awareness that you are absorbing what it offers. It has almost nothing in common with the divine *cultus*, the earnest worship of God that peoples of every culture in every age have, with varying degrees of success, attempted to offer. To the extent that this is true, there is little in the new liturgy that can powerfully *attract* a serious pilgrim in search of the living God—a Muslim whose overwhelming desire is to adore the Almighty Lord of heaven and earth, a Buddhist monk intent on the silent pursuit of enlightenment, an orthodox Jew whose life is consumed by reverence for the Law of the Most High. If such pilgrims are still to be found attracted to the Catholic faith as embodied in contemporary parish life and even converting, this is a sheer mercy of God, whose grace oversteps the limits of nature and culture. The new liturgy is a negligent midwife in this birth. One may contrast this sad fact with countless stories of preconciliar converts who, like Charles Péguy, were attracted to the Catholic faith first, or most deeply, in and through the sacred liturgy as it was once celebrated throughout the world.

The Law of Diminishing Returns

The adoption of the Novus Ordo and the effective abolition of the Gregorian liturgy was *particularly* foolish from an "ecumenical" point of view.[3] The classical liturgy throws down the gauntlet. It asks: Do you believe what the Church believes, or not? Its very *form* demands an answer, and many converts have come to the Church through her worship because they were provoked by it to make a decision. The revised form of Mass, on the contrary, has by design a Protestant feel to it.[4] A relaxed Protestant might even feel as comfortable at the Novus Ordo as he does at his own service. Accordingly, there is much *less* reason for a Protestant to convert, there is much less reason to be attracted to the Faith in its *distinctiveness* and its fullness of truth. At a time in history when Protestants are either fading away into a liberal twilight of the gods or returning to

---

3. For more discussion of the problems raised in this section, see chapter 11, "The Liturgical Reform's Long-Term Effects on Ecumenism."

4. Cardinal Ottaviani's opusculum is well known, but he is far from alone in perceiving the Protestant influences on the Novus Ordo. The two most comprehensive studies of the changes in *theology* in the texts of the liturgy are Lauren Pristas's *Collects of the Roman Missal: A Comparative Study of the Sundays in Proper Seasons Before and After the Second Vatican Council* (London: T&T Clark, 2013) and Anthony Cekada's *Work of Human Hands: A Theological Critique of the Mass of Paul VI* (West Chester, OH: Philothea Press, 2010). While I do not agree with all of Fr. Cekada's arguments or conclusions, both he and Dr. Pristas have established beyond reasonable doubt that the Consilium intended to change—and did, in fact, change—the theology that the liturgy of the Mass conveys to the people of God, by altering or suppressing elements long established in the Roman Rite.

strict Lutheran and Calvinist error, why would we want to pay them the compliment of imitation? We should rather show our love for the immortal souls of our separated brethren by inviting them to join the one true Church founded by Christ on the Rock of St. Peter—and by worshipping in a manner consistent with our 2,000-year-old tradition.

Even more tragically, consider an Eastern Orthodox Christian. If he is even a little bit open-minded toward the West, it is possible for him to *see* in the Western Church's traditional worship something ancient, solemn, and beautiful, evoking the spirit of the early Church, the era of the Martyrs and Confessors. "No one loves who has not been first delighted by what he has seen," observes Aristotle. But our myopic dismantlings and innovations only go to confirm the severe judgment passed by Orthodox theologians, namely that the Western Church is in the grip of rationalism, which is the source of our plague of modernism. For the Orthodox, a basic problem with the West is that our theology is a "thinker's theology": we come up with new theories, we get enamored of them, and then we start changing around our customs, practices, and even our liturgy to fit our theories. In the East, what takes precedence is the Tradition handed down from generation to generation; this must be the ultimate measure of our present attitudes and thoughts, and if we find ourselves straying from it or rebelling against it, we need repentance, conversion of mind. Now, having seen how easily perverted into blind pride the "Mount Athos" attitude can become, I do not praise the Orthodox for their fidelity to Tradition; in some respects they have betrayed it even worse than the West has done. What I do admire is their fundamental *attitude* vis-à-vis the inheritance they have received: they want to be faithful to it as the precious divine gift it is, and *that* is a spiritually healthy stance—far better than the attitude of Western "reformers," whether of the 16th or of the 20th centuries, for whom Catholic Tradition is a kind of market from which one chooses ingredients that suit one's taste.

How could we have moved so much further away from the Byzantine Divine Liturgy, just when relations with the Orthodox have begun to show a potential for rapport that has not been seen for centuries? In spite of its many obvious external differences, in its spirit the old liturgy—especially when celebrated as a Solemn High Mass—is immediately accessible to an Eastern Christian. It speaks the same language of reverence, solemnity, beauty. As a confirmation of this, I have noticed in my travels that Eastern bishops, priests, and monks are attracted to and at peace in Western monasteries that have preserved the primacy of the liturgy, of chant and other sacred symbols, and are living the contemplative vocation with seriousness and fervor.[5]

Thus, the undeniable postconciliar crisis has to be traced back, in large measure, to the liturgical revolution, the dismantling of the traditional worship of the Catholic Church. The Mass is the quintessence of the faith; when *it* is strong, the lives of the faithful can be centered on the King and Center of all hearts, our Lord Jesus Christ. When it is strong, the missionary impulse must be strong: the desire to bring Protestants to the fullness of the faith by their personal conversion, the desire to seek a true union between East and West based upon a common spiritual patrimony.

Scripture: Quantity or Quality?

One excellent illustration of the profound differences between the two forms of the Roman Rite can be seen in how each incorporates the greatest text or word of all: the divinely inspired Scriptures.

In the traditional liturgy, Sacred Scripture is omnipresent in memorable lines, short enough to be remembered, pondered, and woven into one's prayer life: the Introit, the Gradual and Alleluia, the Offertory, the Communion. . . . The Word of God is *prayed* and prayed deeply in the ancient Mass, as befits a rite that was shaped by a culture of *lectio divina*. In the best of circumstances (but no less normatively on that account), the Word of God is *sung*, with tones exquisitely matching the poetry of the Latin language. In this valley of tears (which we moderns, looking for more stress, have turned

---

5. My comments also apply to those rare places (e.g., Stift Heiligenkreuz, or the Oratories in London, Oxford, and Vienna) where the new liturgy is celebrated in a manner so continuous with the old liturgy that the differences are likely to be unnoticed by someone, let us say a visiting Eastern monk, who is not already well versed in the Roman Rite.

into a valley of speedy highways and instant emails), what are the texts we would take the trouble to slow down for and *sing*? As Augustine said, "Only the lover can sing." We sing words we are in love with, or rather, words that remind us of the one we are in love with. Whenever the Epistle or the Gospel is chanted at a Tridentine Mass, it makes my heart race; it is a love-song, a song of the human heart caught up in romance with the eternal Word. In the new liturgy, by contrast, the Bible is nearly always merely *read out*. There is no love affair; it is a sedate meeting where a certain amount of business has to be gone through.

Contrary to prevailing wisdom, the Ordinary Form also offers the faithful *less* Scripture, qualitatively speaking. The old liturgy is saturated with Scripture, not only in the proper antiphons and prayers but in the unchanging prayers as well, and for this reason it carries greater force in the scriptural formation of the worshiping soul. The Epistle and Gospel of the old rite are almost always shorter, pithier, more directly relevant to the feast itself, and in this way, more pedagogically effective.[6] The old liturgy thus lends itself extremely well to scriptural preaching and meditation. But note that it is successful just by being what it is: liturgy thick and rich and full of religion; it does not seek to be a sort of Bible study.

According to the editors of the Novus Ordo Lectionary, the goal was "more Scripture," so as to "feed the people from the word of God." Yet the ancient rite is far more *steeped in Scripture,* in a living appropriation of scriptural language, rhythms, themes, than is the Novus Ordo, which races through the "liturgy of the word" without any of the *lingering* that goes on in the ancient rite and makes it a perfect ongoing catechizer to those who yield themselves to the prayers and readings. Even though the reading of the Gospel is reached in five to ten minutes in both the Extraordinary Form (when recited) and in the Ordinary Form, with the former one has been better *prepared* for it: one's soul has been tilled by Psalm 42, by

---

6. An exception are the readings of the Passion accounts in the traditional liturgy of Holy Week, where all four Evangelists are read each year on different days. In the new lectionary John retains his Good Friday position but the Synoptics take turns over a three-year period.

the double *Confiteor,* by the exchange *Ostende nobis,* by the ascent of the altar with its two rich prayers, and by the multifaceted collect that says so much in so few words. In the Ordinary Form, however, this portion is rapid and disjointed: sign of the cross, greeting, Kyrie (often without a Confiteor, which has, in any case, been crippled), and collect. There is little sense of a natural motion, an organic whole; it is more like going through an agenda. Then *wham,* the reading—always done by a layman, a woman more frequently than not, who is dressed so as to be obviously *non*-ministerial, as if to represent that the readings are not part of the rational worship that has its pinnacle in the offering to God of the Word made flesh through the ministry of the priesthood.[7] The traditional liturgy is more profoundly scriptural because it has *internalized* the words of Scripture: the Psalm-based prayers at the foot of the altar; the fiery coal prayer before the reading of the Gospel; the Offertory with its many allusions to the Epistles; the psalm recited during the washing of hands; the final reading from the opening chapter of the Gospel of John—all this, even in a *Low* Mass. The Solemn High Mass breathes still more the letter and spirit of scripture. The word of God is woven into the fabric of the ancient liturgy, bone of its bone, flesh of its flesh.

The role and "weight" of Scripture in the old and new forms of the Roman Rite deserves far more attention than it has received up to now, and we will return to it in chapter 9, where a number of concrete examples will illustrate and extend the more general critique offered here.

The Reform that Failed the Council

In view of the reasons for which the Second Vatican Council was

---

7. When a subdeacon or tonsured monk reads the epistle in the ancient liturgy, he is doing so as having an inherent *ordering* to the priesthood; he is not doing so qua layman. The reason is that the readings are understood to be truly a part of the Mass (as the classic division "Mass of the Catechumens" and "Mass of the Faithful" bears witness), although the homily is *not*—at least not in the same way. I would also add that there are some parishes and chapels where the readings from the Lectionary are done by male servers vested as such, which seems a reasonable if temporary solution in the context of the Ordinary Form.

convened by St. John XXIII—to reconcile to the Church all her straying sons and daughters and to reach out to a modern world that was thought to be thirsty for meaning, hungry for truth, ready to be swept off its feet by Christian witness to the authentic dignity of man—few worse things could have been done than to change the liturgy in the manner in which it was changed. The serious young people I have met are hungry for the mystical, the numinous, the "different," in short, the sacred, in whatever guise they stumble upon it; they are thirsty for symbolic ritual. Until quite recently, such things were almost banned in the Church for four decades or more. How many times have I seen the wonder and awe with which people my age or younger (born, than is, after 1970) react to their first Solemn High Mass! The ancient Roman liturgy powerfully answers their deepest spiritual desires, as it has always done for believers down through the centuries, even as it had the power to do during the "scientifically-minded" nineteenth and early twentieth centuries when so many converts came to the Church through her liturgy.

Josef Pieper comments on a story told in Plato's *Phaedrus* about a mythical Tammuz, inventor of the alphabet:

> This story … makes the eternally modern point that technical improvements which to all appearances facilitate man's participation in reality and truth actually do just the opposite: they hamper and possibly even destroy that participation. The ease of communication abolishes real communication.[8]

Sacrosanctum Concilium called for clear and simple rites that would require little explanation. Even by this dubious criterion, the classical Roman rite catechizes more effectively than its successor, without the need for admonitions, instructions, or explanations outside of the homily. In its very spirit, its prayers, its rituals, its majesty, its silence, its entire ensemble of elements, the Tridentine Mass *is* mystagogical catechesis—the offspring of a blessed marriage between the sublime theology of the Church Fathers and the intense monas-

---

8. *Enthusiasm and Divine Madness: On the Platonic Dialogue "Phaedrus,"* trans. Richard Winston and Clara Winston (South Bend, IN: St. Augustine's Press, 2000), 101, citing *Phaedrus* 274c5.

tic and popular piety of earlier ages. It teaches *by example*, by sign and symbol; it teaches *by word*, with prayers and readings that are rich and unfathomable, but not excessive. One comes to the old Mass year after year, always able to derive more fruit from the lush garden of the Church.

The liturgical reformers claimed that their sole intention was to give people solid spiritual nourishment—as though we did not already have it *plentifully*. Instead we were given poor modern food that cannot sustain. Catholics who oppose the Consilium's concoction feast at the banquet of tradition. The recovery of traditional Western liturgies, broadly speaking, is a condition for the very survival of Catholicism. Emboldened by Benedict XVI's legislation and example, blessed by rapid growth in adherents, the traditionalist movement is taking its rightful place at the vanguard of true reform and renewal, which consists above all in a jealous love for the Lord's house, the place where his glory dwells (Ps 69:9, Jn 2:17, Ps 26:8), and fidelity to our glorious inheritance, our birthright in Christ Jesus.

3

The Symbolism of
Silence and Emptiness

One aspect that we must foster in our communities with greater commitment is *the experience of silence*. We need silence "if we are to accept in our hearts the full resonance of the voice of the Holy Spirit and to unite our personal prayer more closely to the Word of God and the public voice of the Church." In a society that lives at an increasingly frenetic pace, often deafened by noise and confused by the ephemeral, it is vital to rediscover the value of silence. The spread, also outside Christian worship, of practices of meditation that give priority to recollection is not accidental. Why not start with pedagogical daring *a specific education in silence* within the coordinates of personal Christian experience? Let us keep before our eyes the example of Jesus, who "rose and went out to a lonely place, and there he prayed" (Mk 1: 35). The Liturgy, with its different moments and symbols, cannot ignore silence.

JOHN PAUL II[1]

I n the ancient Roman liturgy, *silence itself is a symbol*. As Dionysius the Areopagite teaches, we attain most of all to the knowledge of God when we strip away all our inadequate conceptions and insert ourselves into the "darksome light" of God through an intensely sacramental worship.[2] Dionysius would agree with Fr.

---

1. Message *Spiritus et Sponsa*, for the fortieth anniversary of the Constitution on the Sacred Liturgy *Sacrosanctum Concilium* (4 December 2003), 13.
2. See *The Ecclesiastical Hierarchy*, in Pseudo-Dionysius, *The Complete Works*, trans. Colm Luibheid (Mahwah, NJ: Paulist Press, 1987), passim.

David Vincent Meconi: "Silence is the most forgotten of the divine names. Our world has grown too loud to appreciate the veneration that is silence."[3] In his eloquent defenses of the traditional Mass, Dietrich von Hildebrand speaks often of the need for an *attitude* of reverence prior to all acts of worship; he appeals to the influence of silence on the human soul, which, after the Fall, tends to be in a state of noisy flux. The liturgy exemplifies the truth that in love, silence speaks louder than words. The silence *is* the fullness of speech—the *Logos* of God who, in the Godhead, is the speechlessly understood Word of the Father. And this is why St. Thomas Aquinas, among the most voluble and certainly the most gifted of the Church's theologians, ended his career of service to the Word not by dashing off another treatise or disputed question, but by entering childlike into an oasis of mute wonder. We have already seen earlier how Josef Pieper interprets the life-changing vision Thomas experienced during Mass on December 6, 1273:

> The last word of St. Thomas is not communication but silence. And it is not death which takes the pen out of his hand. His tongue is stilled by the superabundance of life in the mystery of God. He is silent, not because he has nothing further to say; he is silent because he has been allowed a glimpse into the inexpressible depth of that mystery which is not reached by any human thought or speech.[4]

The silence of the Tridentine liturgy[5] gives the Christian soul room to make its own the mysteries God graciously reveals, room to

3. David Vincent Meconi, S.J., "Silence Proceeding," *Logos* 5.2 (Spring 2002): 59–75, at 59.

4. Josef Pieper, *The Silence of St. Thomas,* trans. John Murray and Daniel O'Connor (New York: Pantheon Books, 1957), 45. The vision on the Feast of St. Nicholas and its significance is discussed in my article "Golden Straw: St. Thomas and the Ecstatic Practice of Theology," *Nova et Vetera* 2 (2004): 61–89.

5. It is obvious that the low Mass has plenty of full silence, but even the normative and perfect style of celebrating—high or solemn Mass—can and should have moments of silence, too, if it is being celebrated with a good liturgical sensibility. Organists and choir directors need not fill every moment with a hymn or audible doodle. See James Hitchcock, "The Voices of Silence in the Liturgy," *Communio* 5, no. 4 (1978): 352–62.

reflect upon how Jesus comes to us in the ineffable gift of the Eucharist. Those who are accustomed to the classical rite of Mass know how clearly and vividly one can see with one's own eyes, in the very drama unfolding quietly in the sanctuary, that Jesus the Lamb of God, "for us men and for our salvation," is making himself *present upon the altar of sacrifice*. The sacrificial nature is loudly declared by the altar's ornamentation, by the priest's orientation, and by the dignified solemnity of the rubrics, all of which draw the mind insistently to the *mysterium fidei*. The importance of silence here cannot be overemphasized, for it plays a genuine liturgical role, it is not a mere "add-on" (or, perhaps, "take-away"). The silence is necessary precisely to allow the faithful to become aware of the renewal of the sacrifice of Calvary, to open up a "space" within our hearts to welcome its fruits, to make the mind of Christ our own, to unite our thoughts and desires to the divine Victim and, with him, to become an offering to the Triune God.[6] In the quieted soul prepared for its Lord, he will find—he will *make*—a place where he can rest with us. This is necessary above all for Western man with his incessant being-in-motion and garrulous talk, all of which is compounded a thousandfold by the soul-numbing, socially isolating effects of ever more invasive technology. In people almost addicted to shifting around and making noise, there is a need all the more profound for stopping, taking a deep breath, quieting down, settling into silence, listening, *being with* the Lord—and, at times, a specific need to *kneel* in front of him, a posture of humility and vulnerability.

Communicatio in Sacris

Communication presupposes, fosters, and lives upon silence. Silence is the most essential food of the discursive soul, without which it perishes in a waste of words and noise. "Silence is so powerful a language that it reaches the throne of the living God. Silence is His language, though secret, yet living and powerful," writes St.

---

6. As Ven. Pius XII instructs us to do in his Encyclical Letter *Mediator Dei*: see, inter alia, nn. 71, 80–81, 85–93, 98–99.

Faustina Kowalska in her *Diary*.[7] As her ancient Latin liturgy reveals, Holy Mother Church understood that we need both music and stillness, beautiful melodies and a beautiful absence of sound. Even if the laity are praying their own prayers of preparation and are thus plunged into a discursive mode of prayer, nevertheless the prayers inhabit a vast space of tranquility, which dwarfs them, gives them due relativity, highlights their inadequacy. The ancient liturgy forces us to be aware of our *inadequacy*, of our "innumerable sins, offenses, and negligences," and at the same time of our interior greatness before the God who makes his servants great by offering them a share of his life in the deiform virtues of faith, hope, and charity. Modern man in particular seems aware neither of the depths of his sinfulness nor of the grandeur of his destiny; his misery and his promise alike are hidden to his own eyes. Such a man desperately needs an awakening to reality, the reality of who and what he is before God, an opportunity for "coming to himself" and so, for coming to the God who is "nearer to me than I am to myself" (St. Augustine). For the Christian as for Plato, the Delphic oracle's counsel "Know thyself" is good counsel. But it is also a difficult and painful path, and a person only really strikes out on it when he has begun to break free from and to leave behind worldly ways of thinking, talking, acting. The same person continues on the path and reaches its goal only if he is continually plunged into that invisible world whose atmosphere is the Holy Spirit and whose center of gravity is the divine Humanity of Christ.

The traditional liturgy is a treasury of symbols whose meaning is grasped by a soul that is *awake*. True liturgical reform would mean helping people to wake up and stay awake, rather than dumbing things down so that they might remain asleep. The words and actions should not become an autonomous function or feature that draws the attention of the worshipers away from the mystery celebrated upon the altar; they must be *transparent* to the divine archetypes, letting them shine through text, song, gesture, clothing, and yes, absence of text and song. The liturgy ought to be a window

---

7. Saint Maria Faustina Kowalska, *Diary: Divine Mercy in My Soul* (Stockbridge, MA: Marian Press, 2003), §888.

through which the light of the divine shines, *dum medio silentium,* in the midst of the great silence of the winter's night when Christ was born; it ought to be a mirror in which the life and death of Christ is reflected with mystic verisimilitude, reverently hymning its Exemplar. If there is going to be singing and speaking during Mass, all of this ought to be ritually determinate and focused entirely on the mystery—as it is in the Eastern liturgy, with its repetition and escalating waves of prayers, or in the Western solemn High Mass, when Gregorian chant and dignified ceremonial combine to place the devout soul outside of time, outside of place, into the very Heart of Christ, the eternal Teacher. What certainly does *not* promote our illumination in Christ is a mere multiplication of words, as if the more we say, the more truth we will convey. On the contrary, as St. Thomas soberly remarks, "an infinity of human words could not adequately reach the one Word of God."[8] We are nearer to the truth when we drop our improvising pretenses and wait on the Lord, reverently reciting the hallowed words of Christian Tradition, letting them lead us into the ineffable mystery that gave birth to them.

This Thomistic insight is echoed in Ludwig Wittgenstein's statement: "If only you do not try to utter what is unutterable then *nothing* gets lost. But the unutterable will be—unutterably—*contained* in what has been uttered."[9] As Catherine Pickstock has argued, the traditional liturgy, with its repetitions, lacunae, ambiguous attributions of agency, superimposing of private and public, complex ceremonial, manages to *mean* and *communicate* a lot more than a liturgy engineered and fabricated by a committee of "experts" bent on a product that is tidy, orderly, and "rational." The classical rite can utter the unutterable because it is not preoccupied with verbalization and participation, but rather, fixed earnestly upon the mystery—which, of course, is the way to find the right words and the right kind of participation. For this reason it knows when to speak,

---

8. St. Thomas Aquinas, *Super Evangelium S. Ioannis lectura* 21, lec. 6, §2660: "Infinita enim verba hominum non possunt attingere unum Dei Verbum." The sense of *attingere* is "reach thoroughly to" or "securely gain."

9. From a letter of Ludwig Wittgenstein, quoted by John Saward, "Towards an Apophatic Anthropology," *Irish Theological Quarterly* 41 (1974), 234.

when to chant, when to whisper, when to ring bells or clink thurible chains—and when to keep silent.

One Word in Two Books

According to the medieval theologians, God has authored two books: the Book of Nature and the Book of Scripture. Creation is the first revelation of God; it is the Word spoken to each being, the participation in the Word that *is* each being. We could not understand the words of Scripture unless God had first created *things* by which and about which he could then speak to us of himself. The dignity of classical philosophy consists in the bold witness of its greatest teachers—Socrates, Plato, Aristotle, Plotinus—to the *meaningfulness* of that world, that cosmos, through the contemplation of which we gain a glimpse of the divine foundation of all reality: the simple Presence of all beauty, goodness, and truth concentrated in the Source of all. This meaningfulness is reflected in the meaningfulness of words, of language,[10] which in turn makes possible the friendly relations of human beings living together in society. The foundation of society, of friendship, language, contemplation, worship, of all human activity, is thus the Word, the Word of inexhaustible fecundity out of which pour forth the forms of all creatures. This is what we read in the first verses of the Prologue of the Gospel of John, recited quietly at the end of the Tridentine Mass: "In the beginning was the Word, and the Word was with God, and the Word was God. He was in the beginning with God; all things were made through him, and without him was not anything made that was made. In him was life, and the life was the light of men" (Jn 1:1–4).

If this is true, the "Liturgy of the Word" of the Novus Ordo Missae is ineptly named. The "Word of God" is first and foremost the eternally-begotten Word of God, the natural Son and perfect Image of the Father. Thus the phrase "Liturgy of the Word" ought to refer primarily to the Eucharist, which *is* this Word-made-flesh for our

---

10. Book IV of Aristotle's *Metaphysics* is like a prose-hymn to the stable and rich meaningfulness of language. The relativist breaks his head against the rock of apprehended unity.

salvation, and only secondarily to the divinely-revealed thoughts that find their verbal expression in holy Scripture. The Word of God is Jesus Christ, not a book, not even an inerrant and infallible book, for a book—be it ever so wise and true—is a lifeless thing, but a person is alive, and a divine Person gives life to all spirits that serve Him. The purpose of proclaiming Scripture at Mass is to *prepare* the worshipers for communion with the Word, the source of the written word and the everlasting meaning of both the Book of Scripture and the Book of Nature. The liturgy is a kind of cosmic writing on the soul, a re-creation of the soul after the manner of the unimpeded original Word which has become blurred by "misinterpretation"—sin, error, ignorance, coldness. The traditional division between the Mass of the Catechumens and the Mass of the Faithful brings out the intrinsic ordination of the parts, whereby the first part represents the soul in process of conversion to Christ, hearing his word as yet from the outside, while the second represents the lover of Christ filled with his light and life, feasting upon the Word, letting It permeate body and soul. The new division, far from bringing out this order, obscures it.

Sanctuary for the Soul

At a traditional Mass in an "unrenovated" chapel in Steyr, Austria, many years ago, I came to understand for the first time how important, how significant, it is that church sanctuaries used to be so empty of furnishings—that there was a large *open space* between the communion rail and the high altar, a space in which the priest and ministers could freely move, performing their "sacred dance," as Monsignor Robert Hugh Benson called it.[11] This open area accentuates the magnitude of the mystery, not by putting it at a distance, but by giving it ample *room*, so to speak, *to descend into our midst*. There is a certain solemnity in the very absence of objects, an absence that

---

11. Of course, he said this long before the days when silly "liturgical dances" were attempted. Benson's point will not be lost on anyone who has paid close attention to the beautiful ceremonial "choreography" of the classical Roman rite. At a solemn High Mass, the interplay of the priest, deacon, and subdeacon is like a hieratic mystery play, a dance of David in sober style.

suggests very strongly the divine Presence, as with the mercy seat of the ark of the covenant. When a table is brought in, and with it various other objects like chairs and pedestals and lecterns, the space is suddenly shrunk down to human proportions, it becomes a kind of holy lounge where the business of the liturgy is conducted. Even in the most magnificent cathedrals of past centuries, with their elaborate sanctuaries, tabernacles, and furnishings, there was still, in the center, a broad and open space within with the liturgical action was to take place, all the more accentuated by the ornate surroundings. In many new or renovated churches, gone is that awaiting emptiness of the stable of Bethlehem, the emptiness of the wounds in Mary's heart, the emptiness of conceptual understanding in Joseph's mind, the emptiness of the world awaiting its longed-for Savior—this pregnant and richly-decorated *emptiness* is gone, filled instead with clutter.

In the old structure of the sanctuary, everything leads the eyes and the soul up to the majestic altar of God, where our youth is replenished, where the Lion of Judah, with all the roaring of silence, descends in a flash of invisible light. There, in the empty and silent sanctuary, is the symbol of the soul thirsting for God, the soul which lacks and knows where to find its plenitude. In the space, the very *space* is a home for the homeless God who dwells everywhere and nowhere, who dwells in inaccessible light. Moreover, the priest standing at the altar, the small priest swallowed in the empty space and in the silence, his arms raised in a solemnly hushed prayer of sacrifice, represents the ultimate smallness, one might even say the nothingness, and yet the infinite dignity and incomparable glory of man incorporated into the Mystical Body of Christ, offering the very sacrifice of Jesus Christ (*per ipsum, et cum ipso, et in ipso...*)— he is a true participant in the cosmic liturgy, where earth and heaven unite in the person of Jesus Christ, the Eternal High Priest. This one lowly man, ordained to mediate as a living sign of the sole Mediator, stands there at the juncture of every ontological axis. He is, for a moment, the centermost point of the cosmos, in imitation of Christ, the Word through whom all things live and move and have their being.

The traditional liturgy thus shows forth the priest as a true sacramental image of the God-Man; there he stands, beneath the over-arching reredos, in the vastness of the sanctuary, swallowed as it were by his vestments, by the altar, by the beauty of the Lord's house, and yet it is *he,* truly this one individual man, unique, with all his particularities, who thus unites God and man, who thus stands with Jesus and enacts, by his power, the sacrifice that sanctifies the world. The cosmic liturgy of the Mass exhibits simultaneously the insignificance and the immortal grandeur of the individual as he stands before the God who is incalculably distant and unspeakably intimate, the God who is wholly Other and wholly *mine,* transcendent in his immanence and immanent in his transcendence. Look at him, the priest with his back turned, with his face, his hands, his heart fixed on the mystery of faith—he disappears, to be replaced by Christ; he vanishes, and yet he is more himself than ever. Despite his littleness—the littleness of a child, unable to speak, unable to express what it wants to express, except by imitating words handed down to it and accepted without any choice, without the freedom of "originality"—he is the very agent and medium through which the Lord acts to unite, sanctify, and recapitulate all things in himself, and is thus, after all, "original," for he is at the source whence the cosmos originates in a way incomparably greater than any work of art originates from any artist, greater than all human works of all ages. Look at him, the flash of flame—there heaven and its holiness, earth and its neediness, are joined and blend their voices! In this way the cosmic liturgy is perpetuated and perfected even as it is already completely finished and admits of nothing more. There is *nothing* to be added, a nothingness loudly expressed by the silence and the empty space of the sanctuary—but there is *everything* to be gained, a gift that is all gifts and more than all gifts because it is their very giver. This everything is quietly announced, as is fitting, in silence and empty space, because any sound or any representation would be idolatrous, would not be able to express even the syllable let alone the word or its meaning. And in the quiet and the void comes to us the Word who is the music of the Father, the Word who is *full of grace and truth,* and he has been given the *aural and visual room* to present himself in the humblest food, the white host, thin and frail, and the chalice, shimmering with gold and silver, far more precious than unconsecrated wine, but veritable dust compared with the Blood this wine becomes.

"A Still, Small Voice…"

There is rich meaning, a world of meaning, in every aspect of the traditional Roman liturgy, and in the architecture, the music, vestments, vessels, the space and silence it created for itself as the Holy Spirit brooded over the Church, century after century, with his broad and merciful wings. We know that the Church of Jesus Christ, in these our times, is sorely beset from without and within, as is her sacred liturgy, which always shares her fate, for better or for worse. We know that the rich meaning of her liturgy and the whole Catholic culture to which this *cultus* gave birth began to be systematically dismantled half a century ago by a brigade of modernists; we know that the result has been the marginalization, suppression, at times destruction of much that was precious, traditional, and sacred. We know that there is still a danger of irreversible amnesia and permanent oblivion. All this causes us much suffering that we can and must offer up to our Lord, for the purification and reform of his Church; all this compels us to realize how vital for the health of the Mystical Body are our prayers for the Church's pastors, our fidelity to Catholic Tradition, and our efforts to understand better the mighty gifts we have received from them and from it, so as to hand down these gifts to others with conviction and joy. It is a challenge fit for saints—for those who can believe without seeing, who can hope against hope, who can love in spite of all disappointment, scandal, and persecution. Truly, no one but lovers of silence and prayer will be able to survive this age and meet such challenges.

> The greatest things are accomplished in silence—not in the clamor and display of superficial eventfulness, but in the deep clarity of inner vision; in the almost imperceptible start of decision, in quiet overcoming and hidden sacrifice. Spiritual conception happens when the heart is quickened by love, and the free will stirs to action. The silent forces are the strong forces.[12]

---

12. Romano Guardini, *The Lord*, trans. Elinor Castendyk Briefs (Chicago: Regnery, 1954), 13.

4

Contemplation
of Unchanging Truth

I T HAS BECOME FASHIONABLE among Church historians to
deny that there ever existed a heresy called Americanism, at least
on the shores of America itself. The usual line is that it was only
ever a living idea in *France*, and even there, it meant little more than
the liberalism of advocating the absolute separation of Church and
State. If, however, one looks carefully at the Americanist ideas cri-
tiqued in Pope Leo XIII's letter *Testem Benevolentiae*, addressed to
James Cardinal Gibbons on January 22, 1899, one can see readily
enough where they finally came to roost: the Novus Ordo Missae.
Like prominent preconciliar European clerics in general, Annibale
Bugnini and his companions on the Consilium were cultured and
educated men who could not have failed to know, and know well,
the ideas that were branded as Americanism. In any case, the ideas
are plainly manifested in their work.

Near the start of *Testem Benevolentiae* Leo XIII identifies "the
underlying principle of these new opinions" in words that are chill-
ingly prophetic of certain tendencies among the liturgical reformers:

> In order the more easily to attract those who differ from her, the
> Church [so the Americanists maintain] should shape her teach-
> ings more in accord with the spirit of the age and relax some of her
> ancient severity and make some concessions to new opinions.
> Many think that these concessions should be made not only in
> regard to ways of living, but even in regard to doctrines which
> belong to the deposit of the faith. They contend that it would be
> opportune, in order to gain over those who differ from us, to omit
> certain points of her teaching which are [said to be] of lesser

importance, and to tone down the meaning which the Church has always attached to them.

After repudiating this opinion with a quotation from the First Vatican Council, Pope Leo then castigates those who omit certain principles of Christian doctrine or pass over them in silence, for, he says, "all the principles [of Christian doctrine] come from the same Author and Master.... They are adapted to all times and all nations." As liturgical scholar Lauren Pristas has documented, the Novus Ordo Missae exhibits a systematic effort on the part of its compilers to downplay or eliminate elements of worship and piety that were pervasive in the Roman liturgical tradition embodied in the old Missal—elements the reformers considered out of date or even offensive to "modern man."[1] In short, to borrow Leo XIII's language, the new Missal often relaxes severity, makes concessions, tones down meanings, and, no other method availing, resorts to silent omission.

The second major Americanist idea censured by Pope Leo, and regarded by him as "even a greater danger and a more manifest opposition to Catholic doctrine and discipline," is that "such liberty should be allowed in the Church that, her supervision and watchfulness being in some sense lessened, allowance be granted the faithful, each one to follow out more freely the leading of his own mind and the trend of his own proper activity." Wait a minute, the modern reader says; what is so objectionable about that? We are steeped in the view that each man is a kind of law unto himself and is free to do as he pleases, provided he harm no one else's body or property. But this is a peculiarly modern view, characteristic of our Enlightenment frame of reference. Catholics understand freedom to be not a brute fact, like the color of one's skin, but a moral accomplishment, one that is secured by adherence to the true and the good. In other words, the only way a son of Adam can achieve lasting happiness is by allowing his free will to be shaped and disci-

---

1. See Lauren Pristas's book *Collects of the Roman Missal*, complemented by her "Theological Principles that Guided the Redaction of the Roman Missal (1970)," *The Thomist* 67 (2003): 157–95; for detailed discussion of the change in the orations, see Cekada, *Work of Human Hands*, 219–45.

plined by divine law and divine grace. Apart from these there is no freedom worthy of the name, but rather a slavery to sin (see Jn 8:34). What Pope Leo is condemning is the view, nowadays taken as self-evident, that each man knows best what is best for him and that he ought therefore to be left "free" to experiment with different ways of life, to combine and divide ideas, to form and dissolve relationships at will. Transposed into the liturgical domain, Leo XIII would be talking about the parish liturgy committee "putting together" Sunday's Mass according to their own "lights" and "inspirations," if one may be permitted to use traditional words for such a novelty. No, this is all wrong; for good reason must the Church exercise supervision and watchfulness over Catholic life. The Mass, above all, should be something we *receive* in all its integrity and splendor, something we guard and preserve as our dearest inheritance, humbly handing it on to the faithful who come after us.

Next, Pope Leo XIII addresses the Americanist claim that we are entering into a "new age" in which (in Leo's words) "the Holy Spirit pours richer and more abundant graces than formerly upon the souls of the faithful." The pontiff asks if "anyone who recalls the history of the apostles, the faith of the nascent Church, the trials and deaths of the martyrs—and, above all, those olden times [of the Middle Ages], so fruitful in saints" could "dare to measure our age with these, or affirm that they received less of the divine outpouring from the Spirit of Holiness?" This is vintage Leonine material: the High Middle Ages, in his estimation, are the pinnacle and model of what Christian society is meant to be and must always strive to be. He then argues that the Spirit does not act independently of the Church established by the Son of God, but works through "the aid and light of an external teaching authority." The conclusion: We are *not* better than our predecessors when it comes to living the Gospel, and we, as private individuals or clotted into committees, do not enjoy ecclesiastical authority. If ours is a new age, its novelty consists rather in the magnitude of disbelief and the boldness of hostility toward the Faith than in any warmth of welcome to the truth of Christ. In light of such reflections, one might think again about the manifestations of the charismatic movement in the Church; the innovations introduced by certain ecclesial movements such as the

Neocatechumenal Way, claimed to be inspirations of the Holy Spirit; the "spirit of Vatican II," so ready to claim the Holy Spirit as its futuristic source, so ready to detach itself from and even hold in contempt the Council's promulgated teaching; the ominous omission of so many feasts of ancient and medieval saints from the revised liturgical calendar (one thinks of the suppression of the age-old *cultus* of certain popular saints); and so forth. That is, we are living in times, after the Second Vatican Council, when people are even more likely to indulge in the fantasy of a "new age," with all the mindless and heartless destruction it has visited and still visits upon the treasures of Tradition.

The last major error of the Americanists discussed by Pope Leo XIII is their exaltation of activity over contemplation, natural over supernatural virtues, "active" over "passive" virtues. Some people, says the pope, claim that so-called "natural" virtues make a man "more ready to act and more strenuous in action" than supernatural ones and that the modern age demands a more "active" approach to life and sanctity than the predominantly contemplative and, as it were, receptive attitude of ages past. In keeping with these novel notions, a secluded life of prayer is felt to be an unproductive relic of the premodern past. Leo XIII expresses his concern that such views are contributing to the ever-lessening esteem for consecrated religious life. Leo's pessimistic warning, one that could have seemed so far-fetched in a church flourishing with religious vocations, became bitter fact in the years immediately following the Council, characterized as they were by a massive defection from religious orders, a monstrous repudiation of countless vows solemnly made, in a desperate and self-defeating effort to be "up to date." For its part, the Americanist exaltation of activity, of keeping busy and productive, anticipates and informs a number of catastrophic liturgical principles, such as the superficial notion of "active participation" that gained ascendancy during the revision of liturgical texts and the consequent rejection of contemplative, serene, subtle, and poetic elements, anything that savored of long maturation, profound meaning, and effort-asking asceticism, all written off as relics of the monastic and medieval past. A prejudice in favor of external activism and against contemplation merged with iconoclasm and bad taste to leave us with the liturgical wasteland that is now the ordinary lot of the vast majority of Catholics in the world.

According to Leo XIII's letter, the basic problem of the Americanists is a naïve reconciliation with modernity that takes the form of accommodation to a prevailing *Zeitgeist* rather than confrontation and conversion of culture. For the Americanist, the Catholic has to modernize, get up to date, embark on a project of *aggiornamento,* if he expects to remain "relevant" to the people of his time. The irony, of course, is that modern converts to the Catholic Faith were often drawn to it precisely because it offered a profoundly sane *alternative* to the madness of the modern world, not because it was smartly attuned to its rhythms.

Clear and Distinct Ideas

Critics of the Pauline Mass note the many respects in which it is a product molded by Cartesian principles.[2] The New Mass was to be like the New World: every city a grid pattern with straight streets and efficient apartment blocks. Descartes complained that old European cities, which are the result of a slow, gradual development involving many builders, have meandering streets going this way and that, with buildings everywhere, even on top of one another; they are not scientific but organic. These cities are reminiscent of the world of nature, the "dappled things" and the "gear and tackle and trim" praised by Gerard Manley Hopkins: "All things counter, original, spare, strange."[3] Descartes, in contrast, said he would prefer a city created by one designer according to a single "rational" plan, a city in which everything is symmetrical and predictable.[4]

2. See, for example, Jonathan Robinson, *The Mass and Modernity: Walking to Heaven Backward* (San Francisco: Ignatius Press, 2005); Aidan Nichols, O.P., *Looking at the Liturgy: A Critical View of Its Contemporary Form* (San Francisco: Ignatius Press, 1996); the essays in *Looking Again at the Question of the Liturgy with Cardinal Ratzinger,* ed. Alcuin Reid (Farnborough, UK: Saint Michael's Abbey Press, 2003).

3. From "Pied Beauty," in *Poems of Gerard Manley Hopkins,* ed. Robert Bridges (London: Humphrey Milford, 1918).

4. See René Descartes, *Discourse on Method,* Part II, in *Discourse on Method and Meditations on First Philosophy,* trans. Donald A. Cress (Indianapolis: Hackett, 1998), 6–13.

There would be no clutter. Functionalism would make our lives easier and more productive. Is it not amazing how Descartes could have been describing the difference between the old Mass and the new Mass? For Bugnini et alia, the liturgy was poised at last to embody the method of modern Western man: clear and distinct ideas. Here, too, the connection with America is hardly fortuitous. Tocqueville famously wrote:

> America is therefore the one country in the world where the precepts of Descartes are least studied and best followed. That should not be surprising. Americans do not read Descartes's works because their social state turns them away from speculative studies, and they follow his maxims because this same social state naturally disposes their minds to adopt them.[5]

Now, in comparison to, say, the Byzantine Divine Liturgy of St. John Chrysostom, the predominant Western liturgy—the Tridentine Mass—is already short and pithy. Its texts are notable, on the whole, for their recollected sobriety, elegant diction, and concentrated, lapidary style. If this Mass is made any shorter, clearer, or cleaner than it already is, the very spirit of the liturgy is threatened, and the proper character of the Mass as such is seriously compromised. The liturgy is a complex whole, complex because the great mystery it contains and communicates is so intensely simple that the human mind cannot fathom it, cannot experience it, except by means of diverse approaches and through diverse concepts. Participation in the Eucharistic liturgy finds itself in the very same predicament as theology striving to speak of the divine nature. To remain true to the God who stands beyond being and beyond all language, theology must avail itself of a great multitude of diverse names drawn from all ranks of being, as Dionysius the Areopagite tells us in *On the Divine Names*.[6] In like manner, the sacred liturgy demands a variety of hierarchical ministers, gestures, prayers, chants, vestments, vessels, furnishings, and so forth, with all possible beauty and

---

5. Alexis de Tocqueville, *Democracy in America*, trans. Harvey C. Mansfield and Delba Winthrop (Chicago: University of Chicago Press, 2000), vol. II, pt. I, ch. 1, 403.

6. *On the Divine Names*, ch. 1, in Pseudo-Dionysius, *The Complete Works*, 49–58.

elaborateness, if it is to pay worthy homage to the *sacra mysteria* in their sublime simplicity.[7]

The new liturgy is a kind of Cartesian attempt to intuit the whole of the mystery in a simple act, a single *argumentum*, instead of the multiple interlacing layers of analogy by which the human spirit must ascend to the divine simplicity in, as Dionysius would have it, a composite motion formed of spiral, straight, and circular motions. It is true, thanks to God's mercy, that the new liturgy retains some share of analogous cognition due to the elements of the ancient liturgy that have been preserved in it; but it is also true that the pervasive influence of "Cartesian angelism" has yielded a system of worship in which there are no natural patterns of irregularity and complexity, such as one finds in the whole of the cosmos God has created—the controlled chaos of a river or a forest or a mountain, the massive coherence formed by forces more meandering as one approaches utmost particularity. Ideals such as "clarity," "simplicity," "accessibility," are intrinsically ambiguous and ambivalent; they are two-edged swords that can either protect or destroy the faith and its ritual embodiment.[8]

Confessing the Faith

St. Thomas states that "religion is a protestation of faith, hope, and charity, whereby man is primarily directed to God."[9] Since the Mass is the highest act of worship—that is, the highest exercise of the virtue of religion, which binds us back to God—it follows that the best form of the liturgy is that which contains or elicits the greatest

7. See my "Doing and Speaking in the Person of Christ: Eucharistic Form in the Anaphora of Addai and Mari," *Nova et Vetera* 4 (2006): 313–79, for an extended treatment of the question of sacramental signification and, in particular, how a liturgy suspends ordinary temporal and spatial rules of discourse in order to reach beyond the confines of creation to the uncreated source and, at the same time, to welcome into our midst the irruption of a miraculous presence that resists linear description.

8. See the extensive critique of Cartesian idealism, rationalism, and dualism in Jacques Maritain's *The Dream of Descartes*, trans. Mabelle L. Andison (New York: The Philosophical Library, 1944) and *Three Reformers: Luther, Descartes, Rousseau* (New York: Apollo Editions, 1970).

9. *ST* II-II, q. 101, a. 3, ad 1.

protestation of faith, hope, and charity. A liturgy that is steeped with exhortations and opportunities to exercise these three virtues will, *ipso facto,* be a superior expression of religion. The traditional form of the Roman rite is a seamless garment woven from top to bottom of rich golden threads of faith, hope, and charity. Furthermore, if the Eucharistic sacrifice stands to the Mass as the Mass stands to all other forms of worship (that is, the Eucharist is the heart of the Mass, its meaning, purpose, goal, sun, furnace, just as the Mass is the center of the sacramental life of the Christian), then that form of Mass will be superior which more clearly underlines and exalts the Eucharist, which gives It the most honored place, which prepares for and reacts to the divine mysteries in the most fitting manner. Our acts of faith, hope, and charity are to be directed to God primarily *in the Holy Eucharist,* and thus the same argument applies: a liturgy permeated with promptings to exercise these virtues specifically toward the Blessed Sacrament is, *ipso facto,* a superior expression of the heart of the Catholic faith.

Concerning the commandment against taking God's name in vain, St. Thomas writes: "All inordinate taking of the divine name is forbidden by this commandment."[10] This statement forbids not only perjury, which is the sort of thing Aquinas has in mind, but also forbids any practice of sacred theology lacking in due reverence and faith—and, for the same reason, any practice of liturgical worship lacking in the same way. There is a kind of liturgy that is almost indistinguishable from taking God's name in vain, namely, when his holy Name is invoked without the proper honor, reverence, solemnity, and piety; when it stands like a jewel without a gold or silver setting worthy of it. The new liturgy in its protean adaptability often leads to a situation where God's name cannot be sufficiently honored because it is thrown out into the midst of an ocean of trivial verbiage, horizontal self-affirmation, and ritual poverty. In contrast, the Mass of the ages is careful to honor the Name of God—especially the Name of Jesus and the "Name" of the Blessed Trinity—to the utmost. Given that we are *obliged* to reverence God's Name, the old liturgy's frequent repetition of the doxology makes

10. *ST* II-II, q. 122, a. 3, ad 2.

perfect sense, for example in the set of prayers leading up to the priest's communion. If *Sacrosanctum Concilium* had such things as the ninefold Kyrie or the threefold *Domine, non sum dignus* in mind when it recommended removing "useless repetition,"[11] one can only say it is most unfortunate that some people fail to see the importance of announcing the ultimate mysteries of the faith by speaking, softly and reverently, the divine Name over and over again, repeating what is most holy and therefore most salutary to a soul awake. Repetition is an integral part of human existence—of memory and learning, of the language of lovers, of the language (and non-language) of prayer, as with the Rosary or the Jesus prayer or litanies, or many of the psalms and canticles of the Bible.

Indeed, one can go further: *meaningful* repetition—exactly the opposite of the "vain repetitions" Jesus speaks against (Mt 6:7, KJV)—is worthwhile for its own sake, in the same way that certain kinds of knowledge are worthwhile for their own sake. One could never tire of speaking the sweet Name of Jesus, *if* one understood that this Name contains everything and brings everything back to unity in the divine oneness. The Fatherhood of the Father and the Sonship of the Son are, in a sense, repetition infinitized into an eternal simple act of giving and receiving, begetting and being begotten; "Thou art My Son, this day have I begotten Thee" is the defining word of the Father, "I am Thy Son and Thou art My beloved Father" the defining word of the Son. A *meaningless* repetition of elements is rightly avoided as irrational. How different is the chanting of the Litany of the Saints or the Litany of Loreto, the Paters and Aves counted on the beads of a well-loved rosary, or the cascading Kyries of a Byzantine Divine Liturgy! Of such insistent pleading, it is Our Lord himself who offered the definitive example in the Garden of Gethsemane: "He left them again, and went away and prayed a third time, saying the same thing once more" (Mt 26:44; cf. Mk 14:39).

11. The pertinent passage in the Constitution on the Sacred Liturgy reads: "The rites should be distinguished by a noble simplicity; they should be short, clear, and unencumbered by useless repetitions; they should be within the people's powers of comprehension, and normally should not require much explanation" (§34).

Acknowledging God as God

St. Thomas gives us another important principle: "One must first of all acknowledge God with a view to worship, before honoring him whom we have acknowledged."[12] The Eucharistic liturgy must be ordered in such a way that it "brings" God, who is always already present everywhere, before the conscious mind of the worshiper, so as to be vividly present *to the worshiper;* for we cannot honor God unless we first acknowledge him, and not merely "acknowledge" as we might tip a hat to a passerby, but acknowledge *with a view to worship.* The presence of God should be introduced to us in such a way that we are disposed immediately to pay homage to him and carry out the act of loving adoration or adoring love which is man's highest and most divine act—an act *in* man but not merely *of* him.

The prayers at the foot of the altar—*Introibo ad altare Dei*—immediately summon us into the context of the divine mysteries about to be celebrated; the Kyrie and Gloria continue in an even stronger and more direct vein (*laudamus te, benedicimus te, adoramus te, glorificamus te*). At a sung Mass, the chanted Introit serves the same purpose as the prayers at the foot of the altar. The old rite introduces us somehow both gradually and suddenly into the mystery; the sign of the Cross is immediately followed by *Introibo ad altare Dei,* providing a context for the Name of the Trinity. There must be small steps toward the mystery, approaching and receding, at once confident and contrite, praying in order that there might be praying, ascending the altar while humbly begging the grace to serve there. There has to be an earnest activity of preparing that is somehow also a sign of being prepared as well as a sign that no one can be prepared for what God will do, a drawing away (*Confiteor Deo…*) that is at the same time a forward motion toward the irresistible majesty of God (*Deus tu conversus vivificabis nos*). The classical Roman liturgy is structured and worded in such a way that it is undeniably more oriented to the pure worship of God, to his glorification, and to our subjective sanctification through that very

12. *ST* II-II, q. 122, a. 3.

activity of adoration. In other words, it is inherently vertical, unreservedly theocentric.[13]

For God or For the People?

The traditional Latin Mass is celebrated *for God,* on *his* account, as an act of profound worship directed to Him. The new Mass, as it has been allowed to be celebrated around the world, often looks like an exercise mainly for the sake of the people—almost as if the people are the point of the Mass, and not God.

Are "for God" and "for the people" necessarily in conflict? No, but *only* if what is truly to the people's benefit is borne in mind; then there is no conflict. The way the liturgy should be for the people is by turning their minds and hearts toward God (*versus Deum*), aiding them to reach contemplative and sacramental union with God. If worshipers strive to be united to the Lord in charity, this charity cannot but affect their relationships with one another; loving adoration of God becomes love toward the neighbor. Perfecting the social life of Christians is a secondary end of communal worship, and follows from it naturally if first things are kept first. "Seek first the kingdom of God and his righteousness, and all these things will be added unto you" (Mt 6:33). This primacy of the kingdom of God, which is nothing other than the eternal and adorable mystery of the Trinity and the communion of saints gathered into that mystery in the "liturgy" of the heavenly Jerusalem, is *not* well expressed by a liturgical form that emphasizes community and communication, the circle of believers, to such an extent that the inherently vertical essence of adoration is lost sight of, is no longer manifestly *central.*

Recall how vehemently the reformers both of the sixteenth century and of the twentieth attacked the idea of a "private Mass," where a priest and server offer the sacrifice without a congregation. And yet, if the *essence* of the Mass is an act of profound adoration of the Holy Trinity, in the shadow of Whose wings the priest then intercedes for the good of the entire Church and the conversion of

---

13. See Raymond Leo Cardinal Burke, "The Theo-Centric Character of Catholic Liturgy," *The Thomist* 75 (2011): 347–64.

the world, nothing could be better than the multiplication of such Masses devoutly offered. The critique of the private Mass runs parallel with the demise of the contemplative religious life: a nun or monk in a cell seems useless "for the people," even though in reality such a person's prayers are the only reason the Church does not collapse in a minute, the blood of martyrs run dry, or the world vanish in a flash of fire.[14]

I remember the blessed early mornings I spent at the monastery of Le Barroux in France, watching in the dark Romanesque church as the monks and their acolytes silently processed, one by one, out of the sacristy, each toward a separate side altar, where they began to whisper the prayers of the immortal Mass. The few visitors present would choose a chapel among the many being used, kneel on the hard stone floor, and follow along in their handheld missals, while hearing faintly the tokens of many Masses being said simultaneously in the same vaulted space. I will never forget the moment of consecration at my anonymous monk's chapel, when, in the midst of a quiet as thick and beautiful as I imagine heaven must have in store for us after this noisy world, I heard not only the nearby acolyte's bell ring brightly into the emptiness, but also, and nearly at the same time, a chorus of other acolytes' bells ringing throughout the church as dozens of priests genuflected before the sacred Host and Chalice, and elevated the precious Body and Blood of our Lord in the sight of the Most Blessed Trinity, witnessed by countless angels and few mortal men. I remember being filled with an irrefragable sense that it was the Holy Sacrifice offered by these dutiful monks and others like them that could be the only reason the sun continued to rise and set, the only reason Almighty God had not yet extinguished the life of this guilty planet as he extinguished the life of Sodom and Gomorrah.

What I experienced, beyond all words, was the absolutely God-focused meaning of the Mass, and the God-pleasing effect of the same. This visit to Le Barroux made me realize how wrongheaded the Bugninian reformers were, not just on the matter of private

---

14. I pursue this defense of the private Mass in chapter 10.

Masses but on the matter of the very *purpose* of liturgical worship, and therefore all the accoutrements and accidents that belong to it. What I saw, to revert to the beginning of this chapter, is that the only real alternative to modernism is monasticism, understood as the model of what the Christian life essentially is: to be "hid with Christ in God" (Col 3:3) and to spend our life on earth preparing for the world to come, which is our true life (cf. Col 3:4; 1 Tim 6:19). Obviously not every Christian is literally a monk or nun, but to be Christian at all is to be single-hearted about the kingdom of God, and that is what the monastic life vividly proclaims and embodies in the purest way. Put simply, we must be monastics in our deepest spiritual desires, or we are divided, half-hearted, lukewarm, not convinced that God alone is our portion and cup.

This is the challenge that the traditional Roman liturgy makes to us again and again, in its prayers, its ceremonies, its calendar, its ethos. It is not accommodated to our worldly compromises. It does not try to adapt itself to where we are. It stalwartly proclaims the Kingdom of God in a rigorous purity that can be rather daunting, even off-putting, for those who are new to it. It proclaims unequivocally the primacy of things heavenly and spiritual. It is the luminous expression of an ageless tradition of worship, as carried out by men and women who made this worship their primary work in life. As such, it does the opposite of pandering to us moderns; it confronts us with our need for radical conversion. The old Missal is the unwavering, undying repository of the radical message of Jesus Christ, our Lord and God. Are we ready to hear this Gospel and take up the Cross?

That is a question posed not only to laymen, but to the Church as a whole and especially to her bishops, to whom the Church's mission is entrusted. Will we be *liturgical* Americanists who whittle down our Tradition and change our Faith to accommodate the world, or will we be Catholics who revere and hand on our Tradition so that the Faith may flourish anew in ages to come?

With moral certainty that the great pope who wrote *Testem Benevolentiae* is a saint interceding for us in heaven, I turn to him and pray:

Pope Leo XIII, pray for us; pray for the Church on earth that once you governed as Vicar of Christ; pray for Francis, your Successor in the Chair of St. Peter. Obtain for us the grace to recognize and resist the Americanism that has inundated our churches, and plead with the Lord God of hosts for us, that the restoration of the sacred liturgy may be seen even in our days, for the glory and honor of the Most Holy Trinity, who is God ever blessed, to endless ages of ages. Amen.

5

The Liturgy Forms Christ in Us: "He Must Increase, I Must Decrease"

J UST AS THE VIRGIN bears Christ in her womb and presents him to us, so the liturgy bears Christ and gives him to us. We go to him through her—*ad Jesum per Mariam*—and he comes to us through the Church and her worship as through a mother. We know that the connection of Mary, the Church, and the sacraments is omnipresent in the Church Fathers.[1] The Virgin Mary is the Mediatrix of all grace; the liturgy too is this mediatrix, in its own line of efficacy. The Holy Eucharist is the focal point, the radiant center, of the grace that passes through the queenly heart of the Virgin Mary, thence to be poured out over the world; she is the Mediatrix because she bore Christ within her womb and soul, and continues to bear him for the world by her unequaled love for mankind. In this sense, the Virgin Mary prepares for us the body which becomes the heart of the Mass. Likewise, one sees the *throughness*, so to speak, of the liturgy—its need to be transparent, to be a vehicle that hides itself in the presence of the mystery of the Word made flesh. This is also Mary's vocation, her personality at its most beautiful: a transparent receptivity and openness that lets the glory of Christ, the glory of his merciful love, shine through into the world.

To say, then, as so many Catholics do, that the *form* of the liturgy

---

1. See Hugo Rahner, *Our Lady and the Church* (Bethesda, MD: Zaccheus Press, 2005). For many precious texts on the connection between the Virgin Mother Mary, Holy Mother Church, and the birth of Christians into the divine life of Christ the Son, see Luigi Gambero, *Mary and the Fathers of the Church: The Blessed Virgin in Patristic Thought*, trans. Thomas Buffer (San Francisco: Ignatius Press, 1999).

does not matter that much ("because, after all, Christ is truly present when the consecration is valid; what difference ultimately should it make? Should so much trouble be made over Tridentine versus Novus Ordo, when we just ought to be humbly grateful that our Lord is truly present?") is like saying it doesn't matter what kind of mother Jesus has, what kind of woman or what kind of character Mary has—virginal, sinless, graceful, gentle, or their opposites—for these things would be accidental, incidental, not of the essence of the Christ who comes to us through her. The evident falsity of this position becomes apparent the more one sees the deep connection between, on the one hand, Mary's sinlessness and the glory of the Redeemer, and on the other, our heavenly mother Mary and our sacramental mother, the Mass. It was not long before early Protestantism, having severed the connection between the believer and the visible Church, severed also the profound connection that conciliar dogma and popular piety had always perceived between the Savior and his Mother. This led finally to the callous revisionism of liberal Protestantism: Mary was a Jewish girl like any other, had several children from ordinary marital relations, and didn't know that her Son was divine or had a world-altering mission; the story of the Annunciation is a mythic parable from "Luke's" overactive imagination, and so forth. As St. Cyprian wrote and the Church has always taught: "A man cannot have God for his father who does not have the Church for his mother"[2]—the Church that gratefully and lovingly receives into her womb the divine Word of revelation and takes it for *truth*. One must also add: "A man cannot have Jesus for his brother who does not have Mary for his mother." And one may complete the analogy: A man will not attain the full stature of perfection if he does not worship God in spirit and in truth, in the way God has deigned to reveal to us and to develop over the course of our history as his priestly nation.

Babylonian Captivities

The liturgy has two purposes: to worship God with all due reverence and love, and to feed, nurture, shape, and perfect the wor-

---

2. See St. Cyprian of Carthage, *On the Unity of the Catholic Church*, §6.

shiper. God is not changed or moved for the worse by our bad liturgies; it is we, the Christian people, who are deformed by the Novus Ordo Missae as it is celebrated in most of our churches. God does not suffer if we refrain from attending a superficial ceremony that verges on mockery of his Son and does violence to Catholic worship as it has *always* been known. It is true that there are times when it is necessary to attend even a most disgracefully celebrated liturgy in order to fulfill one's obligation to the Lord, and at this time one ought to go with the express purpose of suffering for one's own sins. It is true, too, that we can and must seek our consolation in the wondrous presence of our Lord Jesus Christ in the Blessed Sacrament, a presence so much beyond all that we can deserve no matter how beautifully and reverently we sing the songs of Sion. Still, there is far more to the substance of liturgical *cultus* than merely the provision of a moment's adoration in the midst of an ocean of banality and noise; the liturgy, both as a whole and in each of its parts, is not *itself* supposed to be a mortification, a cause of pain, but a consolation, a reservoir of peace and joy for building up the inner man. The purpose of the liturgy is to form our souls in the beauty of holiness; and if the human elements of the liturgy are, on the contrary, deforming our souls, then we must not allow it habitually to do so unless, as was just said, we have no choice in a given situation.[3] The "spirit of the liturgy," rightly understood, cannot change; that is why the new liturgy, insofar as it is an experimental and non-traditional liturgy, must either be brought firmly back into conformity with tradition, or be suppressed utterly. In a sense, these amount to the same thing, for to bring the Novus Ordo back sufficiently to its roots would be to abolish it in its current form, even as one who has to relearn a subject from the roots has also to unlearn the faulty version he got first. When push comes to shove, it is not tradition but the departure from tradition that has to go.

3. What I mean is that if a family were to find itself in a situation where the only Mass available was one that was celebrated so badly that it could not help but foster bad religious habits, and where the family's chances of either contributing to or at least witnessing significant positive change were slender, it would be an obligation for that family to move to another diocese, or at least another town, where better options were available.

By attending poor liturgy one implicitly accepts it—that is, one says to it: "Shape me, shape my soul, form my spirit. Make me like yourself." But this is what one must not allow to occur with experimental, horizontal, anti-sacral liturgy; *its* habits, as it were, must not become *my* habits. Sadly, the vast majority of Catholics who still attend Mass, including their bishops and priests, have been habituated precisely to this poverty, so much so that it is no longer possible for most people to be made aware of the impoverishment, let alone convince them of its remedies. This is one among many reasons why the Church, for all who have eyes to see things as they are, has entered upon a second and more perilous "Babylonian captivity," from which she cannot be liberated until the empire of rationalist liturgiology and neo-modernist theology crumbles under its own dead weight. The captivity of the Jews lasted some seventy years (ca. 586 to 516 BC); the Avignon papacy lasted for nearly the same (AD 1309–1378). Will we be delivered from disgrace by the year 2040? It is too soon to tell, or even to guess. What is certain is that we have no more excuse for despair than had the Jews or our brethren six and a half centuries ago. The arm of the Lord is not shortened, however crippled his earthly members may seem. We are in a waiting pattern where humility and patience, longsuffering and prayer, are the lessons we are forced to learn, if we wish to remain faithful to the Lord. Triumphalism is not a bad word, but it happens, at the moment, to be an archaic one. Perhaps the day will come even in our lifetime when the liturgy of our forefathers is born anew, thrives, and embraces countless souls in its maternal bosom, while the children of Holy Mother Church rejoice in a triumph as sweet as it is unexpected. For now, there is the hard, dusty road of privation, a road stretching through a wilderness, and we need—and need to ask for—the grace to persevere along this way until it reaches the destination God in his mercy has already provided. We are not alone on this way, for it is the way of the Cross trodden by Jesus Christ in his Passion. It is the way, in short, of the holy sacrifice. And so we are participating in the spirit of the Mass even in the darkest period of liturgical anarchy and deprivation.

Humility in the Face of Mystery

Reflect on the ethos of humility inculcated by the traditional form of Mass. In the classical liturgy, all the "weight" is on the priest and the sacred ministers. This is a good thing entirely, though a difficult one for fallen nature. It is good because it enables the faithful to lean upon their priest, to go with him to the altar; the liturgy is not suddenly thrown into their hands, but paradoxically, because of the centrality of the cleric, the faithful are able to enter more deeply into the sacrifice "under his wing," like the nameless faithful crowding under the copious mantle of the Blessed Virgin in medieval paintings. The reason is that the objective place of worship is the sanctuary with its sacred ministers, but subjectively everyone can place himself into this place and follow in his heart the offering made by the priest—there is not a false shift to the "heart of the individual believer," as in Protestant worship. The focus remains on Jesus Christ, Head of the Mystical Body, because the focus remains on his sacerdotal icon, the priest, who is the self-sacrificing image of the one High Priest.

One might object (and many did object in the 1950s and 60s): Does not all of this place too much weight on the priest, too much of a psychological burden? The answer is obvious: the priesthood is the most sublime, the most arduous, the most demanding of all vocations—that is how it should be; in fact, it cannot be otherwise, as we learn from authors as diverse as St. John Chrysostom, St. John Fisher, St. John Mary Vianney, and Pope Pius XI. When Christ is present in our midst, the right reaction is to worship *him*, not one another. The priest "disappears" into the Holy Sacrifice when he faces *ad orientem* and offers the sacrifice with his face invisible to the people. Jesus alone is the center, the one Sun whose light illuminates all the worshipers, including the priest. In this sense, the ancient liturgy places at once *all* the emphasis and *none* of it upon the priest; he is the most visible and the most invisible, central and at the same time peripheral. He is central as an icon of Christ, he is peripheral as Jones or Smith. In the reformed liturgy, arguably, things are reversed: Jones or Smith, "this man," is central; what has become peripheral is the unique Mediator between God and man. As St. Thomas Aquinas explains,

The *action* performed by the angel who is sent proceeds *from God* as from its first principle, at whose nod and by whose authority the angels work; and is reduced *to God* as to its last end. Now this is what is meant by a minister: for a minister is an intelligent instrument; while an instrument is moved by another, and its action is ordered to another. Hence angels' actions are called "ministries"; and for this reason they are said to be sent "in ministry."[4]

The angels are the very model of the sacred ministers at the altar: they must make themselves invisible servants, intelligent instruments, of Jesus Christ. When James Likoudis reported on a retreat speaker who preached that Christ was a layman, he was pointing to more than a topical or regional heresy; for this may well be called the evil *par excellence* characteristic of the "New Mass mentality": the laicization of Christ and his priesthood, and the clericalization of the laity.[5] John Paul II and Benedict XVI denounced this trend for many years, it is true, but as long as a compromised liturgical form continues to shape the minds and hearts of the faithful, we may very well see no end of the ongoing desacralization. It remains to be seen whether the current Holy Father and his successors will have the wisdom to recognize how desperately the Church needs to abandon her failed experiment and likewise have the courage to lead Christ's flock to abundant pastures of Eucharistic life.

A friend of mine once remarked that the ancient form preserves the important act of the priest *praying with* the people, at the end of a low Mass when all kneel toward the tabernacle to recite the Hail Marys and other Leonine prayers. It struck me powerfully the other day that at a Novus Ordo Mass, it is possible for the priest *never* to be standing otherwise than toward, which is to say, over against, the people—which, in an ironic twist, *increases* the hieratic distance in

---

4. St. Thomas Aquinas, *ST* I, q. 112, a. 1.

5. I put the phrase in quotation marks because I do not question the validity of the *Novus Ordo Missae* nor the possibility of its being celebrated in a manner worthy of the Roman liturgical tradition (witness the Oratorians at their best), but only pointing out that there are features of its very structure—its linear verbosity, theological minimalism, plethora of options, ceremonial looseness—and even more, habits long tolerated as to its actual celebration, that ignite and fuel serious deviations of belief and praxis in the Catholic Church.

an artificial way and makes the priesthood seem like a political office rather than a sacred weight. In the context of the classical liturgy, it is clear that everyone is focused on one and the same act of worship: the priest *in persona Christi* and the people by their baptismal participation in Christ's priesthood.[6] The roles are vividly distinct yet seen to be convergent and harmonious because all are facing *ad orientem* in common, and at the end of Mass all are praying together, beseeching the Mother of God for her protection. The anonymity of the priest in the traditional rite both increases his visibility as minister of the sacred mysteries and *hides* him, *decreases* his idiosyncratic presence as this individual man: "He must increase, I must decrease." This is what the entire ancient liturgy does in every respect: it brings forth Christ the Lord and suppresses the fallen ego that wishes to assert itself.

The popes of the last two centuries warned again and again that modern man was plummeting down a path of egoism that would trample all before it—the rights of God and of the Church, the legitimate rights of individuals, families, peoples, and nations, the hard-won morality of the Commandments and the Beatitudes, the sublime secrets of deity confessed in the Creed, the treasures of cult and culture laboriously built up and refined over the span of ages. Their warnings have come true before our eyes, as the process of suicidal secularization continues at an accelerating pace. Who could have believed, what pope would have dared imagine, that the Mass—that fixed star in the majestic firmament of Catholic life—would itself one day be caught up and swept away in this tempest of mindless change, this relentless dialectic of dehumanization which inevitably follows upon the refusal of divinization in Christ? This ego is its own worst enemy, a "free" branch that, in the pride of its vitality, cuts itself off from the vine to exult for a moment in free fall, before it settles in soil and rots. This ego may not love itself,

6. See St. Thomas, *ST* III, q. 63 on sacramental character, where the Angelic Doctor explains that all Christians participate in the one priesthood of Christ through the character imprinted on the soul at baptism. This character is a power of *receiving* divine realities from God through the ministers of his Church. The sacerdotal character is, in contrast, a power of *giving* divine realities to the people, not by an independent authority, but by sharing in Christ's unique authority.

that is obvious, but neither is it hopeless, its condition incurable. For there is One who loves us still and always, for he is Love without end; who calls us back to the right path on which we shall find not only the suffering from which we can never escape in this life, but also the consolation and eternal life that no creature can give to itself; who holds in his infallible and changeless Mind all the good that we have abandoned, and is ready to bestow it again through his faithful servants in the Church. I speak of the One whom our brothers in Christ, the Greek Catholics—heirs and guardians of an unbroken liturgical tradition—so beautifully and humbly invoke in their Divine Liturgy:

> O Lord our God, accept this fervent supplication from Thy servants, and have mercy upon us according to the multitude of Thy mercies; and send forth Thy compassion upon us and upon all Thy people, who await the rich mercy that cometh from Thee. For Thou art a gracious God and lovest mankind, and unto Thee we render glory, Father, Son, and Holy Spirit, now and ever, and forever.

6

Offspring of Arius
in the Holy of Holies

I N THE NEW TESTAMENT two basic "orientations" of prayer are
displayed and inculcated: first and foremost, in keeping with
Jewish tradition, prayer addressed to "God" or "Lord" (into this
category may also be placed the altogether novel way in which our
blessed Savior intimately addresses his "Father," as we see, for example, in the farewell discourses in the Gospel of John),[1] and occupy-
ing a secondary but still important place, prayer addressed to Jesus
Christ himself. To the former and more familiar Jewish practice,
Jesus adds a new and crucial element that concerns the very essence
of the revelation he embodies: God is to be invoked *in Jesus' name*,
for the Son of God is now the Son of Man, the one and only Mediator between God and man, through whom all our prayers ascend to
the Father and all his graces are given to us in the Mystical Body.
Hence the Lord teaches his disciples: "You did not choose me, but I
chose you and appointed you that you should go and bear fruit and
that your fruit should abide; so that whatever you ask the Father *in
my name*, he may give it to you" (Jn 15:16), and again: "Truly, truly, I
say to you, if you ask anything of the Father, he will give it to you *in
my name*. Hitherto you have asked nothing in my name; ask, and
you will receive, that your joy may be full" (Jn 16:23–24). Such
teachings are the revealed foundation of the Church's custom of
concluding her prayers *per Christum Dominum nostrum,* a formula
we already see frequently in St. Paul, whose letters are full of liturgi-

---

1. Another example would be Matthew 11:25: "I thank thee, Father, Lord of
heaven and earth..."

cal language: "I thank my God *through Jesus Christ* for all of you, because your faith is proclaimed in all the world."[2]

Nevertheless, our Lord also taught his disciples to address *him*, the Son and Savior, in prayer: "Whatever you ask in my name, *I* will do it, that the Father may be glorified in the Son; if you ask me anything in my name, I will do it" (Jn 14:13–14).[3] When Jesus says: "You call me Teacher and Lord; and you are right, for so I am" (Jn 13:13), he affirms that his followers are right to turn to *him* as the ultimate authority, the Holy One of Israel. Events, especially miracles of healing, confirmed the truth of these words. "The centurion answered him, 'Lord, I am not worthy to have you come under my roof; but only say the word, and my servant will be healed'" (Mt. 8:8).[4] "The crowd rebuked them, telling them to be silent; but they cried out the more, 'Lord, have mercy on us, Son of David!'" (Mt. 20:31). There are the words of the thief: "Jesus, remember me when you come into your kingdom" (Lk 23:42), and the words of the doubter: "My Lord and my God!" (Jn 20:28). Again, the spontaneous exclamations of the early Christians are a precious witness that

2. See, e.g., Romans 5, vv. 1, 11, 15, 17, 21, etc.—the Epistle to the Romans is full of the "through Jesus Christ" formula (as well as the related "in Christ Jesus"). Cf. Pius XII, Encyclical Letter *Mediator Dei*, nn. 144–46.

3. The Greek of Jn 14:14 says: *ean ti aitēsēte me en tōi onomati mou egō poiēsō*, which the Vulgate accurately renders *si quid petieritis me in nomine meo hoc faciam*. Part of the manuscript tradition of the NT lacks the *me* of 14:14, but it is the preferred reading, faithfully reflected both in the Vulgate tradition and in patristic writings. In any event, the phrase "in my name" establishes the point, too, because the thrust of the statement is that the Father will glorify the *Son* by showing the Son's divinity, i.e., his power to save the one praying; it is the Son ("I") who will respond to the prayer. Of course, the Son never responds apart from the Father and the Spirit, but it is important *for us* that we address all three Persons of the Trinity.

4. There are, of course, countless texts in the Gospels in which Jesus is addressed as Lord, *kyrie* in the vocative (*kyrios* in the nominative), which means master, lord, owner, sir—but which can also mean Lord in the proper theological sense, for this usage had already been solidly established in the Septuagint, where the God of Israel is referred to as *kyrios*. In certain passages of the Gospels it is clear that people who address Jesus as *kyrios* are not confessing his divinity but using an honorific title, much as the German title *Herr* means both "Mister" and "Lord." But there are other places where a confession is implied, and one of them is this famous statement of the centurion, whom Jesus praises for his faith in the Master's power to heal, which is a divine attribute.

Christ, as true God, was the *addressee* of many prayers, not only a mediator through whom one had access to the Father. "As they were stoning Stephen, he prayed, 'Lord Jesus, receive my spirit'" (Acts 7:59). "To the church of God which is at Corinth, to those sanctified in Christ Jesus, called to be saints together with all those who in every place call on the name of our Lord Jesus Christ, both their Lord and ours: Grace to you and peace from God our Father and the Lord Jesus Christ" (1 Cor 1:2–3). More important than any one verse, however, is the general *tenor* of a number of texts, for example chapter 10 of the Epistle to the Romans, where St. Paul writes:

> If you confess with your lips that Jesus is Lord and believe in your heart that God raised him from the dead, you will be saved.... The scripture says, "No one who believes in him will be put to shame." For there is no distinction between Jew and Greek; the same Lord is Lord of all and bestows his riches upon all who call upon him. For, "every one who calls upon the name of the Lord will be saved." (vv. 9, 11–13)

Here, in typical rabbinic fashion, the Apostle to the Gentiles weaves together citations from the Old Testament that are manifestly speaking about the one true God, the God of Israel, and applies them to Jesus Christ. In this way he is not only clearly asserting Christ's divinity, but also urging the Christians who receive his letter to confess this mystery with their lips (a reference to liturgical worship) and to invoke Jesus as God in their prayers.

In the end, both ways of praying are given a succinct endorsement in the solemn words of Jesus that have echoed down the centuries: "I am the way, and the truth, and the life; no one comes to the Father, but by me.... He who has seen me has seen the Father" (Jn 14:6, 9). By saying that he is *the way,* he self-effacingly presents himself as Mediator, the Word made flesh, the only way to reach the Father; by saying that he is *truth and life,* consubstantial with the Father, he presents himself as he truly is in the Father's glory— namely, as the Son who, together with the Father and the Holy Spirit, lives and reigns, *one God,* forever and ever. Hence, there can never be any tension, much less contradiction, between praying to the Father and praying to Jesus. For Jesus is Emmanuel, God-with-us, and whoever sees or speaks to him has seen or spoken to the Father.

In regard to ways of praying, it comes as no surprise that traditional liturgies of all rites, Eastern and Western, closely adhere to the witness of the New Testament and the practice of the ancient Church. The classical Roman liturgy—viewed in terms of ethos, ceremonial, spirituality, and the dogmatic theology expressed in the texts—shares much more in common with the Byzantine liturgy than it does with the Novus Ordo Missae.[5] Perhaps nowhere is this fact more obvious than in regard to the presence, in liturgical texts and ceremonies, of solemn Trinitarian affirmations and their counterpart, a thoroughgoing Christocentrism. Indeed, there could hardly be a more insistently Christ-confessing liturgy than the Divine Liturgy of St. John Chrysostom. In this liturgy there is a constant hymning both of Christ as the one true God and of the indissoluble unity of the Trinity: "Let us commend ourselves and one another and our whole life to Christ our God"; "For You, O God, are gracious and You love mankind, and to You we render glory, Father, Son, and Holy Spirit, now and ever and forever." Right before the Nicene Creed is recited, the priest sings: "Let us love one another, so that with one mind we may profess"—and the people finish his sentence: "The Father and the Son and the Holy Spirit, the Trinity, one in substance and undivided." Immediately after the consecration the priest sings: "We offer to You Yours of Your own, on behalf of all and for all," to which the people respond: "We praise You, we bless You, we thank You, O Lord, and we pray to You, our God." One of the most beautiful texts in the Divine Liturgy is an ancient hymn that perfectly illustrates the point we are making:

> O only-begotten Son and Word of God, Who, being immortal, deigned for our salvation to become incarnate of the holy Mother of God and ever-virgin Mary, and became man, without change. You were also crucified, O Christ our God, and by death have

5. See chapter 11, "The Liturgical Reform's Long-Term Effects on Ecumenism."

trampled death, being One of the Holy Trinity, glorified with the Father and the Holy Spirit, save us.

The Byzantine liturgy is overflowing with such texts, boldly confessing the divinity of Christ and the perfect unity of Father, Son, and Spirit.

Now, even if the classical Roman liturgy, with its comparative sobriety and simplicity, is not "overflowing" in the same way as Eastern liturgies tend to be, it too conveys the same theological message, and with many of the same expressions and gestures. It clearly belongs to and derives from the same ancient Christian heritage, where chanting the praises of the divine Word-made-flesh and falling in adoration before the Most Holy Trinity were the pith and purpose of liturgical life.

In marked contrast, the Novus Ordo Missae displays an insistent "Patricentrism" or generic Theocentrism that is characteristic of *no* historically well-established liturgical rite. In its official texts and ceremonial the Novus Ordo exhibits what can only be called a certain Arianizing *appearance* or *tendency*.[6] The presbyter Arius of Alexandria (ca. 256–336), after whom the heresy of Arianism is named, taught that Jesus Christ is not truly and properly divine, but rather, a highly exalted creature and specially favored servant of God—a "son" or "god" by grace, not by nature.

Before discussing this issue, let us lay down some principles:

1. Properly speaking, the Holy Sacrifice of the Mass is offered by Jesus Christ *to the Blessed Trinity*, Father, Son, and Holy Spirit. It is not offered by Christ to the Father "apart from" or in contradistinction to the Son and the Spirit, for the Three are always One in their divinity and never separated, although it is the *Son of God* who offers his human life on the cross, as the Byzantine hymn quoted above so clearly confesses.

2. Our Lord offers the sacrifice of himself in his human nature,

---

6. There is an abundance of material on the questionable theological tendencies of the members of the Consilium; see, for instance, Roberto de Mattei, "Reflections on the Liturgical Reform" and Dom Charbel Pazat de Lys, O.S.B., "Towards a New Liturgical Movement," both in *Looking Again at the Question of the Liturgy with Cardinal Ratzinger*.

which is immolated on the Cross (since the divine nature as such cannot suffer); the sacrifice is infinitely pleasing because the human nature is hypostatically united to the Son of God, so that, as the Liturgy of St. John Chrysostom expresses it: "It is You who offer and are offered, You who receive and are Yourself received, O Christ our God."

3. It is also true to say that the sacrifice is offered *to the Father, through the Son, in the Holy Spirit*; and other formulae express other true aspects of the mystery. As Bertrand de Margerie explains: "In conformity to the two equally legitimate patterns of Christian prayer, the pre-Arian and post-Arian, the Mass can be seen as a sacrifice offered to the Father by the Son in the Holy Spirit or as a sacrifice offered to the Father, to the Son, and to the Spirit."[7] The Roman Canon—so ancient that it antedates the Arian controversy itself—is addressed *to* the Father *through* the Son ("Te igitur, clementissime Pater, per Iesum Christum Filium tuum, supplices rogamus, ac petimus"); the oblation is offered to the Father on behalf of the salvation of the world, with Christ as the Mediator between God and man. Pope Pius XII in *Mystici Corporis* §90 says that this is a reasonable way of praying, given the mystery of the redemption and the role in it of Christ as Mediator and High Priest.

4. Jesus Christ is, however, *true God*, the natural (not adopted) Son of God; the Catholic faith is unwavering in its confession of his eternal divinity, against every form of Arianism that has seduced the minds of men. This means that in all his actions and sufferings—no matter how human or creaturely, even those that are incompatible with the divine nature—it is always the second divine Person who is the *subject* of the acts and sufferings. This is what gives them their infinite worth and power for man's salvation.

5. Given the above points, it is clear that if an Arian were in charge of liturgy, he would wish to get rid of, or decentralize, or at

---

7. *La Trinité chrétienne dans l'histoire* (Paris: Éditions Beauchesne, 1975), 451. The pre-Arian form is referred to as a "subordinating doxology" while the post-Arian (and anti-Arian) form is referred to as a "coordinating doxology." Both forms were defended by the Church Fathers such as St. Basil the Great, but it was the former in particular whose orthodoxy had to be proved and guarded against subordinationism.

least obscure, the confession of Trinitarian equality and majesty (cf. the Preface of the Most Holy Trinity, "Qui cum Unigenito Filio tuo"), and by the same token demote Christ to a sub-divine place—as the one, namely, *through whom* the sacrifice of praise is offered to the Father-God. The Arian would understand "*per* Christum" as an implicit denial of the divinity of Christ. While he would be quite mistaken to think that this is the only meaning the formula can have, or even its proper first-level meaning, he would certainly have lent an Arian coloring to the liturgy if he had simultaneously stripped away unambiguous prayers to the Trinity of Persons as well as prayers directed to Jesus Christ as God.

Consider then the classical Roman liturgy.

In Regard to the Blessed Trinity:

1. A solemn prayer is addressed to the Blessed Trinity both at the conclusion of the offertory and after the postcommunion—to give, as it were, the proper theological setting, the first beginning and last end, of the Eucharistic sacrifice: "Suscipe, Sancta Trinitas" and "Placeat tibi, Sancta Trinitas." These prayers use the *per Christum* conclusion, emphasizing that the sacrifice is offered by Christ in his human nature to the one divine nature, Father, Son, and Holy Spirit.

2. The Preface of the Most Holy Trinity, appointed for all the Sundays after Epiphany and after Pentecost, of which there can be as many as 28, is essentially a summary of the Athanasian Creed, "Quicumque vult," which is itself one of the greatest Trinitarian confessions in the entire Latin tradition.[8]

3. The Gloria expresses, with magnificent beauty, the Catholic confession of the Trinity of Persons in one divine essence. Used in the celebration of every third-class feast (or higher) of a saint or

8. The practice of using this Preface for the Sunday Masses after Epiphany and Pentecost was introduced by Pope Clement XIII in 1759; prior to this, the Common Preface was used. Thus, we are looking at a rather "late" development in the history of the Roman liturgy—an excellent example of the rite's *organic* development, which witnesses gradual enhancements and occasionally prunings (as when many Sequences were no longer included in the 1570 missal), but not sudden and radical alterations in fundamental structure, content, or ethos.

mystery in the life of Christ, the Gloria provides the Church militant a way to participate in the heavenly joy of the communion of saints. In practice, given the large number of third-class feasts (and higher), a daily communicant will often hear the Gloria, even several times a week.

4. The "Gloria Patri *et* Filio *et* Spiritui Sancto" is used three times—after Psalm 42, after the Introit verse, and after Psalm 25—counterbalancing the dominant "per Christum." At the principal Sunday Mass, an additional Gloria Patri would be sung after the verse at the Asperges.

5. The sign of the cross—"In nomine Patris, *et* Filii, *et* Spiritus Sancti," which mirrors the Gloria Patri—is made by *priest and congregation* at many significant moments: at the very beginning, before Psalm 42; at "Adjutorium nostrum in nomine Domini"; at "Indulgentiam"; at "Cum Sancto Spiritu, in gloria Dei Patris"; at "Et vitam venturi saeculi"; at "Benedictus qui venit in nomine Domini"; and at the final blessing.

6. The act of the priest's blessing this or that item with the sign of the cross is frequent throughout the liturgy, occurring dozens of times. For one who is awake and attentive to symbolism, each act of blessing is a visible witness to the power of the cross and a silent invocation of the Trinity.

In Regard to the Divinity of Christ:

7. Confessing the true divinity of Jesus, the Church in her ancient liturgy also prays *to* him, most explicitly in:

   a. the "Christe eleison" of the Kyrie;

   b. the Gloria ("Domine Deus, Rex caelestis, Deus Pater omnipotens. Domine Fili unigenite, Jesu Christe, Domine Deus, Agnus Dei, Filius Patris"; "Tu solus sanctus, tu solus Dominus, tu solus Altissimus, Jesu Christe");

   c. the Agnus Dei;

   d. the three prayers immediately following the Agnus Dei ("Domine Jesu Christe, qui dixisti Apostolis tuis"; "Domine Jesu Christe, Fili Dei vivi"; "Perceptio Corporis tui, Domine Jesu Christe"). [It is worthy of note that, while the conclusion "per Jesus Christum" is used throughout the liturgy, in these three prayers before communion, a shift occurs, as the priest directly addresses the Lord present upon the altar: "Domine Jesu Christe . . . qui vivis et regnas Deus" for the first; "Domine Jesu Christe, Fili Dei vivi . . . qui cum eodem Deo Patre et Spiritu Sancto vivis et regnas Deus" for the second and third];

e. the second prayer of ablution ("Corpus tuum, Domine, quod sumpsi").

8. Moreover, there are times when the Church prays expressly to Christ in the collects and other *orationes* of the traditional Roman rite. Some examples, just from the month of October:

a. Collect for St. Thérèse (Oct. 3): "O Lord, who hast said: Unless ye become as little children ye shall not enter into the kingdom of heaven: grant us, we beseech Thee. . . ."

b. Postcommunion for St. John Leonardi (Oct. 9): "Comforted by the sacred mysteries of Thy precious Body and Blood, we pray Thee, O Lord. . . ."

c. Collect for St. Francis Borgia (Oct. 10): "O Lord Jesus Christ, who art both the pattern and the reward of true humility. . . ."

d. Collect for St. Margaret Mary Alacoque (Oct. 17): "O Lord Jesus Christ, who didst in a wondrous manner reveal to the blessed virgin Margaret the unsearchable riches of Thy Heart. . . ."

e. Postcommunion for St. John Cantius (Oct. 20): "We who have been fed with the delights of Thy precious Body and Blood humbly beg Thy mercy, O Lord. . . ."

9. Finally, nearly every Mass concludes with the Prologue of the Gospel of St. John: "In principio erat Verbum, et Verbum erat apud Deum, et *Deus erat Verbum.* . . ."

In addition, one should attend to the dimension of the ceremonial, because, however justifiably we place an emphasis on liturgical *texts* in order to assess their orthodoxy or their tendencies (as I am doing here), we must not become rationalists who think that texts are the only relevant thing to look at. We are *men*, people of flesh and blood, who perceive and respond not only to words, but also to symbolic gestures, which constitute an even more basic human language that cuts across times and cultures. Thus, in the classical

Roman liturgy, the *stipulated* bowing of the head at the mention of the Holy Name of Jesus, the genuflections before the tabernacle (assumed to be in the center, at the high altar, facing eastwards[9]), the bowing at the "Gloria Patri" and the "Suscipe, sancta Trinitas," the many other bows and genuflections, and so forth—all of these gestures are profoundly theological, conveying in sacred silence a deep Trinitarian and Christocentric meaning; all of them constitute small but true *acts of worship and praise*. When such gestures were radically stripped away in the name of simplification and greater "transparency," the moving musicality of the Mass as an ascending hymn of praise to the Trinity was gravely damaged. It became flattened out and socialized, taken over by a wearisome wordiness that has to *explain* everything from start to finish, usually with a goodly dose of ad libbing. As Pope Benedict XVI has excellently said:

> In our form of the liturgy [i.e., the Novus Ordo] there is a tendency that, in my opinion, is false, namely, the complete "inculturation" of the liturgy into the contemporary world. The liturgy is thus supposed to be shortened; and everything that is supposedly unintelligible should be removed from it; it should, basically, be transposed down to an even "flatter" language. But this is a thoroughgoing misunderstanding of the essence of the liturgy and of liturgical celebration. For in the liturgy one doesn't grasp what's going on in a simply rational way, as I understand a lecture, for example, but in a manifold way, with all the senses, and by being drawn into a celebration that isn't invented by some commission but that, as it were, comes to me from the depths of the millennia and, ultimately, of eternity.[10]

---

9. I am aware that the placement of the tabernacle at the high altar is a relatively late development in the history of church architecture, but unlike the liturgical revolutionaries, I concur with Pope Pius XII's teaching in *Mediator Dei* that the Holy Spirit guides the Church into the fullness of liturgical truth, and that later developments, provided they are in continuity with (one might say, extrapolated from) the Tradition that has come before, are therefore not to be scorned or disapproved of. To *remove* the tabernacle from the center once it has become normal, in contrast, is a theological demotion or deprivation that is quite unlike the mere lack of this norm in earlier times.

10. *Salt of the Earth*, trans. Adrian Walker (San Francisco: Ignatius Press, 1997), 175.

Now, while it is impossible *a priori* for a Catholic to maintain that the new Missal as promulgated by Paul VI or John Paul II is actually (that is, formally) Arian or semi-Arian, one may legitimately ask about the private motives and opinions which led to the following changes.

In Regard to the Blessed Trinity:

1. *Both* the prayer of offering to the Trinity ("Suscipe, Sancta Trinitas") *and* the prayer of homage to the Trinity ("Placeat tibi, Sancta Trinitas") were abolished.

2. The Preface of the Most Holy Trinity is heard extremely rarely in Novus Ordo liturgies; according to the rubrics it is required only for Trinity Sunday itself. As a result, most Catholics will not be formed in any sustained way by the rich dogmatic teaching of this Preface, which demands to be heard many times before one can begin to grasp what it is saying.

3. The recitation of the Gloria has been severely curtailed to Sundays and major feast days.

4. All iterations of the "Gloria Patri" have been abolished from the Mass.[11]

5. The use of the sign of the cross has been reduced to the start of the liturgy and its conclusion.

6. In like manner, the use of the sign of the cross in priestly blessings of objects involved in the liturgy has dwindled to almost nothing.

In Regard to the Divinity of Christ:

7. The prayers addressed *to* Christ have been lessened:

    a. The "Christe eleison" remains, but reduced to a twofold instead of threefold petition[12] (thus destroying its eloquent 3 x 3 Trinitarian structure).

---

11. The Gloria Patri managed to survive in the Liturgy of the Hours.

12. If one is lucky, one might hear a schola sing a threefold Kyrie, since the Ordinaries that require, for musical reasons, a threefold Kyrie remain in the Solesmes books; but singing at that level is rather rarely heard in Novus Ordo parish settings.

b. The Gloria, as pointed out, is no longer frequent.

c. The "Agnus Dei" remains, but the prayers following it have been severely deformed. The missal now instructs the priest to *choose* between the second and third preparatory prayers—he is not to say both. Moreover, the Trinitarian conclusions of these latter prayers have been stripped away.

d. The prayers of ablution are abolished, and the rubrics for cleansing the vessels are less detailed and exacting.[13] In many parishes, the sacred vessels are not even cleansed until after Mass; they are left on a tray that is carried out after Mass into the sacristy. Scenarios like this (or worse) are quite common, and show a massive decline in reverence toward the "divine, holy, most pure, immortal, heavenly and life-creating, awesome mysteries of Christ," as the Divine Liturgy of St. John Chrysostom describes the Eucharist.

8. The Novus Ordo missal appears to have *systematically* abolished prayers addressed to Jesus Christ. Virtually none of these old collects, secrets, or postcommunions remain. In their place are prayers that address "God," "Lord," or "Father" and end with the *per Christum* formula. A notable and welcome exception comes on the occasion of the Solemnity of the Most Holy Body and Blood of Christ, where the collect and postcommunion directly address the Second Person of the Blessed Trinity. In this instance, the redactors of the new missal simply carried over the prayers of the old missal.

9. Last but not least, the customary Last Gospel was dismissed as a medieval accretion, a private pious exercise. As a consequence, the only time a Catholic will hear the sublime Prologue of St. John's Gospel is if he attends the Mass of Christmas Day or the Feast of St. John on December 27th.

---

13. This lends strongly, of course, to the Protestant view that Christ comes to be present in the symbolic action of "breaking and sharing the bread and cup"; once the distribution is over, the bread and wine may be treated as ordinary food, since they are no longer serving a sacramental *function*. So, the priest can leave the vessels on the side table and cleanse them afterwards. This happens to be the Byzantine custom, but in that case it is accompanied by many prayers and much reverence, and is *never* done by laymen.

More could be said, but the above is sufficient for the purpose of documenting the tendency or appearance I have in mind.[14]

Now, what was it that Pope Pius XII had taught in his great encyclical *Mystici Corporis* of 1943? In §90 we read:

> Finally there are those [partisans of the liturgical movement] who assert that our prayers should be directed not to the person of Jesus Christ but rather to God, or to the Eternal Father through Christ, since our Savior as Head of his Mystical Body is only "Mediator of God and men" (1 Tim 2:5). But this certainly is opposed not only to the mind of the Church and to Christian usage but to truth. For, to speak exactly, Christ is Head of the universal Church as he exists at once in both his natures (cf. St. Thomas, *De Veritate*, q. 29, a. 4); moreover he himself has solemnly declared: "If you shall ask me anything in my name, that I will do" (Jn 14:14). For although prayers are very often directed to the Eternal Father through the only-begotten Son, especially in the Eucharistic Sacrifice—in which Christ, at once Priest and Victim, exercises in a special manner the office of Mediator—nevertheless not infrequently even in this Sacrifice prayers are addressed to the Divine Redeemer also; for all Christians must clearly know and understand that the man Jesus Christ is also the Son of God and God himself. And thus when the Church militant offers her adoration and prayers to the Immaculate Lamb, the Sacred Victim, her voice seems to re-echo the never-ending chorus of the Church triumphant: "To him that sitteth on the throne and to the Lamb benediction and honor and glory and power for ever and ever." (Rev 5:13)

As happened also with the same Pope's unambiguous directives in *Mediator Dei* (1947) about many other aspects of the liturgy, the teaching contained in the above section seems to have been not

---

14. There is some consolation to be found in the fact that the new Liturgy of Hours, especially in its official Latin text, contains numerous invocations of Jesus and a fair number of prayers addressed to him. One could more successfully exhibit the Church's faith from these books than from the Missal. This in itself shows the magnitude of the problem: however important the Liturgy of the Hours is (and surely it is important in the lives of thousands of religious, not to mention a fair number of lay people), the Mass is the central act of worship of the Mystical Body of Christ, and perhaps not even 1% of the Christian faithful today will be shaped by the Liturgy of the Hours.

only forgotten, but actively opposed, in the actual execution of the "reforms" that the Fathers of the Second Vatican Council demanded —surely, for the most part having Pius XII's understanding in their minds.

Traditionalist authors have, of course, documented the many different ways in which the Roman Rite was deliberately and systematically watered down, as regards, for example, devotion to the Virgin Mary and to the angels and saints, to the Passion of our Lord, to the Real Presence, and so on.[15] My argument here adds one more confirmation that we are looking at not simply a downplaying of this or that incidental aspect, but more disturbingly, a dechristianization of the liturgy as such, removing from it what is theologically most distinctive of the Christian faith and most central to our corporate worship. What was intended to replace this substance? Man himself, modern man, communal man, the worker, the actor, the self-discovering and self-exulting ego—not the Christian humanism of *Gaudium et Spes* but the Enlightenment humanism of an endless catalogue of unbelievers from Descartes and Newton (who professed himself an Arian[16]) to Kant, Rousseau, Nietzsche, Derrida, and so on. The anthropological correlative to Arianism is Pelagianism. Just as Jesus, for the Arian, is elevated to divinity through his heroic acts, so we, by *our* heroic acts, elevate ourselves to a position of divinity. So false a view is this that it has led not to Christian victory in a renewed evangelization, but to the banality and sterility of what Robert Barron aptly calls "beige Catholicism."

I would go further and point out that the two heresies most "natural" to fallen man are precisely Arianism and Pelagianism. Leave a Christian community to its own devices and you are likely to end up with some kind of Pelagian and Arian understanding of the faith. And one can see the close link between these two: Pelagius teaches that man (the son of Adam) is really a god, whereas Arius

---

15. The prominent place of angels in the old rite of Mass and the diminishment of their presence in the new rite is discussed in my article "A Brief Introduction to Angels," *The Latin Mass* vol. 16, n. 2 (Spring 2007): 34–39.

16. See Maurice F. Wiles, *Archetypal Heresy: Arianism through the Centuries* (Oxford: Clarendon Press; New York: Oxford University Press, 1996), especially ch. 4, "The Rise and Fall of British Arianism."

teaches that god (the Son of God) is really a man. In a certain way, if you combine these heresies you end up with Feuerbach. Fallen man is Pelagian man—Promethean, Cartesian, Baconian man. Fallen man is Arian man: the mystery of Christ is too much for us, we try to downplay it, qualify it, let it slip away into a vague spiritualism, or revert to a more primitive Jewish monotheism. The spiritual life of the Church, as expressed supremely in her liturgy, has always fought against these tendencies. The missal of Paul VI removes huge segments of anti-Arian and anti-Pelagian content.[17] Is this not a cause for the deepest concern—indeed, for the deepest doubts about the "reform" and the new missal it launched against unsuspecting believers?

Moreover, is it not true that the more reverence one has toward Christ, true God and true man, Judge of the living and of the dead, the less one will want to tamper with the Mass in which he is not only worshiped but over which he himself presides as High Priest, in which he himself is offered up as victim, and received as our spiritual food? And is it not true that only a person of Pelagian tendencies would think he could or should be "pro-active" with regard to the liturgy—changing it, reworking it, simplifying here, adding there, as if the responsibility for making it or making it better lay principally with *us*, and not with Christ, the Apostles, and the slow process of time in which the centuries add jewels to a common inheritance jealously guarded? "Jesus Christ is the same yesterday and today and forever. Do not be led away by diverse and strange teachings" (Heb 13:8–9a).

---

17. See Cekada, *Work of Human Hands*, esp. 219–45.

93

7

The Five Wounds
and the Church of the Future

WHEN I READ Bishop Athanasius Schneider's stirring address on the five wounds to the Mystical Body that have been inflicted in the era of the liturgical reform, I realized that I had never seen a more powerful presentation of the very essence of the crisis we are facing. He writes:

> There are a certain number of concrete aspects of the currently prevailing liturgical practice in the ordinary rite that represent a veritable rupture with a constant and millennium-old liturgical practice. By this I mean the five liturgical practices I shall mention shortly; they may be termed the five wounds of the liturgical mystical body of Christ. These are wounds, for they amount to a violent break with the past since they deemphasize the sacrificial character (which is actually the central and essential character of the Mass) and put forward the notion of banquet. All of this diminishes the exterior signs of divine adoration, for it brings out the heavenly and eternal dimension of the mystery to a far lesser degree.[1]

In Bishop Schneider's words, the five "wounds" are, first, "the celebration of the sacrifice of the Mass in which the priest celebrates with his face turned towards the faithful, especially during the Eucharistic prayer and the consecration, the highest and most sacred moment of the worship that is God's due"; second, "com-

---

1. The text of Bishop Schneider's address, "The Extraordinary Form and the New Evangelization," may be found at www.paixliturgique.org.uk/aff_lettre.asp?LET_N_ID=863; it was also published in *The Latin Mass,* vol. 21, n. 2 (Summer 2012): 6–10.

munion in the hand"; third, "the new Offertory prayers"; fourth, "the total disappearance of Latin in the huge majority of Eucharistic celebrations in the Ordinary Form in all Catholic countries"; fifth, "the exercise of the liturgical services of lector and acolyte by women as well as the exercise of these same services in lay clothing while entering into the choir during Holy Mass directly from the space reserved to the faithful." If then-Cardinal Ratzinger was correct in his assessment that "the crisis in the Church that we are experiencing today is to a large extent due to the disintegration of the liturgy,"[2] Bishop Schneider, it seemed to me, had succinctly diagnosed the life-threatening disease and, in turn, identified the cure with luminous clarity: an unabashed, unequivocal return to Sacred Tradition.[3]

As I pondered Bishop Schneider's address, a mnemonic device occurred to me for summing up the five wounds he identifies: (1) Closed Circle; (2) Proud Posture; (3) Obliterated Offertory; (4) Lapsed Language; (5) Malleable Ministries. The last gave some trouble, as Schneider is packing several things into that category. One could also say "Meandering Ministries" because of people sauntering up from the congregation, or "Mixed Ministries" because of the novel involvement of women in roles that are traditionally and rightly connected with the all-male priesthood.

This chapter will reflect on four of the five wounds so well identified by his Excellency, omitting the Obliterated Offertory because I wish to concentrate on problems that originate in habits of bad practice and rubrical violation.[4] The matter at stake in regard to each of these wounds is something far greater than a debate over personal tastes in spirituality or aesthetics. Our Lord Jesus Christ

---

2. *Milestones: Memoirs 1927-1977* (San Francisco: Ignatius Press, 1998), 149.

3. Here is how, according to Vatican Radio, Kurt Cardinal Koch expressed himself at the theological faculty of the University of Freiburg: "Since the crisis of the Church today is above all a crisis of the liturgy, it is necessary to begin the renewal of the Church today with a renewal of the liturgy."

4. The new Offertory rite (or, to be precise, Preparation of the Gifts) is a case of mandated liturgical rupture and discontinuity, and thus far more grave than any mere abuse or violation. For a close comparison of the old Offertory rite with the new Preparation of the Gifts, see Cekada, *Work of Human Hands*, 275–304.

has, and has shared with his Church, but one mission in this world: to save souls for the glory of God, to make men sharers of his divinity and his beatitude. The devil has but one mission of his own: to lure as many souls into sharing his damnation, for misery loves company. Both are thirsty for souls: Jesus because he loves us; Satan because he hates us.

The changes in the liturgy after the Council produced a novel liturgical theory and praxis that introduced toxins of heresy and sacrilege into the blood system of the Catholic world. The more this novel theory conquers minds and the more this novel praxis gains normative status, the less effectively will the liturgy sanctify souls and transform the world for Christ the King. All the changes mentioned by Bishop Schneider show the signature of evil angels vastly more intelligent and powerful than their human allies; all of the changes bring benefit, if we may call it that, to the devil's empire. It can hardly surprise us that Satan is fighting tooth and claw against the reform Pope Benedict XVI set in motion.

Closed Circle

Let us begin with a principle that has always been and must always be unshakeable for Catholics: the principle of continuity with Tradition. This principle has been given consummate expression by Saint John Damascene (d. 749), a Father of the Church who devoted his entire life to its articulation and defense:

> For as what is small is not small, if it produces something big, so the slightest disturbance of the tradition of the Church that has held sway from the beginning is no small matter, that tradition made known to us by our forefathers, whose conduct we should look to and whose faith we should imitate.[5]

In the same work—a defense of holy icons against the iconoclasts— he takes up the same theme more than once: "Nor can one word overthrow a tradition of the whole Church, which stretches from

---

5. St. John Damascene, *Three Treatises on the Divine Images,* trans. Andrew Louth (Crestwood, NY: St. Vladimir's Seminary Press, 2003), 20.

one end of the earth to the other."[6] He cites in support a magnificent text by Saint Basil the Great (d. 379):

> Of the dogmas and preachings preserved in the Church, some we have from the written teaching, others we received from the tradition of the Apostles, handed down to us in secret, both of them having the same force for piety. No one who has the least experience of the laws of the Church will object to these, for if we try to dismiss that which is unwritten among the customs as of no great authority, then without noticing it we shall damage the Gospel.[7]

Saint Basil goes on to mention three examples of the "dogmas and preachings . . . received from the tradition of the Apostles" that are *equal* to the canonical scriptures in their "force for piety": the threefold immersion in baptism; praying facing East; and the "tradition of the mysteries," i.e., the divine liturgy or sacrifice of the Mass itself. We know that the threefold immersion or ablution with water in baptism has never been denied or abandoned; we know that the liturgy of the Eucharist has been celebrated from age to age as a sacred duty never to be compromised for any reason. Basil sees praying eastwards, *ad orientem,* to be exactly equivalent in force, and even argues that "no one who has the *least experience* of the laws of the Church will object to these [practices]" and that rejecting them would "damage the Gospel." Indeed, Basil chose these three examples because he wanted to invoke practices already totally familiar to his readers and not subject to quibbling.

Saint Basil the Great and Saint John Damascene are only two of the cloud of witnesses to the universal Christian custom of praying facing the East, from antiquity onwards.[8] Of the many more one could cite, Saint Germanus, Patriarch of Constantinople from 715 to 730, speaks particularly eloquently about the reasons for the custom:

---

6. Ibid., 39.

7. From St. Basil the Great's treatise *On the Holy Spirit,* quoted by St. John Damascene in *Three Treatises,* 37.

8. The evidence is discussed at length in the finest work to date on the subject, Uwe Michael Lang, *Turning Towards the Lord* (San Francisco: Ignatius Press, 2004); see also the illuminating chapter "The Altar and the Direction of Liturgical Prayer" in Ratzinger, *Spirit of the Liturgy,* 74–84.

Praying toward the East is handed down by the holy apostles, as is everything else. This is because the comprehensible sun of righteousness, Christ our God, appeared on earth in those regions of the East where the perceptible sun rises, as the prophet says: "Orient is his name" (Zech 6:12); and "Bow before the Lord, all the earth, who ascended to the heaven of heavens in the East" (cf. Ps 67:34); and "Let us prostrate ourselves in the place where his feet stood" (cf. Ps 67:34); and again, "The feet of the Lord shall stand upon the Mount of Olives in the East" (Zech 14:4). The prophets also speak thus because of our fervent hope of receiving again the paradise in Eden, as well as the brightness of the second coming of Christ our God, from the East.

Let us go all the way back to the temptation in the Garden of Eden. The serpent was trying to persuade Adam and Eve to think of God as a being on the same playing field, as "one of us," and therefore somehow in competition with us. Traditional Christian liturgies of East and West dramatically emphasize God's transcendence over us and our duty to worship him by offering rational sacrifice with contrite and humble hearts. It was therefore much to the devil's advantage to turn the priest around toward the people, creating a pleasant circle of neighborly affirmation that brought the Mass down to the level of a horizontal exchange, a back-and-forth in everyday speech. Nothing transcendent about that; on the contrary, God is domesticated—not a receiver of sacrifice but a subject of conversation. The use of the vernacular obviously contributes to this phenomenon as well, a topic I will take up later.

Pope Benedict XVI has written eloquently about *ad orientem* worship and has celebrated the Mass eastwards as Pope.[9] Here is how Ratzinger the theologian encapsulates the problem with our current situation:

---

9. The unusual orientation of Saint Peter's Basilica misled scholars in the last century to hypothesize that Saint Peter's reflected an older tradition of Mass facing the people—an argument now thoroughly discredited. For an account of this perplexing situation and how scholars were accustomed to mentioning Saint Peter's layout as justification for redesigning churches and sanctuaries, see the two books mentioned in the preceding note.

The turning of the priest towards the people has turned the community into a self-enclosed circle. In its outward form, it no longer opens out on what lies ahead and above, but is closed in on itself. The common turning towards the East was not a "celebration towards the wall"; it did not mean that the priest "had his back to the people": the priest himself was not regarded as so important. For just as the congregation in the synagogue looked together towards Jerusalem, so in the Christian liturgy the congregation looked together "towards the Lord." As one of the Fathers of Vatican II's Constitution on the Liturgy, J.A. Jungmann, put it, it was much more a question of priest and people facing in the same direction, knowing that together they were in a procession towards the Lord. They did not close themselves into a circle, they did not gaze at one another, but as the pilgrim People of God they set off for the *Oriens*, for the Christ who comes to meet us.[10]

Restoring for the entire People of God the hitherto unbroken apostolic tradition of worshiping eastwards is not a mere pious desideratum; it is an absolute necessity for healing the subtle narcissism that has crept into the very temple of God, the Western humanism that has pulled rank on the Orient. In the words of Fr. John Zuhlsdorf: "*Ad orientem* worship is one of the most important re-reforms [i.e., returns] we can implement because the turning around of altars after Vatican II was perhaps the single most damaging change to Catholic identity that was forced on the Church."[11]

Proud Posture

The practice of layfolk receiving communion in the hand while standing[12] is, once again, a disruptive novelty, introduced by ecclesiastical authorities who sought to overthrow a longstanding, unchal-

---

10. *Spirit of the Liturgy,* 80.

11. wdtprs.com/blog/2008/04/update-turning-the-altar-around-in-greenville-sc-its-time/, accessed June 20, 2013.

12. I would not maintain that standing can never be a legitimate posture for receiving communion. In the Byzantine tradition it has always been customary to stand throughout the entire liturgy, including the consecration. However, the Eastern Christian layman, while standing, receives the Sacrament directly into the mouth, tilting his head back, *never* handling the consecrated species, and a napkin

lenged, and wise discipline.[13] In his demented way of thinking, Satan derives particular pleasure from seeing the Eucharist profaned and desecrated. This happens in two ways: through negligence, as when people carelessly drop fragments of the host or spill the precious Blood; through contempt and blasphemy, as when people receive "without discerning the Body and Blood" and so "eat and drink condemnation" to themselves, as Saint Paul says (1 Cor 11:29), or when they deliberately carry away hosts in order to destroy them, use them in Satanic worship, or sell them online.

Reports of sacrilege increase every day. The most notable incident I have heard of was the religion-hating professor who posted on YouTube videos of him violently disposing of hosts he had carried away from Masses. In one video he drove a nail through the host before throwing it away; in another, he flushed a host down the toilet. It seems hard to believe that he bought himself unconsecrated hosts and merely pretended to do all this. It is far more likely that he was, in fact, collecting hosts at Masses, because there is rarely any vigilance when it comes to who receives, who doesn't, and what happens to hosts. All of this, including thousands of carelessly lost fragments of consecrated hosts, has been made possible by that most foolish, most nearsighted of all decisions—to allow communion in the hand.

When we ponder the awesome mystery that the Eucharist is really, truly, substantially *Our Lord Jesus Christ,* in his body, blood, soul, and divinity, the above-mentioned facts should cause us immense pain, anguish, sadness, and anger. Now, it is important to see that our Lord himself is beyond suffering; he is not directly

---

is held below his mouth to guard against profanation of the Sacrament. Besides, the overall ethos of the Divine Liturgy is so pronouncedly sacred that there is absolutely no way to see this mode of reception as "casual."

13. See the masterful treatment of the question by Bishop Schneider himself, *Dominus Est—It is the Lord: Reflections of a Bishop of Central Asia on Holy Communion,* trans. Nicholas L. Gregoris (Pine Beach, NJ: Newman House Press, 2008), as well as the thorough treatment by Most Rev. Juan Rodolfo Laise, *Communion in the Hand: Documents and History* (Boonville, NY: Preserving Christian Publications, 2011).

harmed when the Blessed Sacrament is harmed. He is present in the sacrament as the *Risen* Christ seated at the right hand of the Father; after the resurrection he cannot suffer or die, but lives in the glory of immortality, bestowing immortality on all souls that receive him worthily, and, sooner or later, on their bodies as well. The person who is harmed by desecration is the *desecrator*—and this shows us why Satan so delights in the vastly increased incidences of desecration (including Black Masses) and, in general, of unworthy, inattentive, casual, or altogether indifferent receptions of communion. Those who perform such acts are committing the sin of Judas, the crime of betraying that which deserves our utmost fidelity, the crime of hating that which most deserves our love, the crime of holding in contempt that which deserves our profound adoration on bended knee. At best, it is treating the Savior of the world as if he were a morsel of common food, to be handled as we please; at worst, it is spitting in his very face, a rejection of the salvation he and he alone can bring to us, and therefore also a rejection of the Father who sent Him. In all these ways, the devil is eager to see the host treated carelessly, disrespectfully, or blasphemously, for these are steps along the same continuum.

Dangers of sacrilege aside, there is a more basic question of *reverence*. The priest's hands are specially consecrated with holy oil— why? So that he may rightly and fittingly handle the Blessed Sacrament; that he may handle *God Incarnate*. His hands are sanctified in view of touching and administering the holy gifts. A layman's hands are not consecrated in this way. We *receive* the Blessed Sacrament from the hands of the priest, like a baby bird being fed in the nest by its parent. From this symbolic vantage, it is utterly inappropriate that the priest put the host into *our* hands, so that we may then administer communion *to ourselves*, symbolizing that we owe our nourishment to our own action, as dutiful democratic Pelagians would have it. Such a gesture says: "I'm grown up and can feed myself, thank you very much, and my hands are just as good as the priest's." This, as we know, is false; the priest is a man set apart by Holy Orders, and his hands, too, like the rest of his powers of body and soul, are dedicated to sacred service. Communion in the hand, therefore, helps create and support that noxious atmosphere of egalitarianism, horizontalism, and activism that has stifled the Church's spiritual life in the past half-century.

In addition to the proper *manner* of receiving the Lord, we must also consider the proper *posture*. In his commentary on the Epistle to the Ephesians, St. Thomas Aquinas has this to say about the significance of kneeling:

> Humility makes a prayer worthy of being heard: "He hath had regard to the prayer of the humble: and he hath not despised their petition" (Ps 101:18). And, "The prayer of him that humbleth himself shall pierce the clouds: and till it come nigh he will not be comforted" (Sir 35:21). Therefore, he immediately starts his prayer in humility, saying *For this cause,* that you fail not in the faith, *I bow my knees to the Father.* This is a symbol of humility for two reasons. First, a man belittles himself, in a certain way, when he genuflects, and he subjects himself to the one he genuflects before. In such a way he recognizes his own weakness and insignificance. Secondly, physical strength is present in the knees; in bending them a man confesses openly to his lack of strength. Thus external, physical symbols are shown to God for the purpose of renewing and spiritually training the inner soul. In the prayer of Manasse: "I bend the knee of my heart. . . ." "For every knee shall be bowed to me: and every tongue shall swear."(Is 45:24)[14]

Are we among those who bend the knee before God, or those who remain standing? Will our posture when we come before the Sovereign Lord of heaven and earth be one of proud control and self-sufficiency, or one of humble submission and intense adoration?

Lapsed Language

Latin is the language proper to the Roman Rite, the fertile human soil in which a luxuriant garden of liturgical prayers, readings, and hymns grew up; it is the "catholic" language of Christendom, rising above all nations, peoples, cultures, and ages. For a variety of historical reasons, Latin became, and was always retained as, the vehicle of formal, public worship in all the particular churches gathered around the Throne of Peter in the Western part of the quondam

---

14. *Super Epistolam B. Pauli ad Ephesios Lectura,* cap. 3, lec. 4, n. 166.

Roman Empire. Its antiquity and breadth of use, clarity and stability of meaning, and subtle beauty of expression imbue Latin with all the qualities requisite for a public *cultus* that is ever ancient, ever new, noble and solemn, utterly free from the vagaries of worldly fashion. All these qualities render Latin a precious treasure of which all Latin Rite Catholics should be justly proud—a familiar, one might even say maternal, presence for the faithful everywhere in the world, yet accompanied withal by a sacred aura and majesty that demand reverence.

Far from strengthening the hold and influence of liturgy on the lives of Catholics, the sudden vernacularization of the liturgy, bringing with it the illusion of easy understanding and passivity, has made it far more difficult for people to achieve a sustained interior awareness of the depth, magnitude, seriousness, and urgency of the action in which they are engaged. The priest's facing the people, even for the moment of the divine sacrifice, has, together with the use of the vernacular, reinforced the impression of something plain and simple going on—not the awesomeness of a hushed mystery vis-à-vis God. While a priest's capable reading or singing of liturgical texts can make a big difference in this regard, it is still the case that the Ordinary Form is top-heavily verbal, didactic, and linear in a way that is strangely foreign to the liturgical Tradition as a whole, Eastern or Western, and it is no less certain that the use of the vernacular has greatly contributed to the obvious loss of sacrality and common Catholic identity across the globe.[15]

Malleable Ministries

Many Catholics have heard that all the baptized share a common priesthood of the faithful. This is entirely right and orthodox and traditional, coming straight out of sacred scripture, as we read in 1 Peter 2:9: "You are a chosen generation, a kingly priesthood, a holy nation, a purchased people, that you may declare his virtues, who

---

15. For more reflections on language and liturgy, see chapter 1, "Solemnity: The Crux of the Matter," and chapter 12, "Latin, the Ideal Liturgical Language of the West," as well as Uwe Michael Lang, *The Voice of the Church at Prayer: Reflections on Liturgy and Language* (San Francisco: Ignatius Press, 2012).

hath called you out of darkness into his marvellous light."[16] We find the priesthood of the faithful amply proclaimed by the Fathers of the Church and expounded upon by St. Thomas Aquinas in his sublime writings. What saddens me, however, is how poorly some Catholics understand this magnificent truth. There are few topics more urgent for priests to preach about than this one, because it touches on the fundamental meaning of the Christian life: to be a priestly victim in union with Jesus for the salvation of one's soul and the souls of others. If a layman cannot explain why being conformed to Christ as priest, prophet, and king in virtue of his baptism is the single most important thing in his life, then he doesn't know even the basics of his faith, the ABC's of his catechism. For in this mystery of baptismal conformity lies the whole secret of the Christian hope in the promises of the Gospel.

First, to be a priest in the universal (baptismal) sense is to have died and risen with Christ Jesus, the Eternal High Priest. We are thus made Christ's; we die to sin and rise to new life. Our participation in the resurrection comes about in this way and only in this way.

Second, our sufferings are made fruitful by the Cross of Christ. The *only* way suffering can be redeemed and become redemptive is by this sharing in Christ's priesthood. Otherwise, suffering is, so to speak, "wasted." And is this not, together with death, one of the deepest questions fallen man has? "Why suffering? Why evil in the world? Why sickness, old age, and finally death?" Apart from Christ, there is no answer; and apart from Christ, there *is* no point, no

---

16. Douay-Rheims translation. This teaching is rooted in the Old Testament, where we hear God say to Israel: "You shall be to me a kingdom of priests and a holy nation" (Ex 19:6). Nevertheless, Israel had a similar distinction between the layman and the ministerial priest: the layman brings his sacrifice, which is truly *his,* but there is a limit to what he can do; another must actually offer it for him. How great is our dignity as Christians, that we can approach the Holy Place, the very edge of the sanctuary, in a way that no Israelite apart from the priest could ever dream of doing! The greatness of approaching the altar to receive our Lord himself is actually diminished when people downplay the sublime dignity of the ministerial priest and the special area of the sanctuary, the Holy of Holies. Our true dignity is seen in the very fact that we can be present where this sacrifice takes place and can receive its supernatural fruits.

fruit, for us. Because of our share in Christ's priesthood, we are able to die in union with him so as to enter into eternal life. Our death changes from being a curse to being a grace, a blessing, a gateway. It remains a curse for nature, but the curse is transformed into an occasion of final sanctification, and so, of salvation.

Third, by being united with the Head of the Mystical Body, we are made partakers of one another's triumphs and sufferings: we share in the communion of saints. We profit from all the good works and merits of all the members of the Mystical Body. Here is how the Angelic Doctor expresses this wondrous truth:

> Not only is the strength of the Passion of Christ communicated to us [through the Sacraments], but also the merit of the life of Christ; and whatever good all the saints accomplished is communicated to those who live in charity, because all of us are one .... Thus it is that whoever lives in charity participates in all the good that is done in the whole world.[17]

Nothing is inherently more important, more weighty and decisive, than the sacramental character received in baptism, with its eternal consequences for good—or for ill, if the vows that bind us to our merciful Savior are found to be broken at the point of death. Not even the *priest's* special sacramental character, as necessary as it is for the common good of the Church and as crucial a role as it plays in his spiritual life, is as decisive for his final destiny, since he will be saved or condemned *as a Christian,* that is, based on how he personally lives the life of faith, hope, and charity infused into his soul at baptism. Put differently, nothing that a Christian can ever do or become will equal, in supernatural dignity, the gift of divinization and conformity to Christ he received at the baptismal font. We can see, then, how tragically mistaken are the desires and efforts of lay people to perform the functions that more properly belong to the clergy, as if doing so were somehow a greater, more important exercise of their baptismal priesthood than receiving the sacraments

---

17. *The Sermon-Conferences of St. Thomas Aquinas on the Apostles' Creed,* trans. Nicholas Ayo (Notre Dame: University of Notre Dame Press, 1988), 138–39; translation modified in light of the Latin.

devoutly, striving to live a holy Christian life, and converting the world outside the church doors.

There is a fine passage on the priesthood of the faithful in Fr. Antonio Rosmini, who, on this matter, nobly voices the traditional view:

> With regard to liturgical power, the faithful as such do not possess the faculty of *immolating* the victim of the New Testament through the consecration of bread and wine, but they have the faculty of *offering* that victim to the eternal Father. In addition, they have the faculty of immolating *themselves* by their union in spirit with the victim of propitiation for the world's salvation. The Christian's self-immolation comes about through his sacrificial love, which keeps him constantly prepared to undergo actual death for the sake of witness to Christ, for justice and the increase of God's kingdom. In the same way all the prayers and actions offered to God by the faithful acquire special efficacy and value through the priestly character with which the faithful are invested by God himself.[18]

As St. Thomas explains, the priesthood of the faithful, which encompasses *all* Christians, has to do with *receiving* divine things; the ministerial priesthood, which is proper to those who have received Holy Orders, has to do with *giving* divine things.[19] Any liturgical ministry that involved bestowing God's sacramental gifts was, therefore, traditionally reserved to the ordained clergy. As we know, there are cases where it is canonically permissible for lay people to exercise some of these functions; but in such cases, it is imperative that the lay people in question be at least *conformable* to the priestly office. This means they should be male and should be

---

18. *The Philosophy of Right,* vol. IV, trans. Denis Cleary and Terence Watson (Durham, UK: Rosmini House Publications, 1995), sec. 3, ch. 3, art. 2, §2, nn. 897–899. For similar language, see Vatican II, *Presbyterorum Ordinis,* §2, 4.

19. *ST* III, q. 63. In a. 3, Aquinas comments that the baptismal character deputes the baptized to a twofold end: eternal life and liturgical worship, wherein they either *receive* or—should they have the character of Order—*bestow* things pertaining to the worship of God. This theology of sacramental character is expounded in the *Roman Catechism* in Part II, ch. 1, ¶5, as well as in *Lumen Gentium,* in the passage quoted elsewhere in this chapter.

properly vested for their functions, because the things they are doing are *priestly in nature*, even if not always reserved to priests. This connection of minister and function is founded, in turn, on a more basic principle: our actions contain and convey meanings; our *ritual* actions communicate *religious* meanings. It is not "all the same" whether a priest or deacon, a layman, or a laywoman distributes the Precious Blood; nor is it all the same whether the one doing so is dressed in ritual vesture, formal but non-clerical clothing, or casual dress; nor is it all the same whether they who carry out liturgical functions are seated in the sanctuary or in the congregation's part of the building. There is an objective language of the body and sexuality, of clothing and office, of architecture and position, that we cannot simply ignore, or worse, manipulate in pursuit of a political agenda.[20] Hence, on those rare occasions when there might be a genuine need for an extraordinary minister of holy communion—I say rare, given that reception under one species is altogether sufficient, and that reception by intinction allows for the distribution of the Body and Blood of Christ without needless lay involvement—the ones called upon to meet this need should be *men* who are appropriately *vested*.

We can see the deeper rationale for distinctions in liturgical roles between the ordained and the non-ordained, as well as between men and women, if we place ourselves at the foot of the Cross with our Lady. The Lord Jesus is doing the priestly act *par excellence,* offering himself in sacrifice, and to this extent he stands over against the Church, represented by the Blessed Virgin Mary. Our Lady does not do what the priest does, nor is it her blood that saves us, or her cross that is our hope—she is not the priest, the victim, and the altar of sacrifice—but we know at the same time that she *is* perfectly offering up her Son in her heart by an interior union of love with him, in a manner so pleasing to God and so meritorious

---

20. For theological arguments in support of this common sense view, see Manfred Hauke, *Women in the Priesthood?: A Systematic Analysis in the Light of the Order of Creation and Redemption* (San Francisco: Ignatius Press, 1988) and Sara Butler, *The Catholic Priesthood and Women: A Guide to the Teaching of the Church* (Chicago: Liturgy Training Publications, 2007).

for sinners that she deserves the unique title Coredemptrix.[21] The Virgin Mary embodies the fundamental vocation of the Christian, the role each of us is called to play in the Church: to hear the Word of God and keep it in our lives by remaining faithful to the one who is our Head. In that sense, *all* of the baptized are both "sons in the Son"—sons adopted by the Father in his only-begotten Son—*and* "brides of Christ," espoused to the soul's divine Bridegroom (cf. 2 Cor 11:2). The ministerial priest, on the other hand, is a member of the baptized who has been called forth to serve God's people by being endowed with the power to act as "another Christ," *alter Christus*, one who can offer sacrifice and bestow divine gifts in the manner of Christ. His distinction of office is at the service of everyone, as the Second Vatican Council teaches:

> Though they differ from one another in essence and not only in degree, the common priesthood of the faithful and the ministerial or hierarchical priesthood are nonetheless interrelated: each of them in its own special way is a participation in the one priesthood of Christ. The ministerial priest, by the sacred power he enjoys, teaches and rules the priestly people; acting in the person of Christ, he makes present the Eucharistic sacrifice, and offers it to God in the name of all the people. But the faithful, in virtue of their royal priesthood, join in the offering of the Eucharist. They likewise exercise that priesthood in receiving the sacraments, in prayer and thanksgiving, in the witness of a holy life, and by self-denial and active charity.[22]

In light of so beautiful and rich a teaching, we may lament that so much of our ancient tradition has been swept away in the tides of egalitarian leveling and feminist ambition, while communities of Catholics, whether from ignorance or indifference or both, lethargically settle into illicit and invalid routines that wear away the foundations of the Faith day by day, year by year. "When the Son of Man comes, shall he find faith on the earth?" (Lk 18:8)—not a faith of

21. In fact, as Saint John Vianney says, Our Lady could look upon her Son on the Cross and truly say: "This is my body, this is my blood," for his body and blood had been derived from her virginal flesh at the moment of the Incarnation.
22. *Lumen Gentium* §10, 2.

our own inventing, but the Faith delivered to the Apostles and handed down by the Church.

Regarding the worst of the persistent abuses, we know that the Vatican has repeatedly asked that the habitual use of extraordinary ministers of Holy Communion be avoided or, where it has become established, discontinued. The disciplinary statements on the subject are consistent, recurrent, and unambiguous.[23] Unfortunately, we see here a phenomenon familiar throughout the past several decades: neither the Vatican nor, with a few exceptions, the episcopacy seems to have an efficacious will to enforce the discipline. Judging from parish customs across the United States, one might be forgiven for never knowing that Rome had said *anything* on the subject, let alone handed down a restrictive judgment. It may be supposed that the fundamental problem is the radical shift toward "creativity" in the liturgy, which, combined with the potent drug of "active participation" wrongly understood, has made any and all liturgical discipline nearly impossible to maintain.

As Bishop Schneider notes, it is the common practice in the Ordinary Form for lay people simply to walk up from the part of the church designated for the congregation and enter into the sanctuary area that is reserved for the celebration of the sacred mysteries. It is as if there is no recognition whatsoever of the differentiation of sacred space, function, meaning, and purpose. There is a kind of profanation of the sanctuary by the obliteration of the distinction between the sacred and the secular, which in turn destroys the symbolic value of the sanctuary as an image of heaven, of the Holy of Holies, of salvation coming from Christ alone. The traditional Roman liturgy, with its sobriety and sanctity, continually reminds us of this truth in the prayer said by the priest as he ascends the altar: "Take away from us our iniquities, we beseech Thee, O Lord,

---

23. See my "Extraordinary Ministers of the Eucharist," *The Catholic Faith* 6.6 (November–December 2000): 34–42, still available online via EWTN. A Vatican instruction that appeared subsequent to this article, *Redemptionis Sacramentum* (2004), issues a clarification that we are *not* to call laypeople "ministers of the Eucharist" but rather "extraordinary ministers of holy communion" (§154); the language in my article from 2000 is therefore inaccurate in this regard.

that we may be worthy to enter with pure minds into the Holy of Holies: through Christ our Lord, Amen."

Tradition is Our Only Future

Quite apart from the battery of theological or historical arguments that can be and have been made against the liturgical "reform," there are always the acutely *practical* arguments. During the 1960s and 70s, cultural anthropologists, psychologists, and sociologists were pointing out, for anyone who would listen, that the demolition of a centuries-old liturgical life was guaranteed to produce cataclysmic consequences.[24] Sudden and significant changes in the manner of approaching the Most Holy Eucharist, for example, would weaken and might even destroy Eucharistic piety and sound belief. They noted that repetition and reiteration are essential elements of pedagogy for all human beings—whether the reiteration in question is the numerous side-altars in a large church, the threefold repetition of the Kyrie and the *Domine, non sum dignus,* or the almost daily use of the Gloria. They were also in a position to observe that modern congregations, full of literate people who can follow the Mass in their missals while hearing the prayers and chants taking place in the church, will end up knowing the liturgy backwards and forwards, because it has seeped into their bones from attentive listening and reading. These observers knew that such things as the burning of incense, the ringing of bells, and the wearing of beautiful vestments did not find their way into the liturgy by accident but were developed out of the very nature of the sacred action, and had long since embedded themselves deeply in the Catholic imagination. Indeed, anyone could have seen that the virtual abolition of Gregorian chant and Latin, or the solemn High Mass with its visible reflection of the Church's hierarchical structure, would have catastrophic effects on the faith and unity of the Church, the solemnity

---

24. Cultural anthropologist Mary Douglas's work on the meaning and conditions of ritual is particularly well known and appreciated in this connection, but one can find similar critical observations in authors as diverse as C.G. Jung, Mircea Eliade, Titus Burckhardt, Dietrich von Hildebrand, Josef Pieper, Evelyn Waugh, Louis Bouyer, Jacques Maritain, Klaus Gamber, and James Hitchcock.

and majesty of divine worship, the noble ideals for which the Latin Rite was once famous.

There was a time, even until fairly recently, when it seemed that a spell of blindness had been cast upon the Church, so few were the Catholics who could *see* these uncomfortable truths, or seeing them, could face them head on and seek remedies. Today, thanks be to God, we are a substantial minority whose number, influence, and activity are growing every day; and yet, too many members of the hierarchy are slow to recognize where the Spirit is blowing—namely, back to the eternal Now of the Church's glorious heritage, and not to the eternal Yesterday of the dingy, dreary, dated liturgical reform of the 1960s and 70s.

In one of his many quotable articles, D. Q. McInerny had this to say about "The Past":

> The second way we can mistreat the past is to pretend that it is something which can be blithely discounted, as having no practical applications to the present. . . . Generally, we must continuously go back to the past in the sense that we must keep in constant touch with it, habitually refer to it, consult it, review it, all for the sake of our own edification and education. . . . Let us say that, with regard to this or that matter, where we presently find ourselves is not where we really should be. Somewhere in the past, distant or proximate, we took a wrong turn, and ended up on a road which led us to a rather bad situation. . . . We would need to retrace our steps, go back to that fork in the road where we took the wrong turn. . . . To continue to follow a road which has brought us to an admittedly bad situation would be only to bring us eventually to even worse situations. . . . There are times in life when the only responsible and rational way we can go forward is by going back, returning to the point where we became disoriented and started going in the wrong direction.

This advice, which fits the present liturgical situation hand in glove, echoes Bishop Schneider's insistence that the only way we will overcome the contemporary crisis in the Catholic Church is by reconnecting with her authentic Magisterium and liturgical Tradition. We made a wrong turn. We need to go back and take the right path—the path of continuity with Tradition.

8

A Rite Histrionic and Disoriented

THE TITLE OF THIS CHAPTER highlights two aspects of the new form of the Mass. The word "histrionic" refers to the Ordinary Form's tendency to place emphasis on the priest as a talker and performer, with ample room allowed for extemporaneous words and free-form bodily posture, in contrast to the Tridentine rite's insistence on the priest as an "animate instrument"[1] who fulfills a definite hieratic function at the altar through his recitation of ecclesiastically determined sacred speech and his careful observance of detailed rubrics fraught with inherited meaning.

The word "disoriented" refers specifically to a Mass turned away from the East and toward the people, thus toward the West. Since, for all the Fathers and Doctors of the Church, the East represents Christ the Daystar who rises into our world and receives our worship,[2] while the West represents the darkness and those who love the dark by fleeing from God's light, this turning of the priest's back to the cosmic symbol of Christ and his second coming and toward the people is code language for anthropocentrism, the worship of man's inner potentiality, and the subordination of the immutable

---

1. St. Thomas, *ST* III, q. 64, a. 8, ad 1.
2. *ST* II-II, q. 84, a. 3, ad 3: "There is a fittingness in adoring eastwards—first, because the divine majesty is indicated in the movement of the heavens which is from the east; second, because paradise was situated in the east according to Gen 2:8 (Septuagint), and so we signify our desire to return to paradise; third, on account of Christ, who is 'the light of the world' (Jn 8:12; 9:5) and is called 'the Orient' (Zech 6:12), who mounts above the heaven of heavens to the east (Ps 67:34) and is expected to come from the east, according to Mt 24:27, 'As lightning cometh out of the east, and appeareth even into the west; so shall also the coming of the Son of Man be.'"

divine source of perfection to the ever-changing human "experiment."[3] St. Thomas quotes St. Augustine: "The East (that is, Christ) calleth thee, and thou turnest to the West (namely, mortal and fallible man)."[4] By contrast, in the words of Diderot, encyclopedist of the Enlightenment, "Man is the single term from which one must begin, and to which all must be brought back."[5]

Research on the new liturgy by such mainstream theologians as Aidan Nichols, Lauren Pristas, and Jonathan Robinson, building on the work of earlier critics like Klaus Gamber, has established the deep and pervasive influence of Enlightenment theory upon the members and fellow-travelers of the Consilium, the team that produced the new liturgical books.[6] It is no surprise that a liturgy set within this Enlightenment context, which at once accentuates the people and invites the priest to become a presider over or president of this republic, cultivates a distinctive celebrity ethos, the aura of the politician who, in modernity, is not so much a moral agent as an amoral actor. The presider or president is the center of attention and must act and react accordingly; he is, more than ever, the man in charge, the holy politico. According to Cardinal Ratzinger, the

3. It may be objected that moderns are so "cosmologically challenged" that they no longer register any of the significance of these things; Ratzinger, in *The Spirit of the Liturgy*, observes that city-dwellers are hardly aware of the rhythms of sun and moon, stars and seasons. True indeed; but actions are symbolic, and liturgical actions doubly so. We cannot effect a 180° change in priestly position (not to mention every other aspect of liturgy) without profoundly altering the subliminal *and* conscious messages transmitted thereby. In reality what occurs is the substitution of a *new* worldview to replace the old, cosmically-rooted one; it is an essentially anthropocentric, technocratic, rationalist worldview, where man ignores not only nature but the God who is the author and redeemer of nature.

4. *ST* II-II, q. 189, a. 10, corp. Elsewhere, in *Contra retrahentes*, St. Thomas cites the passage again: "St. Augustine, in his book *De verbis Domini*, has this passage: 'The Orient calls thee; wilt thou wait for the West?' Now by the Orient is meant Christ, as we know from the words in Zech 6:12, 'Behold a man, the Orient is his name.' By the West is signified man, declining to the grave, and liable to fall into the darkness of sin and ignorance."

5. Cited in Dena Goodman, *The Republic of Letters: A Cultural History of the French Enlightenment* (Ithaca: Cornell University Press, 1996), 26.

6. One need only read the superb studies of Lauren Pristas to see how deep was the influence of modern(ist) thinking on the composition of the missal's prayers.

feminist clamor for women's ordination could have occurred only after the lowering and lessening of the priestly office to a vehicle of community power. If he would lord it over the congregation, a priest should stay as far as possible away from the *usus antiquior*, with its sober beauty, classical restraint, and ascetical attention to details unseen and unheard.

The Tridentine liturgy stresses the unworthiness of the priest himself and continually asks that he, and the rest of us, be made worthy by a divine initiative of mercy. The priest may well be vain or egoistic himself, and that may affect his entire ministry, especially outside of liturgical functions; yet the classical order of Mass goes constantly against the grain of fallen nature, it constantly asks of the priest a self-abnegation out of obedience to the law of the liturgy, it almost forces him to enter its own rhythm and the lilt of its language, so dominating is the ceremonial aura. It would take a fairly corrupt priest to ignore, trifle with, or undermine the old *ordo Missae*. Think about it: in the traditional rite, the priest himself, splendidly attired, set apart as a consecrated mediator, of whose superior status there never was the slightest doubt, nevertheless beats his breast, bows low, asks for the grace to offer the sacrifice worthily, purifies and prepares himself throughout the liturgy until the act of consecration, when Jesus speaks *in propria persona*—as though the liturgy were saying: "You, O human priest, in spite of all your prayers, are still unworthy; I, the Incarnate Word, the Eternal High Priest, must step in and act for you, offering myself to the Father." The old liturgy in its solemn silence almost shouts that the priest bears the burden on his own shoulders, as Christ bore the weight of the rood. What lay person would stand up and say, "Give that great burden to me, it is my right, it is unjust for you to hold it to yourself"?

In the new form of the Mass it is altogether different. First, for all intents and purposes, it is taken for granted that everyone is completely worthy, "on top of it," since, apart from a couple of fleeting references (*agnoscamus peccata nostra, ut apti simus ad sacra mysteria celebranda...*; *Domine, non sum dignus*—said once only), mention is hardly made of sin and repentance. The missal could be (and sometimes is) read out by anyone; the rubrics, said to be "simplified," are in reality inadequate and unstable, allowing opportunities for the celebrant to show his stuff, to pepper the Mass with personal messages; the vestments, liturgical furnishings, and architecture follow suit, in a crescendo of banality.

Victims of the Vernacular

In direct contradiction of the Second Vatican Council's Constitution on the Sacred Liturgy, which advocated a moderate use of the vernacular and warned against needless and inorganic changes, Church authorities imposed a totally vernacular liturgy on the Latin Church with sudden and iconoclastic absoluteness. The result was not the linguistic nobility of Byzantine or High Anglican services but a horizontal, superficial, chatty atmosphere, lacking in spiritual savor. Given the prevailing absence of spiritual discipline—an absence sadly epitomized in the new Missal's glaring rubrical minimalism, which, in turn, forms a lackadaisical clergy—the vernacular cannot but encourage emotionalism by taking one into the realm of the subjective. The more a celebrant "gets into" the texts, glossing, doctoring, riffing on them, the more artificial and staged and self-conscious the whole thing seems. It becomes like a one-man show or a stage act, not a sharing in the "past perfect" of Calvary or the "future perfect" of the Kingdom made present here and now. A priest who simply reverently reads the old *Missale Romanum* and makes those prayers his own, subordinating himself utterly to the ritual of Holy Mother Church, becomes the mouthpiece of a living Tradition emanating from the living Lord. This requires asceticism from the priest, yes, but it requires the same from the congregation: they too must deny themselves, take up their missal (as it were), and follow the priest, in order to enter the mystery of the cross reenacted on the altar of sacrifice. No one gets to shine or warble; everyone has to kneel and adore.

The new liturgy almost cannot help drawing attention to the *personality* of the celebrant because the vernacular is his comfort zone, the realm of his daily speech, and if there is one thing he has been encouraged to do from day one in the seminary, it is to "connect with the people," to "speak to them where they're at," to "be one of them." So he must also offer Mass in that same spirit, filling it with familiarities, colloquialisms, witticisms, anecdotes, holiday greet-ings, bits of news—and from there the infection takes hold of fixed parts of Mass, too, whose formulations begin subtly to reflect what-ever pastoral or theological perspective the priest happens to have developed. The problem has obvious roots: in the West, for over a thousand years, no systematic attempt was made to employ a noble vernacular in our rituals[7]; hence we did not develop the Eastern cus-tom of total reverence toward liturgical texts in the local tongue.[8] In fact, one of the colossal mistakes of the failed reform was thinking that just because vernacular worship with lots of congregational singing works in the East or among Protestants, it would therefore work fine among Catholics, which ignores the towering fact that for centuries the Catholic soul had been formed by silence, reverence, kneeling, gazing, and, in a way that was far more profound than any of the reformers realized or cared to admit, by the Latin language itself, and to a lesser extent, by Gregorian chant, its connatural com-panion. To make a sudden shift away from these habits of soul was to ensure not only discontinuity with the past but also a death by starvation of those spiritual *virtues* specific to the Western Church. She went from having *some* virtues to having *none*.

As Robert Hugh Benson once wrote, the Tridentine Mass is a sacred dance that requires utmost concentration in its execution, and begs for careful preparations beforehand, not to mention years of preparation for the major ministers. Many older people, whether cleric or lay, would prefer *not* to return to the Tridentine Mass because it is more spiritually and physically demanding. The Novus

---

7. I am not implying that the West was mistaken in not having employed the vernacular in her rites; quite the contrary, as St. John XXIII argues in his apostolic constitution *Veterum Sapientia* of February 22, 1962. My only point is that Roman Catholics were never accustomed to a fixed and solemn vernacular, unlike, for example, the Anglicans with their Elizabethan translation of elements from the Latin liturgical heritage.

8. So profound is the respect of the Byzantine priest toward the text of the Mass books that even when he is celebrating the liturgy in his mother tongue, he will never alter the wording or the rubrics; such things are fixed according to rule, as they used to be in the West. The only thing that will ever be "added" are the names of the sick, the deceased, or others who request prayers—and, of course, the homily in his own words.

Ordo is a perfunctory social event that can be performed with comparatively minimal preparation. One sees the same difference between traditional acolytes and contemporary "altar servers." The former have to be well trained, even drilled, in their elegant, synchronized motions, particularly for solemn Masses, whereas the latter can be shown the ropes of the Novus Ordo in a matter of minutes, since it amounts to little more than hoisting a book or holding a cruet. In both the priest's and the server's case, there is a difference too in habiliments. The traditional priest wears many layers of often rich and beautiful materials that have to be worn in a special way, and the server has at least his old-fashioned cassock and surplice, but the modern priest dons a few items topped off by polyester drapery, and his modern male or female assistant wears a robe of some sort that never manages to hide his or her gym shoes.[9]

The manner in which ministers at the altar work, pray, bow, speak, sing, reflects and represents the reality of what is taking place. In the classical Roman Rite, the ministers are clearly *working*, focused intently on something beyond them, beyond the people. Their role is a difficult one, they are about serious business—"the Father's business." They almost always sweat profusely at a High Mass or Solemn Mass. In the Novus Ordo, whether he sweats or not, the priest appears to be going through motions that are aimed at catching and keeping the people's attention and carrying on a sort of dialogue with *them.* I am reminded of an observation of Msgr. Benson's again: at an old Mass, the priest hobbles out, climbs up the steps and goes to work. He has got a serious job to do, and he does it—not primarily for the people, not with a view to them, but with a view to the *work* to be done, the *opus operatum.*[10] He is worshiping the Father in spirit and truth by entering into the supreme

9. As older Catholics know, tastes in vestments, not to mention styles of church architecture and sanctuary design, had begun to be infected by a utilitarian superficiality even before Vatican II. And there have been other eras in the history of the Church where artistic/liturgical styles and tastes had grown decadent. Still, it would be difficult to imagine a more wholesale banalization, a more ruthless sacrifice of substance to ephemeral fashion, than what we see around us today.

10. While it is true that preconciliar times saw a fair share of desacralization in the Roman Rite—when, for example, a celebrant would tear through the Mass at

sacrifice of his only Son on the Cross. This is why he faces eastward, toward the Christ who has come and who will come. Christ is his master, his "employer," if you will. The priest answers to him alone. Is the priest at the new Mass answering, literally or metaphorically, to Christ, or to the people? The priest's physical disorientation, his turning his back to the Orient and toward Man, inverting the priority of Mass and the masses, symbolizes with a poetic justice worthy of Dante the state of the Western soul and the essential crisis of the Roman Church in this Dark Age.

Meals and Mysteries

A feast or a banquet is a real event of human togetherness, of fraternizing at leisure, and, if we are blessed with faith, a true celebration of life as a gift from God. In traditional societies there was always time for a feast, just as there was a place for fasting. Providence would have it so. For its part, the Last Supper was a meal. Yet Christ decided to institute the sacrament of his love in the context of a Jewish feast that was already richly sacramental and formal in its practice, not at all what modern meals are like; and he transformed the elements of the meal into a mystical supper[11] that made present, in anticipation, his death on the cross the following day, thereby fundamentally altering the event from a commemorative feast into a true and proper sacrifice, the sacrifice of Calvary. This was no "ordinary" meal to begin with; it had become absolutely extraordinary by the time it finished. Christ's command gave the Church power to elevate the human banquet into an instrument for making present, and furthering, the Kingdom of God. This consecration of

---

breakneck speed, making the requisite signs of the cross over the oblata so quickly that they were no longer intelligible as signs of the cross—nevertheless there was not a "culture" of banality that choked the church. People, generally, were still able to experience the Mass as a visible source of invisible grace and peace.

11. I take this phrase from the beautiful Byzantine prayer before communion: "Accept me as a partaker of your mystical supper, O Son of God, for I will not reveal the mysteries to your enemies nor give you a kiss as did Judas, but like the thief I confess to you: Remember me, O Lord, when you shall come into your kingdom; remember me, O Master, when you shall come into your kingdom; remember me, O Holy One, when you shall come into your kingdom."

the ordinary had, in turn, a notable effect upon ordinary life, illuminating it with a ray of the Church's holiness, invigorating nature as a basis for grace. For it was the same people who found the meaning of their life at Mass and broke bread at table in the family circle.

The modern meal—a rushed affair of prepackaged microwavable foods and, on the off chance people are eating together, trivial chitchat—has nothing mysterious or even dignified about it. Do we think that our shift away from the family, the home and hearth, and the rhythms of country life have had no effect on our perception and practice of the liturgy? How can we appreciate a sacred banquet (*O sacrum convivium*, St. Thomas sang), if even a worldly banquet is rarely spread? The "desacralization" of ordinary Christian life, the "demystification" of the Mass: which one comes first and brings about the other—or are they simultaneous and co-causative? This much, at any rate, is clear: in the Latin Rite church we have witnessed the reduction of the divine sacrifice, the *sacred* banquet, to a human meal—and, what is worse, not the traditional meal that creates brotherhood, but the fast food and chatter of modernity that leaves our souls alone and untouched, however energetically we twitter and text away our lives.

A Novus Ordo liturgy celebrated in disoriented churches where the altar has been replaced by a mere table and the priest, breaking with nearly 2,000 years of tradition, faces the people and talks to them instead of facing East and speaking softly to the Beloved, is nothing less than a visible betrayal of the invisible essence of the Mass.[12] All oriental and occidental liturgies are absolutely one in regard to the irreducible priestliness of the priest and the "altarity" of the altar. The priest at the altar clearly has a special priestly task

---

12. Joseph Ratzinger and Uwe Michael Lang, among others, have refuted the old argument that saw in the configuration of certain Roman churches, especially St. Peter's, evidence for a celebration *versus populum*. For in these churches, due to historical accidents, the priest, in order to stand *ad orientem*, had also to stand "toward the people" because the church was built backwards, with the altar not up against the east end but all the way back at the west end. The key point was always to face *ad orientem*, to Christ the Orient.

to perform that demands all his attention; he is focused entirely upon it, and thus *sets the right example for all.* He is doing something that no one else can do, yet paradoxically, in doing it properly he opens up the mystery to everyone who participates in the liturgy, and enables them, *through him,* to approach the altar and offer the same sacrifice. But when structure, text, and praxis emphasize the mundane at the expense of the transcendent, the horizontal to the detriment of the vertical, the ceremony becomes a Protestant exercise in commemoration padded with "moving" or "relevant" sermons.[13] What follows is not that everyone finally worships equally, but that no one effectively does so; the single sacrifice that unites heaven to earth gets lost on the table, in the meal, in the neighborly chatter. A high altar or an altar behind an iconostasis, surrounded by sacred ministers dedicating themselves unstintingly to the giving of thanks to the Most Holy Trinity,[14] visibly and vividly expresses what the entire church building, the entire liturgy, and by extension, the entire Church, *are FOR,* and that from which they originate; a table and a platform frequented by a motley assortment of people does not do this and cannot do this. If it is objected that I am criticizing not the Novus Ordo but the way it is currently practiced, my response is that of Martin Mosebach: the very fact that the Novus Ordo, with its innumerable options and inculturations, *permits* all this to occur, and that the Church leaders have seen fit to allow every sort of "adaptation" (including, in rare cases, Latin chant liturgies) in accord with the "genius" of the Missal of Paul VI, proves my point. No authentic liturgy exults in formlessness.

At a Novus Ordo liturgy, with its never-ending verbiage, from the

---

13. Protestantism has historically tended to see or set up an opposition between form, order, and law on the one hand, and freedom and spontaneity ("in the Spirit") on the other. We have seen this opposition revived in elements of the Catholic charismatic movement.

14. *Gratiarum actio ad Trinitatem*—the title of a prayer by St. Catherine of Siena, but also an apt description of the essence of the Mass as a propitiatory sacrifice in which the Son of God, in virtue of his human nature, offers perfect praise, thanksgiving, honor, and worship to the Holy Trinity on behalf of the Church and all creation, thus pleasing God perfectly and communicating that divine delight to all souls in a state of grace.

improvised greetings of Father to the often poorly-coordinated set of Scripture readings to the meandering homily to the "prayers of the faithful" and so on, we are battered and bored with words, words, words, not captivated by the quiet condescension of Christ. We are surrounded by human words that, more often than not, distract us from the incarnate Word of God, from the One who becomes really, truly, substantially present among us as the ultimate *Mysterium Fidei* to which a silent, wonder-filled gaze of worship is the only suitable response. As a consequence, the medieval ritual of elevating the consecrated host and chalice—a drawing or photograph of which was once able to function as the universal symbol or synopsis of the entire rite of Mass—has become, if one may judge from appearances, an irrelevancy, perhaps an embarrassment, for many celebrants. It is inconsistent with the "supper" idea: when you are having supper, you generally don't elevate the food in front of your table mates. Jews during the Passover Seder lift up the matzo, but no one needs reminding that nearly 100% of the Church is Gentile, and that our Lord, the prince of his own people, inaugurated a new form of worship that, in fulfilling the Jewish ceremonies, brought them to an end. For us Gentiles, the symbolism of offering a gift *in sacrifice* to God by raising it up high over the head, toward the heavens, makes good sense. When the priest is *versus populum,* the rationale for such a gesture is much harder to see. As we know, many priests fail to *elevate* the consecrated host and chalice at all; a slight lift of each, and then we speed into the "acclamation." There is no ceremonial slowness, the catch-your-breath-and-cross-yourself interval during which the heart is lifted up in adoration of the crucified and risen Savior, hidden beneath the veil of bread and wine.[15]

15. Historically, the priest began to elevate the host and the chalice in response to a desire on the part of the faithful to see them and worship the true God hidden under the species of bread and wine. Naturally, the elevation of the species resonated with biblical/theological overtones: "As Moses lifted up the serpent in the desert, so must the Son of Man be lifted up" (Jn 3:14); "And I, if I be lifted up from the earth, will draw all things to myself" (Jn 12:32). The strictly theological meaning of elevating the species remains regardless of whether the priest faces *ad orientem* or *versus populum,* but gone, in the latter case, is the supporting context that made the gesture so obviously appropriate.

We have an hour for verbiage, platitudes, and folksongs, but we have not thirty seconds for silent adoration.

One reason the liturgy has become so banal is that the "ordinary mysticism" of Western liturgical life was gradually lost. This was something that was slipping away long before the Council, although not everywhere and certainly not for everyone. Whenever and wherever the faithful are able to be touched in their soul by chant, by a candlelit morning Mass in Advent, by the stillness of the priest praying the Roman Canon, by the simple but poignant gestures of the sacred ministers, by the fervor of the collects and other prayers printed in well-thumbed handheld missals—when things like this are firmly in place and *appreciated* for what they are, there is neither need nor desire for any "reform," excepting the most obvious, and the most miniscule, adaptations for time and place, new saints or new feasts. Making allowance for differences of temperament, state of mind, and degree of devotion, it is plain that the predominantly quiet participation of the faithful is, in healthy circumstances, as deeply *active* as it will ever be. One only makes it superficially active (that is, one actually makes it *spiritually* more passive) by forcing people to stand up and talk, shake hands, lift hands, wave hands, and so on. Man's highest activity is the silent contemplation of divine reality through the power of his mind elevated by grace, and this is the *activity* toward which the liturgy should be leading all of us.

In his hard-hitting *ad limina* address on 9 October 1998 to the bishops of the Northwestern United States, John Paul II spoke about true and false notions of *participatio actuosa* and of the need to regard meditation and listening (to Gregorian chant, for example) as profoundly *active*. The call for the laity to "participate" arose because of the deleterious influence that the *devotio moderna* had on liturgical life, coupled with an approach to liturgy that emphasized the juridical over the artistic, the utilitarian over the aesthetic. If genuine participation was sometimes poor prior to Vatican II, the post-Vatican II liturgical reformers erred grievously by seeking to achieve participation through the deconstruction and minimalization of the liturgy. Many of them appeared to understand active participation to mean *doing* something: singing, reading, helping out with the distribution of Holy Communion. A premium was placed on the doing, even when it meant making the liturgy banal and simplistic to assure that such participation could be actually realized. They seemed to forget that people who go to the opera or the symphony, for example, do not need to be involved with the production of the music in order to be actively participating in the event.

The most community-building activity is the inward contemplation and assimilation of divine truths and divine love, which have power to transform their bearers into icons of Christ.[16] When men have no longer tasted something of the sweetness of contemplation—how revitalizing it can be just to gaze at a crucifix with trust in one's heart, or to make a visit to a church and be at peace before the tabernacle, half-noticing its red lamp flicker—they will throw away or put into a museum anything that relates to it, like ungrateful descendants going through very old family heirlooms who, no longer knowing or caring about their importance, toss them into the rubbish bin with a shrug of the shoulders.

In this period of history, when God in his inscrutable Providence has permitted Catholics to be driven by their very shepherds into an arid spiritual desert, a secular wilderness of jackals and thorns, it is our task to preserve—in the sanctuary of our hearts, if we cannot preserve the sanctuaries of our churches—the treasures that have been handed down to us in better days by better servants, and to keep them safe for a generation that will taste the fruits of a watered garden once more.

16. This description may seem to apply only to the Low Mass, but it does not. Even in a Solemn High Mass with a lot of plainchant and participation in the singing of the Ordinary—the kind of celebration, in other words, that is the norm and the ideal for the Roman Rite—there is plenty of time for meditation, for listening, for quiet prayer; and there is a *spirit* of stillness, too, that goes far deeper than mere absence of sound. In that respect, I do not think that a low Mass, however simple, and a high Mass, however elaborate, differ all that much *in spirit*, great though their external differences may be.

9

The Loss of Riches
in the Sanctoral Cycle

O NE YEAR, a friend and I had the blessing of attending two celebrations of the Feast of St. Thérèse, for in the old calendar her feast is October 3, and in the new calendar, October 1. In fact, neither date is apropos. Thérèse actually died on September 30, but this has long been the feast of St. Jerome, *qui non movetur*, while October 1, which might be styled the first day of her eternal reward, had been occupied by St. Remigius, Bishop and Confessor, the one responsible for baptizing King Clovis, thereby bringing the Frankish kingdom into the bosom of Holy Mother Church. This latter feast was removed from the universal calendar in the 1969 reform. I shall have more to say later about the removal of "obscure" or "local" saints. Meanwhile, to come back to the Little Flower, it was hard not to feel blessed by the opportunity to celebrate her memory twice. Surely, the saint of heroic humility would be smiling at the inopportuneness of both dates.

Still, in the Novus Ordo celebration (which was, I might add, just about as "Oratorian" as could be, complete with a schola singing the chant), it was hard not to notice how unsuitable the readings were; they were simply the readings for the weekday.[1] The reading from

---

1. Admittedly, the celebrant *could* have chosen the optional readings for a Virgin from the compendious new Lectionary—but he did not, and frankly, this option is rarely exercised. It is far less trouble to stick with the daily sequence, the place to which the book is already open, the place where the ribbon was left from yesterday. I have heard some priests say that choosing the optional readings disturbs the flow of the Scripture passages and so should be avoided, unless the feast is so prominent that the Church herself requires different readings.

Baruch had to do with the wickedness of the cities who reject God; the reading from the Gospel was "Woe to you, Tyre and Sidon." Admitting that a preacher with Origen's exegetical ingenuity could make any Scripture passage illustrate any mystery he pleased, the ordinary layman is left asking: Does this really have much to do with Thérèse? In the Tridentine liturgical cycle, the readings *always* link up with the saint whose feast is being celebrated. In the traditional Mass I attended, the Epistle was Isaiah 66:12–14 ("As one whom his mother comforts, so I will comfort you"), and the Gospel was Mt 18:1–4 ("Amen I say to you, unless you convert and become like little children, you shall not enter the kingdom of heaven"). Here we are right in the company of the Little Flower and her rediscovery of all the freshness of the Gospel. The juxtaposition of old and new prompted me to see how great a disaster was the abandonment of the inner unity of Scripture and feast day. It makes the prayers, the readings, and the sacrifice seem like three different things, when they ought to be woven together, as in the ancient cycle, making one seamless garment.

But there was something more, and worse: the proper chants for her feast day, in the new *Graduale Romanum*, are, in some cases (like the Alleluia verse) irrelevant, and in other cases barely relevant—that is, bearing no special relation to St. Thérèse. A comparison with the propers of the *usus antiquior* for Thérèse's feast day will make apparent the magnitude of the loss suffered by the faithful when the ancient liturgy and its organic development were cast aside.

The *Graduale Romanum*, keyed to the Novus Ordo Missae, offers the following propers for St. Thérèse. The *Graduale*, of course, is in Latin, so I offer here a translation:

Introit (Ps 30:7–8, 2)—I however have hoped in the Lord: I shall exult and rejoice in Thy mercy, because Thou hast looked upon my humility. V: In Thee, O Lord, I have put my hope, I shall not be confounded forever; in Thy justice free me. I however have hoped in the Lord: I shall exult and rejoice in Thy mercy, because Thou hast looked upon my humility.

Gradual (Ps 26:4)—One thing I have asked of the Lord, this I shall seek: that I may dwell in the house of the Lord. V. That I may see the delight of the Lord, and be protected by his holy temple.

Alleluia (Ps 116:1)—Praise the Lord, all ye nations, and rejoice in him, all ye peoples. Alleluia.

Offertory (Ps 102:2, 5)—Bless the Lord, O my soul, and forget not all of his gifts: and thy youth shall be renewed like the eagle's.

Communion (Ps 9:2, 3)—I shall tell of all Thy wonders: I shall rejoice and exult in Thee: I shall sing Thy name, O most High.

If I may digress for a moment, the very fact that the altar missal can have still other texts than those given in the *Graduale Romanum*, and ones not especially better than the selection made by the monks of Solesmes, underlines the lack of coordination and unity which has effectively made it impossible to say that the modern Roman rite is unified and universal. Put simply: When I walk into a church anywhere in the world, I do not know what I am going to get, regardless of the so-called universal calendar—there are so many options, dispensations, derogations, cycles, and what have you. This is a deplorable situation. And as part of this digression, I cannot help recalling that the vast majority of the faithful will never hear these propers of the Mass in Latin or in the vernacular, in the resplendent clothing of Gregorian chant or in any suitable musical vesture, since the propers have been almost universally abandoned, replaced by songs or hymns even less relevant to the feast day being celebrated. Thus the faithful are deprived of the benefit that would accrue to them from having in their ears the actual texts of Scripture chosen (for better or for worse) to adorn the various days of the liturgical year in the Ordinary Form. In short, the "reform" has resulted for the most part in a wholesale abandonment of Propers as such, a loss that has severely crippled the integrity, balance, and scriptural language of the Roman rite—a fact increasingly recognized and lamented in the ongoing conversation about what went wrong, although without much evidence yet that the available resources for singing the propers (whether in Latin or in the vernacular) are being widely adopted at the parish level.

But let us return to the texts of the *Graduale*. I will not direct my criticism at poor vernacular music or the unwarranted omission of the propers; my complaint has to do with the normative Latin edition of the Novus Ordo Mass and its propers, as utilized in the best-case scenario. In her masterful studies, Lauren Pristas has helped us to assess and evaluate the radical differences between the old Missal and the new strictly on the basis of the "pure" ground of the Latin *editio typica* of each. This is where I, too, stake my claims, prescinding entirely from translations or abuses.

Now, consider the propers appointed in the old rite for the feast of St. Thérèse. In stark contrast to the situation that obtains with the new rite, in the old rite the propers were *always* recited or sung, because they are, and were treated as, an integral part of the liturgy. Moreover, people often had their handheld missals with them, so that everyone who cared to pay attention—and this was certainly an ever-growing number right up to the eve of the Council—was nourished by these verses from scripture, beautifully applied to the Little Flower:

Introit (Song 4:8–9)—Come from Libanus, my spouse, come from Libanus, come; thou hast wounded my heart, my sister, my spouse, thou hast wounded my heart. V. (Ps 112:1) Praise the Lord, ye children; praise ye the name of the Lord. Glory be. Come from Libanus, my spouse, etc.

Gradual (Mt 11:25)—I confess to Thee, O Father, Lord of heaven and earth, because Thou hast hid these things from the wise and prudent, and hast revealed them to little ones. V. (Ps 70:5) My hope, O Lord, from my youth.

Alleluia (Sir 39:17–19)—Bud forth as the rose planted by the brooks of waters: Give ye a sweet odor as frankincense. Send forth flowers as the lily, and yield a smell, and bring forth leaves in grace, and praise with canticles and bless the Lord in his works. Alleluia.

Offertory (Lk 1:46, 48–49)—My soul doth magnify the Lord, and my spirit hath rejoiced in God my Savior: because he hath regarded the humility of his handmaid. He that is mighty hath done great things to me.

Communion (Deut 32:10, 12)—He led her about and taught her, and he kept her as the apple of his eye. As an eagle he has spread his wings and hath taken her on his shoulder. The Lord alone was her leader.

Comparing the two sets of propers, I ask: Is this an example of liturgical progress, of a "successful" reform? The Novus Ordo propers are vague and generic, ready for application to any female saint; the Tridentine propers are majestic, poetic, and exactly apropos to the Little Flower. They draw, too, from a wider selection of Scripture: six books (Deuteronomy, Sirach, Psalms, and the Song of Songs from the Old Testament, Matthew and Luke from the New) instead of only one (Psalms), a fact that admonishes us to be careful not to assume too quickly that the new liturgy offers a richer banquet of Sacred Scripture. A gourmet meal features many small courses served at a leisurely pace, and that is how Scripture is fed to the faithful in the old rite—not in large chunks in a single helping, before moving on to other things.

The Loss of Liturgically Suitable Readings

Let us turn to the subject of the readings for Mass and how they are to be selected. A first principle for lovers of liturgical tradition is that the cycle of feasts of our Lord, our Lady, and the saints must take precedence over a cycle of scripture readings. Prior to the Novus Ordo, there was no Eucharistic liturgy in existence that privileged a rationalistically-conceived march through books of the Old and New Testaments. All liturgies, Eastern and Western, look to the mysteries of Christ and of his Mother, and to the lives and virtues of that bright "cloud of witnesses" who incarnate, so to speak, the reality of Jesus again and again throughout history. Recitation of the text of scripture is made decisively subordinate to the historical embodiment of Scripture's message in holy persons. The readings serve, in other words, to frame, adorn, and bring to light the face of Christ and the faces of all his imitators. The use of scripture is iconic, not homiletic. We are not being lectured at, but rather summoned to worship, to bow down before mysteries. The readings are to function as verbal incense, not verbose information. That is why a relatively narrow selection of scripture passages, usually shorter rather than longer, is perfectly adequate and even preferable for the Eucharistic liturgy. With all due respect to the inspired word of God, all passages of the Bible are not equally well suited to the purpose of liturgy *per se*—though all of its pages are certainly fertile ground for *lectio divina*, a practice that will make our very participation in the liturgy more fruitful. Traditionally, the place where a great deal of scripture was read was Matins, and the Office of Readings today continues that custom in a modified form. The Church's liturgy is complex and multifaceted: the Mass is not, and should not be, the only place where the faithful encounter scripture.

With these all too brief considerations in mind, we can see the fallacy lurking behind one of the most common complaints the liturgical movement made against the Tridentine Missal, namely that it did not contain a sufficient quantity or diversity of scripture readings. Apart from the general refutation of the argument— namely, that liturgy is not meant to be a scripture study session, that scripture serves an important but still *subordinate* role in the Holy Sacrifice—the real solution would have been to undertake with great patience the long-term task of composing Masses more "proper" to individual saints or liturgical seasons, so that a carefully augmented use of Scripture would have been able to retain the iconic function exemplified in the propers of St. Thérèse. I do not necessarily mean composing new chants, although in some cases this would certainly have been possible, but selecting chants more directly relevant to the life and teaching of the particular saint, and expanding the readings by appointing previously unread passages for the feast days of saints whom they suit the most. Every five to ten years, a supplement could be published, to be used alongside the missal on those particular feast days, until after twenty or thirty years it was time to put all the new propers/readings into the missal itself. One sees in old missals how certain universal or regional feasts were introduced by appendices pasted into the back of the books.

For example, the feast of St. John on December 27 might have been enhanced by the use of a different entrance antiphon than *In medio ecclesiae*. As beautiful an introit as this is, it was used indiscriminately for all the Doctors of the Church, whose numbers have greatly increased in recent centuries, with no attempt made to craft propers for them. I am not advocating liturgical experimentation, needless to say, but simply the augmentation of a Missal left intact in its beauty and riches. This is exactly what the Church herself had been doing for a century and more prior to the Second Vatican Council: new feasts were introduced, often with new propers, with relevant readings appointed, and even new chants composed. Who could not imagine a Mass for the feast of Blessed Teresa of Calcutta, drawing from the sayings of the prophets (such as Amos) and of our Lord on the poor (the episode of the rich young man comes to mind)? Returning to St. John, a properly Johannine introit for December 27 might use verses from his Gospel to refer to the sublimity of his teaching on the divinity of Christ. In general, the feasts of the Evangelists could be elevated simply by making the propers more, if you will, "proper." Or again, why must every holy woman get the *mulier fortis* reading from Proverbs? It seems odd to apply the selfsame reading to very distinctive saints for whom one could find other more appropriate passages. *This* would have been the way to expand the liturgy's readings while respecting the intrinsic connection between scripture and sanctity. As long as you preserve the *mulier fortis* for, say, three women (rather than for twelve or however many!), daily Mass-goers will still hear or read this fine reading every year, but there will not be overkill on the one hand, and undervaluation of the distinctiveness of the saints on the other. The pattern had already been set by the feasts of those saints who, in the Missal of 1955 or 1962, already had a perfectly adapted set of propers special to them: for example, St. Thérèse herself, where, as we have seen, all the chants and readings are exquisitely suitable, or St. Margaret Mary in her special relationship with the Sacred Heart. Yes, to do this would have made the Missal somewhat larger or perhaps demanded its publication in two volumes, but it would have greatly enriched it, and one of the arguably legitimate goals of the liturgical movement—that scripture be more fully represented—would have been satisfied in a manner wholly consistent with the tradition and its best models.

The new lectionary, in contrast, is largely a failure, for three fundamental reasons.

First, the guiding principles were Cartesian. That is to say, they were informed by a desire for a mathematical order, a technical completeness (we have to "get through" the scriptures), and a typically materialistic disregard for the organic unity of the soul-body complex which is the liturgy—its soul being the Eucharistic sacrifice-sacrament, the dual motion of *offering* to the Father and *receiving* in communion, while its body is the surrounding prayers, readings, and chants.

Second, there is the basic human problem of having more than one year's worth of readings. A single year is a natural period of time; it is pedagogically superior, not to mention deeply consoling, to come back, year after year, to the same readings for a given Sunday or weekday. The faithful get to know the Sunday readings intimately. Over time, Sundays begin to be remembered in terms of their readings, chants, and prayers, which stick in the mind all the more firmly because they are both spoken or chanted *and* read in one's daily missal, engaging more of the senses. In this way the traditional Western liturgy shows its affinity to the Eastern liturgies, which go so far as to name Sundays after their Gospel lections or after some particular dogma emphasized. The Fourteenth Sunday after Pentecost has a distinctive identity: *Protector noster,* that is the Introit, and the faithful know its melody, and the whole Mass grows to be familiar, like a much-loved garden or a trail through the woods. Nowadays, to take a contrasting example, it's anyone's guess what the "Tenth Sunday of Ordinary Time" is about! It is certainly never *experienced* as being the same, year after year.

Third, the bloated new cycle of readings was assembled by a committee of "experts," biblical scholars whom one might have cause to distrust when it comes to spiritual matters. A sensible and reverent way of augmenting a missal would be to entrust *to contemplative monks* the task of proposing new readings and propers for certain saints' feasts, for the weekdays of Advent, and so on—to entrust it to traditional Benedictines, Cistercians, Carthusians, experts in *lectio divina,* whose every thought is permeated by the words, the rhythms, the doctrine of sacred scripture. For these men and women, scripture is not a "project," a book to be divided and conquered; it is their food and drink. Feeling the spiritual weight of what they read, they would be able to recommend readings that are most *fitting* for a given saint, or for the ferias of Advent, Lent, and Paschaltide, always with a deferential eye towards the use of scripture already established by centuries of liturgical practice. So the process could have gone like this: monks at many monasteries propose, after much prayer and meditation, new readings for feast days or ferias in the old calendar; then, final decisions are rendered by a board composed of monks, bishops, and experienced preachers.

What are some areas of the old calendar where new readings could be appointed without undermining the spirit, the unity, the internal pedagogy, and the traditional perfection of the liturgy as a whole?

Weekdays during Advent. Fairly early on, the Roman church adopted the practice of daily Mass during Lent at a time when daily Mass, particularly in the East, was still unusual. This explains why Lent possesses a cycle of daily readings; in the Tridentine missal there is no other season with a daily cycle of that kind. The more modern emphasis on assisting at daily Mass, together with the understanding of Advent as a lesser season of penance, suggests the wisdom of enriching this segment of the calendar, too. Here, then, is a beautiful open field for the assigning of Advent lessons from the Pentateuch, the Prophets, and the Wisdom books, and new graduals from the Psalms, all of them pointing as with one voice to the coming feast of Christmas and testifying to the mystery of the Incarnation. The saints' feast days during Advent should not, however, be interfered with; only the "empty" days should have readings assigned to them. If the Church decided to add a new saint's day to the universal calendar, the readings could be adjusted accordingly. And, in fairness, it must be acknowledged that the Advent readings in the new lectionary are some of the most successful, because they deliberately and consistently track the liturgical season and thus underline the intrinsic link between the iconic function of scripture in the Mass and the sacramental presence of the long-awaited Messiah himself.

Weekdays during Paschal time. Again, without prejudice to the celebration of saints' feasts, a cycle of daily readings for Eastertide could be appropriately introduced into the *usus antiquior.* And again, we must acknowledge that the new Lectionary has gathered many fitting lections for this season, although the price to be paid is the Ordinary Form's tendency to run roughshod over the sanctoral cycle and its relationship to the mystery of the Mass.

In general, many of the saints' feast days could be furnished with apposite readings, in the way that, in the *usus antiquior,* St. Monica's feast has the Gospel passage about the widow's son raised from the dead, or St. Gregory Thaumaturgus, a saint famous for having literally moved a mountain, is honored by the Gospel passage about the moving of mountains by men of faith.

Suppressing "Archaic" Saints

The mention of St. Gregory Thaumaturgus leads naturally into a related theme: the suppression in the new Missal of so many saints' days, and their partial replacement with newer saints more "relevant" to our times and to modern Catholics. The fact is, there are thousands of saints; John Paul II canonized hundreds more. There could never be room in the calendar for even the modern saints (19th and 20th centuries), let alone a representative sampling from all centuries. The liturgy's reformers seemed to have acted upon the conviction that the calendar should reflect in almost mathematical proportions, by a quantitative sampling, the various periods of Church history, with weight being given to the modern because it is nearer to us. In doing so, the reform betrays a false notion of sacred time. We are the *contemporaries* of Christ, the Apostles, and the early Christians who died in agony for sake of the faith, and yet we are most likely to forget about them and to need their prayers and their example ever before us. The early Christians are the perennial witnesses to the faith, the first great standard-bearers after its sudden appearance in the fallen world. There is something especially glorious about them, and that is why the old calendar is filled with their names. We are ever being led back to the first ages, the infancy of our faith, the childhood of our religion.

The calendar's main purpose is not to keep up with the ongoing march of saints; there are devotional books, prayer manuals, biographies, and much more to help us deepen our knowledge of that vast assembly. No, the saints whom the Holy Spirit moved the

Church to include in the universal calendar are there for special reasons which cannot be grasped by a sociological or historical analysis; the reasons are intuited by one who prays long and faithfully with the old missal. The very appearance of randomness, of an unlikely gathering of some few more recent saints with the much larger number of saints from the earliest times, gives pause for reflection: Am I numbering myself with the ancients, the wise men, the first martyrs? Am I remembering my forefathers, who would otherwise pass out of human memory? The continual recollection of the earliest saints corrects the modern tendency to think that the new is more real, and the old is a distant shadow no longer distinct and discernible. No, the missal brings us immediately into the company of the Romans and Greeks and barbarians who converted to the faith, who were great bishops or virgins or martyrs, and who bring us outside of our age into the agelessness of the faith, its eternal youth that sings the praises and begs the intercession of these ancient men and women just as though they were sitting next to us in the pew. It ever joins the end to the beginning, and keeps today rooted in the first day; it brings into sharp relief the awesome fact that the Christian religion is ever-present and transhistorical, there is neither yesterday, nor today, nor tomorrow, but Christ is always and forevermore coming to us in the manger and dying for us on the Cross, and his saints, even those whom our human instincts would place at a distance, are not dead strangers but living friends. The old calendar does all this with a remarkable subtlety of force: it works at us day by day, quietly, until we begin to recognize the names, remember the collects, and spontaneously turn to the men and women who bore the names, who are now not only our models but our contemporaries. Clock time loses its hegemony, and sacral time, which participates in the changeless now of God, gains on our soul. *That* is the kind of calendar we need.

One who is attentive to the old liturgical calendar will perceive many instances of the subtle unity and harmony that pervade this noble work of the Holy Spirit, in which many great souls participated but, thanks be to God, no committee had a part. Note, as a palpable but by no means isolated example, the magnificent progression of feasts from September 14th to September 18th, which form a miniature catechesis on the mystery of the passion and death of our Lord and its saving power throughout all ages—beginning with Mary and John at the foot of the cross, and continuing in all the heroic imitators of Christ whom divine grace raises up when the faith has begun to grow cold. I do not reproduce here the texts in full but sketch out each day, to show how well they cohere.

September 14: The Exaltation of the Holy Cross. *Introit:* cf. Gal 6:14: It behooves us to glory in the Cross of our Lord Jesus Christ, in whom is our salvation, life, and resurrection, by whom we are saved and delivered. *Collect:* O God, who on this day dost gladden us by the yearly feast of the exaltation of the holy Cross: grant, we beseech Thee, that we who on earth acknowledge the mystery of redemption wrought upon it, may be found worthy to enjoy the rewards of that same redemption in heaven. Through the same our Lord Jesus Christ.... *Epistle:* Phil 2:5–11: Let this mind be in you which was also in Christ Jesus.... *Gospel:* Jn 12:31–36: And I, if I be lifted up from the earth, will draw all things to myself.... While you have the light, believe in the light, that you may be the children of light.

September 15: The Seven Sorrows of the Virgin Mary. *Introit:* Jn 19:25: There stood by the cross of Jesus his mother, and his mother's sister Mary of Cleophas, and Salome, and Mary Magdalen. Woman, behold thy son, said Jesus: and to the disciple, Behold thy Mother. *Collect:* O God, at whose Passion, according to the prophecy of Simeon, a sword of sorrow pieced the most sweet soul of the glorious Virgin and Mother Mary, mercifully grant that we who honor with devotion her sorrows, may obtain the happy fruit of Thy Passion: who livest and reignest with God the Father.... *Epistle:* Jud 13:22, 23–25: The Lord hath blessed thee by his power, who by thee hath brought our enemies to nought.... for thou hast not spared thy life by reason of the distress and tribulation of thy people, but hast prevented our ruin in the presence of our God. *Gospel:* Jn 19:25–27.

September 16: Saints Cornelius and Cyprian, Martyrs. *Introit:* Ps 78:11, 12, 10: Let the sighing of the prisoners come in before thee, O Lord; render to our neighbors sevenfold in their bosom; revenge the blood of thy saints, which hath been shed. *Epistle:* Wis 3:1–8: The souls of the just are in the hand of God, and the torment of death shall not touch them.... As gold in the furnace he hath proved them, and as a victim of a holocaust he hath received them.... *Gospel:* Lk 2:9–19: They will lay their hands on you and persecute you, delivering you up to the synagogues and into prisons, dragging you before kings and governors, for my name's sake.... In your patience you shall possess your souls.

September 17: Impression of the Holy Stigmata on the Body of Saint Francis. *Introit:* Gal 6:14: But God forbid that I should glory, save in the cross of our Lord Jesus Christ: by whom the world is crucified to me, and I to the world. *Collect:* O Lord Jesus Christ, who when the world was growing cold, in order to enkindle in our hearts the fire of thy love, didst renew the sacred marks of thy passion on the body of blessed Francis: mercifully grant that with the aid of his merits and prayers we may ever bear our cross, and bring forth worthy fruits of penance: who livest and reignest with God the Father.... *Epistle:* Gal 6:14–18: But God forbid that I should glory, save in the cross of our Lord Jesus Christ.... From henceforth let no man be troublesome to me; for I bear the marks of the Lord Jesus in my body. *Gospel:* Mt 16:24–27: If any man will come after me, let him deny himself and take up his cross and follow me. For he that will save his life shall lose it; and he that shall lose his life for my sake shall find it. *Postcommunion:* O God, who in diverse ways didst show forth in blessed Francis thy confessor the wondrous mysteries of thy cross, grant, we beseech thee, that ever following the example of his devotion, we may be strengthened by constant meditation on that same cross. Through our Lord Jesus Christ....

September 18: Saint Joseph of Cupertino, Confessor. *Introit:* Sir 1:14–15: The love of God is honorable wisdom, and they to whom she shall show herself, love her by the sight, and by the knowledge of her great works. *Collect:* O God, who hast ordained that thine only-begotten Son when lifted up from the earth should draw all things to himself, mercifully grant, through the merits and example of thy seraphic confessor Joseph, that we may be lifted up above all earthly desires and be found worthy to come unto him, who liveth and reigneth with God the Father.... (Recall that St. Joseph of Cupertino was especially famous for his much-witnessed levitations that literally lifted him high above the ground, even to the very rooftops. So, the Collect is using the saint's "levity" as a symbol of how we, too, must rise above merely earthly goods and cleave to those of heaven. It is a splendid example of multiple layers of meaning planted in a text, ready to be discovered and delighted in by the faithful.) *Epistle:* 1 Cor 13:1–13: If I should have prophecy, and should know all mysteries and all knowledge; and if I should have faith so that I could move mountains, and have not charity, I am nothing.... *Gospel:* Mt 22:1–14: Many are called, but few are chosen.

This sequence of profoundly coordinated and mutually reinforcing prayers, readings, and propers is only one example among many of the quiet working of the Holy Spirit on the calendar over the centuries, perfecting the liturgical expression of the mysteries of faith and intensifying its pedagogical power on souls. I recall how a highly perceptive priest who had celebrated the Tridentine Mass every morning for years told me that such treasures of beauty and order could be found throughout the calendar. We should not be surprised; we should even have expected that a liturgy that has grown organically for centuries would exhibit refinements of this degree.

Preserve, Study, and Pray

What, then, is the conclusion we can derive from the foregoing observations? First, there is the obvious truth that we must preserve, with all our might, the riches of the Latin liturgical heritage for future generations who deserve to know what the Roman liturgy really is, and who long to worship God in spirit and truth according to his gifts to the Church. The words of John Paul II in *Ecclesia Dei* still ring out with ever-new relevance: "respect must everywhere be shown for the feelings of all those who are attached to the Latin liturgical tradition." And not just their feelings, but their deepest thoughts and convictions. How could anyone fail to be attached to so rich a tradition, and disturbed by so impoverished a revision? The motu proprio *Summorum Pontificum,* beyond all expectation, transformed John Paul II's counsel into a veritable law for the Latin Church, down to each and every parish, and in this way gives the Church's official sanction to the apostolate of a living and life-giving preservation of our inheritance.

Second, and less obviously, we need to take the time and make the effort to *study* the traditional liturgy to the extent that our state in life permits, so that we can peacefully, intelligently, and persuasively defend its superiority, and help those who are unfamiliar with it to see the vital spiritual lessons, the poetic beauty, the catechetical instruction, the consolation of soul it plentifully affords.

Finally, and still less obviously, we need to support with prayers and good will the many priests and laity who are doing their utmost to bring the celebration of the Novus Ordo into conformity with the Latin liturgical tradition, however much this may seem to be a quest to square the circle. Ultimately, for the very survival of orthodox Catholicism, there has to be a return to the ancient heritage that has been spurned, yet this can happen both in a pure way and in a piecemeal way. Many young adherents of the "new liturgical movement" strive with might and main to follow a purer way, one of strict return to the pristine Roman liturgy, but they must not scorn the piecemeal (or "reform of the reform") way, for it, too, is capable of leading souls in the right direction. It is not for us to judge how the victory will be won. Our task is to promote the good we know. May St. Thérèse—and all the saints nourished by the ancient Roman rite—pray for us.

10

The Loss of Graces:
Private Masses and Concelebration

S ITTING AT MY DESK one evening many years ago, I wrote in
my journal about an overwhelming experience:

August 12th. The feast of Saint Clare. Thanks be to God, the greatest and best. This morning, by his unspeakable mercy, I was given
the chance to attend a private old-rite Mass and receive the Lord: a
gift worth more than all gifts. But without my having the slightest
idea it would happen, he also granted me the privilege of serving
this Mass, which was offered by the holy Abbot of Fontgombault.
There is some sort of Benedictine retreat going on here at the Kar-
tause for a week, with oblates from all over Europe in attendance,
and three French abbots and many monks too, and there will be
bishops visiting, etc. It's all rather splendid. Yesterday I'd heard
that a monk was going to say the old rite at 6:00, so I got up and
came down for it, heading into the sacristy. I found out that the
Abbot himself, taking precedence, was going to offer the day's first
Mass before other monks did, and, as I knew how to serve, he
asked me if I would serve it. Laus Deo! It was the most peaceful
Mass I have ever attended. The Abbot lingered over every phrase,
and I honestly thought he was in an ecstasy during the Canon. I
felt there were hundreds of souls and spirits in the chapel with us.
I am speechless. Glory be to God.

That is the kind of thing one cannot forget, but even better, the kind
of thing one really cannot plan, either. The lack of planning is part
of the gift. It comes like a thief in the night. You know you don't
deserve it, and it comes to you anyway, because the Lord is so good
to us sinners.

The Daily Offering

I recount this story not to focus on the experience itself, but rather on what it helped me to see about an important facet of our Catholic tradition, in a lesson that mingled pain with joy. This monk's offering of the holy sacrifice for his own sins and for the sins of the world embodied in its very prayerfulness, by its God-focused intensity, an irrefutable justification for the long-standing custom of private Masses offered by individual monks prior to their conventual Mass, or, for that matter, by any priest who has the possibility of celebrating a daily Mass.[1] I envisioned in my mind's eye all of these monks quietly beseeching the divine mercy all over the world: a small army of Abraham's "just men," placating divine wrath and winning grace for sinners.

Up until the liturgical rupture it was customary for each priest who lived in a monastery or other religious community both to celebrate his own private Mass each morning and to assist at a communal or conventual Mass. The rationale was obvious: the Mass is the foremost act of religion, devotion, prayer, adoration, thanksgiving, and praise that any ministerial priest can offer, since it is none other than the immolation of the High Priest himself. As Venerable Pope Pius XII explained: "It cannot be overemphasized that the Eucharistic sacrifice of its very nature is the unbloody immolation of the divine Victim, which is made manifest in a mystical manner by the separation of the sacred species and by their oblation to the eternal Father."[2] Each and every Mass pours forth the fruits of the sacrifice of Calvary into the Church for the inestimable benefit of all

---

1. Given the confusion surrounding this topic, it is important to define the term "private Mass." Joseph Jungmann's seminal work on the liturgy has this to say about the subject: "From these Masses said in private homes, or on an estate or at a graveside where at least a group of people, however small, attends the service, we must carefully distinguish the *private* Mass strictly so called. This we understand as a Mass celebrated for its own sake, with no thought of anyone participating, a Mass where only the prescribed server is in attendance, or even where no one is present, as was once the case in the so-called *Missa solitaria*. These are Masses—contrasted to the conventual Mass and the parochial Mass—which are most generally referred to in medieval documents as *missae privatae* or *speciales* or *peculiares*" (*The Mass of the Roman Rite* [Westminster, MD: Christian Classics, 1986], 1:215).
2. Pius XII, Encyclical Letter *Mediator Dei* (1947), n. 115; cf. nn. 68–70.

the faithful—for the release of souls in purgatory, for the honor of the saints in heaven, and for the perseverance of souls on earth—and ultimately for the salvation of the entire world.[3] Therefore, objectively speaking, the more Masses celebrated, the better off the world is.

In the maelstrom of postconciliar changes, the private Mass fell under a shadow of suspicion, even contempt. With rare exceptions, individual monks no longer celebrate private Masses. If there are several priests living in one place with one publicly scheduled Mass, they will generally concelebrate it. Surely there is something amiss here. The profound sacramental theology we inherit from the Middle Ages and the Council of Trent teaches us that *each* Mass—or to be more specific, each enactment of the mystical oblation on the altar—is a renewal and application of the saving event of the Cross, and as such, wins further pardon and actual graces for the human race. How, then, can this shift toward the communal be justified? Would not a denial that each priest should celebrate his own Mass each day imply at some level a repudiation of this theology, and with it, a downplaying of the Mass as a true propitiatory sacrifice? I am not speaking of a *formal* repudiation, such as Luther's or Calvin's, whereby the Mass is denied to be a sacramental representation of the sacrifice of Calvary. I mean a repudiation of the truth that *each and every* Mass advances the salvation of the world. If the practice of individual Masses is abandoned, it appears that personnel in the Church have made a decision that affects, nay retards, the salvation of sinners. A monastery in which twelve ordained monks daily offered *hoc sacrificium laudis* is responsible for pouring out the grace of Calvary twelve times upon this timebound and ever-needy world of ours. The one all-sufficient sacrifice with its intrinsically infinite merit was applied concretely to us, to the world of sinners, a dozen times.[4]

---

3. Ibid., nn. 71–75.

4. Note that if there are twelve priests in the community, one of them would not celebrate a private Mass that day in order to be the priest who offers the conventual Mass in the midst of his brethren. No priest celebrates twice a day (bination) unless pastoral need requires it, which would not be the case in such a community.

Colossal Difference

Let us examine the scenario more closely to see if mystical theology and common sense can shake hands. Say eleven of these monks are celebrating Mass at separate side altars each morning, followed later by the conventual Mass that the twelfth monk offers: then twelve re-presentations of the Sacrifice of Calvary take place. It is as if the veil separating earth from heaven were pierced twelve times to let the dew of grace fall through, that it might soak into the soil of our souls. Since the Eucharist as a sacrifice is propitiatory, it accomplishes what it represents: each time the Mass is offered, the fruits of the redemption are extended to souls throughout the world. As Pope Leo XIII stated: "Christ has willed that the whole power of his death, alike for expiation and impetration, should abide in the Eucharist, which is no mere empty commemoration thereof, but a true and wonderful though bloodless and mystical renewal of it."[5]

Now, let's say those twelve monks decide to stop celebrating their individual Masses and come together around the altar for one Mass—a *single* Mass, a single sacramental sacrifice. Certainly there may be several Mass *intentions*; each priest can bring his own intention and even accept a stipend for it. Nevertheless, when it comes to the immolation of the holy Victim, this Victim is made really present only once, and so the salvific *offering* of that Victim is made present only once. Extrapolate over the course of the year. At a more traditional monastery of twelve ordained monks, if we count not only the private *Missae recitatae* (recited or low Masses) but also the community *Missae cantatae* (chanted or high Masses), what do we find? The living symbols of the Lord's Passion, the full dynamism of that mystery, will have been made present upon the altar about 4,800 times each year within the walls of their most fortunate church. At a monastery where the twelve scrapped their personal Masses for concelebrated ones, the number drops drastically, to, let's say, 400 Masses a year. We are looking at a colossal difference in

---

5. Leo XIII, Encyclical Letter *Mirae Caritatis* (1902), n. 18.

sacramental mediation, priestly intercession, the irruption into the world of the Precious Blood that washes away our sins. Several thousand applications of the saving Passion of Christ to a world drowning in sin and suffocating with guilt is a much better prospect for the salvation of men and societies than a few hundred. But that's just the beginning; I limited myself to one small community of monks. Imagine the difference if we multiplied these figures for all Catholic priests across the face of the earth! By the singular privilege of their ordination and its sacred character, *each* of them is able to offer *every* day the one saving Sacrifice of Calvary, but so many, in the past forty years, have chosen instead to limit themselves to a single Mass celebrated *en masse*. Some have objected that this kind of language "quantifies" grace. It does not; rather, we must guard against so "transcendentalizing" grace that it ceases to be connected to space and time.

The Problem with Concelebration

If one denies that the number of Masses has any significance, is he not on the way to denying the truth of secondary causality, the truth of the historicity or temporality of grace, the truth of the ministerial priesthood, the truth that God *cares* for creatures—he cares so much for them that it makes a difference to him whether there are still one or two or five just men in a city of criminals? In the Catholic theology of the Mass, each priest, as *alter Christus* acting *in persona Christi*, renews the one sacrifice of Calvary, in such a way that both sides of the mystery are safeguarded: (1) there is no other and no further sacrifice than that of Christ, which in itself and with nothing else supposed suffices for the salvation of the whole of creation; and (2) there are ordained priests conformed to and participating in the unique office of the High Priest, such that there are *temporally distinct* makings-present or presencings of Calvary, pouring the grace and merit of the High Priest into the hearts of men here and now. If you get rid of (2), you are a classical Protestant; if you get rid of (1), you are a liberal Protestant. If you retain both and see them as mutually reinforcing, you are a Catholic. To separate one from the other destroys the sacramental economy and the truth of the Incarnation no less than if one were to separate the natures and persons in Christ, as Nestorius did.[6]

The abandonment of private Masses in favor of communal Masses, the sidelining of one-priest celebration in favor of many-priest concelebration, implicitly undermines the latter truth, namely, that there are temporally distinct presencings of Calvary which are *in themselves* really and truly channels of grace for the world. This confirms from yet another angle that the direction of the liturgical reform, as Michael Davies and others have long maintained, has an essentially Protestant trajectory.[7]

St. Thomas Aquinas was not unaware of the custom of concelebration, as used on rare occasions. An article of the *Summa* asks "Whether many priests can consecrate one and the same host?"[8] As an argument in the affirmative he brings forward a fact: "according to the custom of certain [local] churches, priests, when they are newly ordained, concelebrate with the bishop who ordained them."[9] The body of the article mentions the same custom, comparing it to the Apostles supping together with Christ at the Last Supper, and notes that when there are many priests, all direct their several intentions to one and the same instant of consecration, so that they share but one intention to consecrate. Replying to an objection, St. Thomas goes so far as to say: "Since a priest consecrates only in the person of Christ, and the many are one in Christ, for this reason it makes no difference whether this sacrament is consecrated [at a Mass] by one or by many, except that it is necessary to observe the

6. Nestorianism is "one of the great heresies of the fifth century, which broke the personal unity of Christ by positing in him two subjects [i.e., persons], one divine and one human" (*Dictionary of Dogmatic Theology* [Milwaukee, WI: Bruce, 1951], 199). In reality there is only one Person in Jesus Christ, the Son of God, who assumed human nature when "the Word became flesh and dwelt among us."

7. While the Eastern churches have developed a different tradition in regard to individual celebration and concelebration, it remains true to say that *in the West*, the widespread repudiation of the doctrine of the Council of Trent concerning the Holy Sacrifice of the Mass together with many of its practical implications is far more indebted to a Protestantizing mentality than to a desire (misplaced as it would be) to emulate Byzantine theory or praxis.

8. *ST* III, q. 82, a. 2.

9. Ibid., sed contra.

rite of the Church."[10] In other words, concelebration involves many priests acting *as one* because they have a single intention to consecrate the Eucharist. There is, then, only one sacrifice taking place when many speak the words of consecration. But precisely for this reason, the Angelic Doctor sustains the common sense view mentioned above, for as he writes elsewhere in the *Summa*: "In many Masses, the offering of the sacrifice is multiplied, and therefore the effect of the sacrifice and of the sacrament is also multiplied."[11] So the next time someone says "There's nothing the matter with concelebration," you might counter: "Sure, it's not morally wrong, but it robs the Church and the world of so many other Masses that could have been celebrated individually by those priests, and so it deprives us of many effects that might have been obtained."

The Popes Weigh In

Is this a view sustained by the papal Magisterium? Although, understandably, Pope Paul VI is no hero among lovers of liturgical tradition, we should not be especially surprised to find him *upholding* the custom of private Masses:

> We should also mention "the public and social nature of every Mass," a conclusion which clearly follows from the doctrine we have been discussing. For even though a priest should offer Mass in private, that Mass is not something private; it is an act of Christ and of the Church. In offering this Sacrifice, the Church learns to offer herself as a sacrifice for all. Moreover, for the salvation of the entire world she applies the single, boundless, redemptive power of the Sacrifice of the Cross. For every Mass is offered not for the salvation of ourselves alone, but also for that of the whole world. Hence, although the very nature of the action renders most appropriate the active participation of many of the faithful in the celebration of the Mass, nevertheless, that Mass is to be fully approved which, in conformity with the prescriptions and lawful traditions of the Church, a priest for a sufficient reason offers in private, that

10. Ibid., ad 2.
11. *ST* III, q. 79, a. 7, ad 3. In this context, St. Thomas explains why receiving many hosts at the same Mass does not increase the effect of the sacrament, whereas many Masses do redound to greater good.

is, in the presence of no one except his server. From such a Mass an abundant treasure of special salutary graces enriches the celebrant, the faithful, the whole Church, and the entire world—graces which are not imparted in the same abundance by the mere reception of Holy Communion.[12]

This passage is from Paul VI's encyclical *Mysterium Fidei*, promulgated in 1965, *after* the promulgation of the star-crossed Constitution on the Sacred Liturgy *Sacrosanctum Concilium*.[13] In it we see reproduced with utter fidelity the doctrine of Pope Pius XII, who treated of the subject at some length in his majestic encyclical *Mediator Dei* of 1947. Two paragraphs in particular come to mind:

> Some in fact disapprove altogether of those Masses which are offered privately and without any congregation, on the ground that they are a departure from the ancient way of offering the sacrifice; moreover, there are some who assert that priests cannot offer Mass at different altars at the same time, because, by doing so, they separate the community of the faithful and imperil its unity; while some go so far as to hold that the people must confirm and ratify the sacrifice if it is to have its proper force and value.
>
> They are mistaken in appealing in this matter to the social character of the Eucharistic sacrifice, for as often as a priest repeats what the divine Redeemer did at the Last Supper, the sacrifice is really completed. Moreover, this sacrifice, necessarily and of its very nature, has always and everywhere the character of a public and social act, inasmuch as he who offers it acts in the name of Christ and of the faithful, whose Head is the divine Redeemer, and he offers it to God for the holy Catholic Church, and for the living and the dead. This is undoubtedly so, whether the faithful are present—as we desire and commend them to be in great numbers and with devotion—or are not present, since it is in no wise required that the people ratify what the sacred minister has done.[14]

One could assemble reams of testimonies from Tradition and tight theological argumentation in defense of what the Popes teach

---

12. Paul VI, Encyclical Letter *Mysterium Fidei* (1965), n. 17.

13. In fact, the Pope is quoting from that constitution in the first sentence of the excerpt, which echoes a similar phrase from Pius XII.

14. *Mediator Dei*, nn. 95–96.

here. That being said, there is something more that we must not forget. When it comes to mysteries beyond the reach of reason, the truth is as much a matter of that mysterious center of the person we call the "heart" as it is of the mind—a matter of whether our spiritual instincts are right, our intuitions sound, and our inmost feelings harmonious with reality. Modernism, though it claims to be from and for our feelings, exudes the lifeless chill of rationalism and freezes whatever it touches. In contrast, the dogmas and practices of traditional Catholicism, though they have at their disposal armies of ironclad scholastic proofs, breathe and sing and sigh like the living presence they mediate to us in flesh and blood.

A Stream of Sacrifice Poured Up

With this in mind, let me return, in the end, to the beginning. In one of Robert Hugh Benson's finest novels, *The King's Achievement* (1904), there is a passage that deeply resonated with me when I first read it a few years ago, as it called back to mind the short but precious time I spent with the monks of Le Barroux as well as that early morning Mass with the Abbot of Fontgombault.[15] At this point in Benson's tale, the character Christopher Torridon, a young monk at Lewes Priory, is reflecting on the daily monastic routine's all-encompassing goal: "the uttering of praises to him who had made and was sustaining and would receive again all things to himself." The monks, he writes,

> rose at midnight for the night-office, that the sleeping world might not be wholly dumb to God; went to rest again; rose once more with the world, and set about a yet sublimer worship. A stream of sacrifice poured up to the Throne through the mellow summer morning, or the cold winter darkness and gloom, from altar after altar in the great church. Christopher remembered pleasantly a morning soon after the beginning of his novitiate when he had been in the church as a set of priests came in and began Mass simultaneously. The mystical fancy suggested itself as the hum of voices began that he was in a garden, warm and bright with grace, and that bees about him were making honey—that

---

15. My experience with the monks at Le Barroux is recounted in chapter 4.

fragrant sweetness of which it had been said long ago that God should eat—and as the tinkle of the Elevation sounded out here and there, it seemed to him as a signal that the mysterious confection was done, and that every altar sprang into perfume from those silver vessels set with jewel and crystal.[16]

There are lots of scholarly studies and popular pamphlets (especially from the 1960s and 70s) questioning or rejecting private Masses and defending concelebration. Earlier still, Karl Rahner had sown seeds of doubt with his dense and subtle speculations. The shelves of seminary libraries groan with such materials. After slogging through page after page of these treatises, however, what I always want to know is this: Why is it so hard for these people to see what Christopher Torridon (that is, Robert Hugh Benson), and generations of simple believers over the centuries have seen? It consoles me to know that every day, every year that passes, slowly but surely, the Eternal High Priest is drawing the hearts of his ministers back to the altar of God, for the service of which they were ordained; that he is calling them to "worship in spirit and in truth" (Jn 4:23). *Introibo ad altare Dei, ad Deum qui laetificat juventutem meam.* As Benedict XVI said in his homily for Midnight Mass of Christmas 2010: "The Liturgy is the first priority. Everything else comes later."

---

16. Robert Hugh Benson, *The King's Achievement,* ed. Francis X. Connolly (New York: P. J. Kenedy & Sons, 1957), 86.

11

The Liturgical Reform's
Long-Term Effects on Ecumenism

THE CLASSICAL ROMAN RITE[1] is the very locus of catholicity and orthodoxy for the West. I mean this on several levels. It expresses the *universality* of the Catholic Church of the Latin Rite, as all the missionaries of former ages could bear witness. It also gives accurate, sublime, and moving expression to her dogma. But even more, it is the very *language* of the Western Church at prayer. Her identity is contained in its every phrase and gesture. It is not merely one prayer among many; it is the Church-at-prayer *par excellence*, engaged in her definitive act of paying homage to the Most Holy Trinity. The purpose of human existence is to worship God, which includes within itself love, obedience, sacrifice, faith, and even vision, for all of these things are ordered to the supreme act of heavenly adoration, as the Book of Revelation shows us.[2] To the extent that this worship suffers in its purity and lucidity, the Church's mystical life is dulled; her life becomes increasingly bureaucratic and pedagogical. The liturgy should be educating

---

1. One may legitimately speak of a "classical Roman rite" for three reasons: (1) in spite of historical development and the accretions of this or that regional tradition, the *core* of what we refer to as the "traditional Latin Mass" is truly ancient, going back substantially to the first millennium and even the first half of the first millennium; (2) I mean to refer rather broadly to the whole preconciliar liturgical heritage and not simply to the Roman Missal codified after Trent; (3) I do not wish to exclude the *possibility* of a reform of the new Missal that would bring it essentially into spiritual conformity with the ancient heritage.

2. See Ratzinger's brilliant essay "Theology of the Liturgy," in *Looking Again at the Question of the Liturgy with Cardinal Ratzinger*, also available at www.pierced-hearts.org/benedict_xvi/Cardinal%20Ratzinger/theology_liturgy.htm.

Christians in the most fundamental sense by teaching them the spirit, the attitude, the mind of prayer; yet only her traditional liturgy did and can do this thoroughly.

In the ancient Roman rite one sees, still present and alive, elements that are common to the historical liturgical rites of all the Eastern and Western churches. The Catholic Church's genuine and prior *orthodoxy,* her pre-possession of all that the separated Orthodox Church still to some extent retains and lives, is located, as in a center-point, in the prayers, rituals, and spirituality of the ancient liturgy, as even a sufficiently open-minded Orthodox bishop would be able to see were he to attend a Solemn Pontifical High Mass with chant and polyphony—something he would *not* be able to see in a celebration of the Novus Ordo Missae except in the most rarefied circumstances, for example at the Brompton Oratory in London, or at the Vatican in the days of Benedict XVI.

Although it may seem ironic to say so in light of the now-distorted understanding of "ecumenism"—a distortion to which the globally adverse reaction to even as tame a document as *Dominus Iesus* bore dramatic witness—it is nonetheless true that the received Western liturgical rites were, and should always be, the means and the focal point of authentic Christian ecumenism between East and West, and, in a different way, between Catholics and Protestants. We seek to bring all Christians, by the path of a conversion of mind and heart, before a common altar of worship ("Introibo ad altare Dei..."), where the natural unity of mankind is elevated to the supernatural unity of the Church, of whose heavenly destiny the earthly liturgy is the foretaste and symbol ("Emitte lucem tuam et veritatem tuam ... in montem sanctum tuum, et in tabernacula tua"). Directly following upon the demise of traditional liturgy is a loss of awareness of the uniqueness of the Catholic Church, an abandonment of *extra ecclesiam nulla salus*—the only position she can take without tearing herself apart into contradiction. Bad liturgy is volatile fuel for false ecumenism. No wonder many priests and bishops no longer speak to us as the Fathers and Doctors of the Church and all the saints down through the centuries have spoken: the latter were formed and nourished by a liturgy that invited continual conversion of heart and mind to the one true faith, whereas the former are now generally celebrating a liturgy that looks rather like the flotsam and jetsam kept by traditional Protestants after the shipwreck of the Reformation. It is as though the Church belatedly "admitted" that she was wrong all along. This, in practice, is the result of the massive changes. In principle, of course, the liturgical changes do not *need* to be interpreted this way. Yet the fact that they *are* interpreted that way by a vast majority should give us cause for serious anxiety. If it takes a doctorate or two in theology in order to figure out the sense in which the Catholic faith is the one true faith, and the Catholic Church is the one true Church of Christ, then our Lord's mission to save mankind by forming us into a visible body gathered around his Vicar on earth will have been a resounding failure, since it would not be possible even to identify this body or to define how one becomes a member of it.

In the *symbolic* value it has come to possess in the postconciliar period, the Novus Ordo Missae is a kind of rough-and-ready repudiation of the Council of Trent, of Boniface VIII's *Unam Sanctam*, of Patristic mystagogy, the antithesis of our ancient and medieval heritage. For all these reasons, it represents a contradiction of the liturgical self-presentation suitable to the true Church in its Western or Latin tradition. False ecumenism will continue to spread and pollute the faith of believers as long as the leaders of the Church keep the faithful in bondage to a "reformed liturgy" of this kind. A war is now taking place between the essence of the Church and her accidents. The accidents want to wrest control of the essence and, as it were, remake it into a different substance. This war is going on all the time, with each new church built in a modernist style, each congregation-facing vernacular liturgy accompanied by the strumming of guitars, each ecumenical prayer gathering that obscures the centrality of the Eucharist, and it may well lead to an unprecedented spiritual cataclysm that will shatter much of the Church on earth. "When the Son of man comes, will he find faith on earth?" (Lk 18:8). He will find faith in unlikely places, but its heart will be the ancient liturgy or at least some vivid simulacrum of it.

Visiting and praying in the glorious Gothic churches with which Europe abounds, and pondering the life of the medieval Catholics who built them and prayed in them, has prompted me more than once to think that we moderns have forgotten what Christian life and divine worship are about. What we need for a sane Christian life together is a truly *noble* simplicity, the silence of anonymity, clouds of beautiful song and incense, a healthy routine of life marked by feasts and processions, a life of worship spent in churches that foster an ecstatic praise of God, bearing witness to his transcendent beauty. This is what the Middle Ages had in abundance, for all that the poor peasants lacked; this is what we fundamentally lack, for all the cleverness and comfort we have. Every time an ugly church is built or the Mass is offered unworthily, faith is endangered, distorted, thinned out. In the Church on earth, half a century out from the great springtime that was supposed to follow the Second Vatican Council, we are in the midst of a darkening Age of Unbelief, a winter colder than the Enlightenment itself.

The principal causes of this darkness are the fatally flawed reform of the liturgy and the apostasy of bishops—two things that are not unrelated. Despite the good fostered by John Paul II during his reign, the liturgical wasteland grows evermore, and the rage for everything modernist continues unabated throughout the Western world, with most people turning a deaf ear to anything the Church may say. And until these wounds are healed, the Church will continue to lose blood—that is, she will lose faith, believers, cultures. Her perennial missionary work is now, in a sense, impeded by the shallow horizontalism of her worship. The Novus Ordo Missae is wanting in substance, in the "thickness" of prayer, and it will be a ball and chain for the New Evangelization.

Let us reflect for a moment on this descriptive term, "thickness." All the great religious traditions of the world have retained a sacred language, at least for some of their rites and chants: for Eastern Christians it is ancient Greek, Church Slavonic, or some other venerable tongue; for the Jews, Hebrew; for the Muslims, classical Arabic; for the Hindus, Sanskrit. They take pride in using this holy language for worship, keeping it alive in scholarly meditation. The common people have heard it for so many centuries that there is no real difficulty presented by its ongoing use. Some kind of sacred language seems almost to be a constitutive component of religion as such. The rhythmic, melodious chanting of sacred texts is also such a component. Dignified ritual motions, priestly vestments, incense —these too seem to be, from the point of view of the phenomenology of religion, intrinsic to the *cultus* of the divine. Now, if we consider the Solemn High Mass of the classical Roman liturgy, we see the sacred text chanted and incense offered, by priests in magnificent vestments; we see ritual motions suitable to the worship of the all-holy God and the Son of God, Jesus Christ.[3] Such a liturgy is naturally accessible to members of the other great religious traditions; the traditional Mass fulfills the longings of the Gentiles for perfect worship. The traditional liturgy is thus the *chief missionary tool* of the Catholic Church, her main point of contact with Jews, Muslims, Eastern Christians, Hindus, Africans, and so on. By jettisoning this liturgy, the Church abandoned a missionary foothold of great value; it is harder for her to show traditional cultures that she is not just another spokesperson for the contemporary West, which has little good to offer to any traditional culture, tending rather to spread the pollution of her atheistic and materialistic worldview. By suppressing the palpable verticality and ritual splendor of the traditional Roman liturgy, she burned the bridge of piety and its manifold expressions that link her to pagan cultures and their own halting attempts to cultivate piety toward the divine.

But now I come back to the theme announced in my title. The banishment of the ancient Roman rite was also one of the most foolish *ecumenical* moves possible. Instead of keeping the traditional liturgy by which we possess a great likeness to the Eastern Orthodox, who are (with the Eastern Catholic Churches) the "other lung of the Church," we now have a liturgy of a more Protestant appearance, in an age when many mainstream Protestant denominations are dying out. In fact, the very changing of the liturgy on a large scale and the repudiation of much that was sacred in it is, in the minds of the few Orthodox who study these matters, decisive proof of papal imperi-

3. Example: a person familiar with Japanese theater and worship would be struck by the uncanny "orientality" of the Solemn High Mass: all the ministers continually and gracefully bowing to one another, incensing one another at the Offertory, etc.—it is like *noh* theater writ large, the Japanese ethos finally transferred into its true home, where it most belongs. Surely this had something to do with the initial successes of St. Francis Xavier and other Jesuits in the Far East.

alism and the adultery the Roman church has committed with modernity. Scrapping a truly ancient liturgy in favor of a pseudo-ancient liturgy convinces an Eastern Christian that the Roman Church does *not* preserve the Tradition intact; and in this instance, however many theological distinctions one may rightly demand, they would score a point or two. It is ironic that the classical Roman liturgy—which, in its fundamental elements, stretches back to the first millennium, displays innumerable points of contact with the Eastern liturgical tradition, and gathers into itself all essential expressions of the human longing for the divine as found in other great religions—was buried under a committee product which is neither ancient nor ecumenical nor notable for its sacrality.

The ecumenism of the new form is nothing other than the horizontal "lowest common denominator" ecumenism so rightly condemned by many popes. It is "ecumenical" by being generic, like prime matter, open to a world of possibilities, lacking form and substance. In contrast, the traditional liturgy emerges from and always points to the heart of the Christian faith, its total nexus of mysteries. This is the quality that makes the *usus antiquior* an invaluable means for the rediscovery of the historical continuity and apostolic foundation of the Catholic Church. The ancient liturgy is profoundly ecumenical in the best sense of the word because it stresses the fundamental truths of faith, which it exemplifies, inculcates, symbolizes. By a quite legitimate paradox, it is exactly the antithesis of what is now meant by "ecumenism," precisely because it best serves the real purpose of all dialogue with non-believers or sectaries—namely, conversion, entrance into the one true Church, the Catholic Church founded on the rock of Peter.

In the end, there are only two possible directions for the soul: either the liturgy shapes one's personality, or one's personality shapes the liturgy. The first is true *formation* in the monastic sense, whereas the second is *reformation* in the Protestant sense. I once heard a Greek bishop express a similar sentiment: "In the East, we think what we pray. In the West, you pray what you think. So, our theology doesn't change because our liturgy doesn't change, whereas when *you* began to change your theology, you also changed your liturgy." This is a true judgment, but it is true only about the *modern* West, for what the good bishop described was the Enlightenment-inspired project of the reductionistic (and eventually victorious) faction of the liturgical movement, as distinct from its dogmatic-mystical mainstream represented by figures like Dom Guéranger. Enlightenment rationalism misunderstands the active power of the intellect and pictures man the thinker as reconstructing and deconstructing reality. It turns away from the *anima fit quodammodo omnia* (the soul becomes, in a way, all things) of Aristotle and St. Thomas, with their teaching that knowledge means a profound communion of known and knower, of the reception of the known into the knower. In the West, too, up to and including the great age of the medieval Doctors, both monastic and scholastic theologians "thought what they prayed"—not just in personal prayer, but also in liturgical prayer. The sermons of the great Cistercians are a tapestry made up of texts expounded with the aid of the liturgy. St. Thomas, St. Bonaventure, St. Albert, and the rest often turn to the liturgy in their theological reflections, and not just on strictly liturgical matters. For instance, Thomas cites one of the collects of the Mass to bring home the truth that God's omnipotence is manifested most of all in his showing of mercy.[4]

These thoughts also convince me more than ever that genuine renewal in theology, the *ressourcement* or "return to the sources" so highly promoted by some at the time of the Council and still championed today, cannot take place unless we return not just to intellectual sources but also to *liturgical* sources—*not* in the antiquarian way condemned by Pius XII and then promptly adopted by Bugnini and the Consilium, but rather, the liturgical tradition as we have received it from Holy Mother Church, from her popes and saints, and under the constant guidance of the Holy Spirit. In many ways, the very idea of a comprehensive reform of the liturgy, "updating it," "modernizing it," is disturbing to anyone sensitive to the fixed nature of the relationship that exists between liturgy and tradition. Tradition is not merely "what dead people used to do or think"; it is the truth handed down to us unbrokenly by the Apostles and their successors, and cherished by the Christian people. It is our lifeline

4. *ST* I, q. 25, a. 3, ad 3.

with the past, our chain to the Apostles and the Lord. It is the source, the contact point, of our living union with the past. Liturgy is not merely "what we do at Mass"; it is the *summa* of our religion, the still-point of the believing soul, the ultimate perfection of faith in this life. Change the liturgy enough and—for all intents and purposes—you have changed the religion. To vivisect an animal is sooner or later to kill it.

Can one imagine Orthodox Christians—or today's Byzantine Catholics, for that matter—radically changing their liturgy? Can one imagine "traditional" Protestants such as High Church Anglicans or conservative Lutherans, radically changing *theirs*? Can one imagine observant Jews or Muslims suddenly changing their customary forms of worship in any substantive way? The thing is impossible. Other religions and other instantiations of Christianity will not abandon their forms of worship, because they consider these forms among the most holy, most precious, most fundamental elements of their religious life. And the same was once true of us, of our traditional liturgy. But we are now in our fifth decade of a dumbed-down ritual and the phenomenon of institutionalized abuse. Benedict XVI, for all his famous criticisms of the new liturgy, seems to have felt his hands tied by the enormity of the problem, as he beheld from the papal throne the devastating carnage of entrenched malpractice that has gained the honorable status of a quasi-tradition.

There is no question that a serious "reform of the reform" could be undertaken such that this quasi-tradition would find itself buried along with the Synod of Pistoia, the Breviary of Quiñones, and other historical aberrations, but this undertaking, so long awaited by traditional Catholics, presupposes a pope who is convinced that the Church simply cannot survive unless she is connected once again to her full liturgical heritage, and who is zealous to see it return; a pope with an iron will, ready to wield his full Petrine authority to undo what Paul VI's misuse of the same authority inaugurated; a pope with diplomatic skill and boldness in the appointment of new bishops and the disciplining of existing bishops; and a network of papal agents and supporters throughout the world to implement swiftly and effectively the course of action decided upon. The Lord who works wonders has wrought many surprises in papal history, as when Cardinal Giovanni Maria Mastai-Ferretti, elected pope with a reputation for liberal sympathies, ended up the 19th century's most infamous and indefatigable opponent of liberalism, Blessed Pio Nono. We might fittingly turn to him in prayer, asking through his intercession for that restoration of the *libertas Ecclesiae* which begins with the freedom to "go unto the altar of God" in just the way our forefathers had done for centuries.

12

Latin, the Ideal
Liturgical Language of the West

M ANY CONVINCING ARGUMENTS can be and have been given in favor of preserving the Latin language in the liturgical life of the Roman Catholic Church—as even the Second Vatican Council's Constitution on the Sacred Liturgy *Sacrosanctum Concilium* (1963) stated that it should be, following close on the heels of John XXIII's remarkable Apostolic Constitution *Veterum Sapientia* of 1962.[1] As we all know, Pope John XXIII's and the Council's reaffirmations of Latin in the liturgy were more or less cancelled out completely by the ill-considered decisions of Pope Paul VI, who once more demonstrated to the world that if the pope enjoys the charism of infallibility when teaching the truths of faith and morals, he enjoys no such gift in regard to particular prudential judgments, including the dispositions of the liturgy in its change-

---

1. *Sacrosanctum Concilium* states: "Particular law remaining in force, the use of the Latin language is to be preserved in the Latin rites" (36.1); "steps should be taken so that the faithful may also be able to say or to sing together in Latin those parts of the Ordinary of the Mass which pertain to them" (54); "In accordance with the centuries-old tradition of the Latin rite, the Latin language is to be retained by clerics in the divine office" (101.1). Even Annibale Bugnini writes in his memoirs: "The conclusion reached in this debate [between partisans of Latin and partisans of the vernacular] was ultimately set forth in Chapter I of the Constitution on the Liturgy, where the question is answered in a way that reconciles the rights of Latin and the need of the vernaculars in celebrations with the people" (*The Reform of the Liturgy* [Collegeville: Liturgical Press, 1990], 25). Would that the rights of Latin had been respected by Paul VI.

able elements.[2] In any case, my purpose in this chapter is not to cat-alog and review the many arguments in favor of Latin, a task that has already been well explored by others, but merely to speak of some of my own personal experiences of where and when the impressive unity of Latin would have made so much more sense in real life than the Babel of vernacular languages.

My wife and I lived in Austria for seven and a half years. Being in Europe convinced me past all doubt that the switch after the Council to an exclusive use of the vernacular for the Mass was the most foolish and nearsighted change that could have been made. Instead of making the Mass more deeply accessible, it localizes, particular-izes, and relativizes it, shutting off everyone who does not speak the local tongue; traveling or immigrant Catholics are thrust into a for-eign environment that alienates them far more than the solemn Latin liturgy ever alienated the simplest peasant. In fact, due to its pervasive aura of sacredness and its perceptible focus on the mys-tery of the Eucharist, the traditional liturgy, even when the words are not fully understood, shapes the soul better than the new liturgy when cerebrally understood.

The irony can be seen on many levels.

First, Latin is universal and is not the daily language of any mod-ern nation or people. There is no cultural imperialism in the use of Latin, but rather a visible sign of the Church of Christ reaching out to all nations, leading them back to unity in one faith, one com-munion, one worship of God. If the use of Latin were argued to be a

---

2. Although I sympathize with many arguments given by supporters of the "reform of the reform," I cannot agree with their contention that Latin has always remained the language of the liturgy. It is, of course, the language of the *editio typica* on which translations are based, but the Vatican has done next to nothing in the past forty-five years to ensure that Latin remain the language of the Novus Ordo Mass *anywhere*. Already when Paul VI introduced the new missal, he lamented the loss of Latin it would bring, and said we ought to consider this painful sacrifice worth it in view of how well the vernacular would serve the contemporary needs of the Church. Whenever John Paul II mentioned Latin, he reserved for it a small place, not the dominant place given it by John XXIII and Vatican II. Nor did Pope Benedict XVI see to it that the Ordinary Form be celebrated far and wide in its Latin typical edi-tion; rather, he encouraged the rediscovery and spread of the Extraordinary Form, which, *Deo gratias*, remains in the Church's mother tongue.

form of cultural imperialism, we would have to go further and say that proclaiming and preaching the Trinity or the Incarnation is a form of *theological imperialism* destructive of pagan African, Asian, and European cultures and religions, or that the very use of the same Mass, the same missal (in however many vernacular tongues), is a form of *liturgical imperialism* destructive of the peculiar ways that an Aborigine might choose to worship Christ. There is no escaping this logic: if you deny the fittingness of a universal presence of Latin, a universality insisted on by none other than St. John XXIII, you are on the road to denying the universality of Christian doctrine and worship as such. Why acknowledge or adhere to *any* type of transcultural and transhistorical unity—why not opt for total pluralism, as postmodernism has done? Or perhaps I should say, as postmodernism has *attempted* to do, since one cannot exalt total pluralism without denying the intelligibility of communication and therefore rendering null and void the entire project.

Second, modern Europeans in general are strongly multilingual, which would make Latin easy enough for them to get used to, as indeed they once were accustomed to it not many decades ago. There has never been an age when Latin would be more accessible than now, precisely on account of the "globalization" taking place. If men of Switzerland or Denmark can and often must speak several languages, what would be the difficulty of liturgy in Latin? It would be a source of international unity among believers, far more than idiosyncratic local liturgies could ever be. In those years in Europe, I participated in many liturgies that would have gone far more smoothly had they simply been in Latin. On my sole visit to Lourdes, I attended a Mass in which the languages were being shifted constantly to accommodate the international congregation, an elaborate show of linguistic gymnastics that I found highly distracting, and it was almost impossible for me to pray. The already overly verbal and self-involved character of the new liturgy was heightened all the more by this preoccupation with proportional coverage of language groups.

Third, and building on the last point, because literacy has spread everywhere, large numbers of people are in a position to follow along with a hand missal or a booklet that reproduces the Ordinary of the Mass. Even the illiterate, who often enjoy (in compensation, as it were) a rich oral culture and a high level of intuitive understanding, will benefit from sermons in their own tongue that explain the Mass, as Romano Guardini explained it to his German congregations. Moreover, as Jacques Maritain says in *Peasant of the Garonne*, the believer who, by simply kneeling at Mass and letting his mind be drawn to heavenly things, is caught up in silent worship of God, does not need words, missals, long readings and sermons; it is enough for him to *be there*. As the peasant in the parish of the Curé of Ars put it: "He looks at me and I look at Him." When the liturgy breaks this immediate spiritual contact in favor of verbal didacticism, it does a disservice to the spiritual lives of believers.

Fourth, the longed-for fraternity of nations and peace on earth— what could serve this aspiration better than a liturgy everywhere the same? An American traveling in France, a German traveling in Spain, an Italian traveling in Denmark, indeed an Asian in Africa or an Indian in Australia, all of them would find themselves "back home" in the local parish church. And given the importance G.K. Chesterton and Gabriel Marcel rightly place on this deep and inexpressibly consoling feeling of "being at home," should not the Church do everything in her power to make the liturgy the very place where one can always be at home, no matter where one is? Not, of course, by making the liturgy chummy and casual, but by ensuring that it remains deeply familiar in its identity, coherence, consistency, and stability. It is, or should be, a single solemn act of adoration of the Blessed Trinity that never varies *in spirit* from the rising of the sun to its setting. As Our Lord says: "Believe me, the hour is coming when neither on this mountain nor in Jerusalem will you worship the Father.... The true worshipers will worship the Father in spirit and truth" (Jn 4:21, 23). This was once a common experience of Catholics. In spite of vast differences of peoples, cultures, and circumstances, the sacred liturgy was truly universal and unified, so that one encountered the beautiful face of Christ in the face of his Church everywhere. Lamentably, the Church of today gives quite a different impression, one of democratic diversity, with many different masters served on as many different mountains.

We are living in the age of travel, the age of the "global village." At least in the Western world, almost everyone travels at some point or another; there has never been a time in the entire history of the world when so large a number of people take trips within their country as well as to foreign countries. How foolish it was to break down the universal mode of worship just when it has become more needed than ever! The *usus antiquior* emphatically illustrates and admirably furthers the purpose of human brotherhood—and, as Henri de Lubac observes, there is definitive brotherhood only in a *common adoration of God.* In the realm of the Novus Ordo, however, the liturgical celebrations illustrate a diversity or plurality that is not traced back to unity and universality, as is painfully evident to a traveler who speaks few or no other languages than his own. Once upon a time, parishes and chapels across the entire globe testified to the profound inner unity of the Catholic (that is, universal) Church; now there is only the Protestant phenomenon of localization.

This last point deserves a bit of development. The era of the traditional liturgy in fact left much room for inculturation or local adaptation, whether in the design of churches, in the style of vestments, in the layout and decoration of sanctuaries, or in popular hymns, carols, and processions. Nevertheless, the one constant axis was the Holy Sacrifice of the Mass, which testified in its very language and ritual to an unbroken unity with Rome, the mystical-historical seat of the Church founded by Christ. The incarnational *scandal of the particular* was never sacrificed in view of temporary and superficial gains; Christ was never declared to be an African or an Asian, a female or a hermaphrodite, in order to win converts from paganism, feminism, gnosticism, etc. The Faith is founded on the rock of Peter, by providence Bishop of Rome, and this utmost particularity will remain until the end of time, as an image of the even greater scandal of the particularity of Christ, a Jewish man born in Nazareth during the heyday of the Roman Empire. The Chinese Catholic, as a man and as Chinese, worships God *in communion with Rome.* This is what the old liturgy proclaimed, in blissful and holy ignorance of the shallow charge of "cultural imperialism," which of course the proclamation of truth can never be, even though the Gospel was given to mankind through the most particular of all particular circumstances.

Some years ago, I was taken aback when a friend forwarded me a discussion by a conservative Catholic apologist who had come out in full arms and armor to defend the vernacularization of the Mass after the Council. My first impression was that his panoply of arguments, though reasonable-sounding, had already been rehearsed by the promoters of the Consilium's "reform" back in the 1960s, and had not gained in truth or persuasiveness with the intervening decades. My second impression was that I was looking at a case of old-fashioned dissent in respect of Pope John XXIII's Apostolic Constitution *Veterum Sapientia*, which declared Latin to be the permanent and preeminent language of the Roman Catholic Church's worship and theology. This Constitution has been endlessly violated since its promulgation, but it has never been rescinded nor its contents abrogated. It may be that a future pope will be able to take it up again with praise when the full effects of *Summorum Pontificum* have permeated the Church.

In any case, the apologist argued that Latin was the common language of ancient Rome, and so we ought to be using the common language of our day and age. Well, Latin certainly was the common language of many members of the Catholic Church once upon a time, in the declining Roman Empire, but already in the early Middle Ages, with the invasions of barbarian tribes speaking a plethora of languages, Latin became more and more a monastic and academic tongue, and at the popular level morphed into early forms of the Romance languages, such as the Italian dialect in which Dante wrote his *Divine Comedy*, or the Neapolitan dialect St. Thomas Aquinas used when preaching in his native territory. Thus, we may safely say that for over a thousand years the Catholic Church was worshiping in a language that had become a fixed, formal, sacred language, just as Hindus use Sanskrit, Jews Hebrew, Muslims Arabic, and so on.

It was also plain silly for this apologist to assert that most people in the old days did not understand what was going on at Mass. From what I can tell, it seems fair to say that far more people in the old days knew what was going on at Mass—essentially—and why it was important, than people know nowadays, even though the Mass is in their own language. Now, I would not blame the language for this; I rather blame the clergy, as well as the wretched translation of the Novus Ordo that was foisted upon the faithful by the original ICEL, malforming congregations for forty years. Still, the tectonic shift in language signified in the popular mind a shift in the very meaning of what was taking place in church, and hence, over time, a further deviation in the faith of the people regarding the Holy Sacrifice of the Mass.

Will it ever be possible to calculate the damage done to the Church by the banishment of Latin from her public worship? I think not. We have little conception of the true extent of the harm, just as we have trouble imagining the size of the earth, the solar system, or the galaxy we are in. By the sudden cessation and replacement of the solemn sacred language that for over 1,500 years had been the tongue, the voice, part of the inmost character, of the Western Church, the opinion already circulating at the time of the Council that the past is meaningless to the present and the present must be liberated from the past was confirmed and, as it were, institutionalized. In the very fact of vernacular worship is embodied the hermeneutic of rupture and discontinuity, a feeling of superior enlightenment and superior mission, as though *now* we finally understand, now we finally know what we are to do in the modern world. "Fools, for they have not far-reaching minds," as Empedocles once said. What we ought to do in the modern world is nothing other than precisely what we have always been doing in every age. The mistake was thinking that we could do better. For our punishment, we have been permitted not only to do much worse, but to burn many of the bridges that lead back to doing better.

Although he hated many features of the Catholic liturgy after his break from Rome, Martin Luther retained respect for the Latin tongue. Actually, the case is even more embarrassing for today's Latin-loathing Catholics, inasmuch as Luther had the basic psychological insight to realize that Latin adds something to the liturgy and that it should not simply be thrown out, as can be seen in his preservation of the Latin language in Lutheran worship—a custom that lasted well into the time of Johann Sebastian Bach, whose more compact settings of the Gloria and Sanctus are not crypto-Catholic oddities but perfectly useful Lutheran church music. Is it not long past the time when the Pope and the appropriate dicasteries at the Vatican should do something about this travesty, this amnesia of our own identity, history, culture, and mother tongue of worship?

Maybe someday historians will be able to look back and see that *Summorum Pontificum* marked a decisive shift in the "language wars"—a phrase by which I advert not to the more pedestrian, albeit still important, question of whether the Ordinary Form is well translated, but rather, to the more intriguing and more consequential question of whether a liturgy that has been cut off from its age-old roots in the Latin language and the piety of the Latin rite can survive in the long run. Maybe the motu proprio marks the beginning of a movement that will culminate, decades or centuries later, in the rightful triumph of the Latin liturgy, the Mass of our forefathers, the Mass of the ages. For this quixotic but, with God's power, manifestly achievable goal, we should certainly not fail to get on our knees to pray: *Miserere nobis, Domine.*

13

Catholic Education and Sacred Liturgy

I N THE YEAR OF FAITH convened by Benedict XVI, Catholics turned their minds toward the Second Vatican Council, commemorating the fiftieth anniversary of its opening on October 11, 1962. As had happened before in 2005 when the Church recalled the fortieth anniversary of the closing of the same Council on December 8, 1965, my thoughts were drawn to many of the themes this council discussed and synthesized in its sixteen documents. The first document to be promulgated was *Sacrosanctum Concilium* (December 4, 1963), and the last, *Gaudium et Spes,* in company with the declaration on religious freedom *Dignitatis Humanae,* the decree on the ministry and life of priests *Presbyterorum Ordinis,* and the decree on the Church's missionary activity *Ad Gentes* (all on December 7, 1965). In an address given when he was still Cardinal, Benedict XVI found special significance in the fact that the first document to be promulgated was the constitution on the liturgy. He then showed its organic interconnection with the other three of the Council's four constitutions:

> The fact that it [*Sacrosanctum Concilium*] was placed at the beginning was basically due to pragmatic motives. But retrospectively, it must be said that it has a deeper meaning within the structure of the Council: adoration comes first. Therefore God comes first. This introduction corresponds to the norm of the Benedictine Rule: *Operi Dei nihil praeponatur.*[1] As the second text of the Council, the Constitution on the Church [*Lumen Gentium*] should be considered as inwardly connected with the text on the liturgy. The

---

1. "Let nothing be placed before the work of God"—the chanting of the Psalms, the celebration of Mass.

Church is guided by prayer, by the mission of glorifying God. By its nature, ecclesiology is connected with the liturgy. It is, therefore, logical that the third Constitution [*Dei Verbum*] should speak of the Word of God that convokes the Church and renews her in every age. The fourth Constitution [*Gaudium et Spes*] shows how the glorification of God is realized in the active life, since the light received from God is carried into the world and only in this way becomes fully the glorification of God. In the history of the postconciliar period, the Constitution on the Liturgy was certainly no longer understood from the viewpoint of the basic primacy of adoration, but rather as a recipe book of what we can do with the liturgy. In the meantime, the fact that the liturgy is actually "made" for God and not for ourselves seems to have escaped the minds of those who are busy pondering how to give the liturgy an ever more attractive and communicable shape, actively involving an ever greater number of people. However, the more we make it for ourselves, the less attractive it is, because everyone perceives clearly that the essential focus on God has increasingly been lost.[2]

The Council also had a great deal to say about education—about its centrality in the life of the human and Christian community, about the urgent task of returning to classic sources in our tradition (including St. Thomas Aquinas[3]) so that we might recover their timeless wisdom in a world much in need of wisdom, and about how to combine the schooling of the mind with the schooling of the *heart*. If we put all this together with Cardinal Ratzinger's point about the primacy of adoration exhibited in the prayer of the Church, above all in her celebration of the sacred mysteries, we might be prompted to ask: What is the connection between education and the liturgy? Could it be said that all education flows from and culminates in liturgy? How might we learn from the Mass and

---

2. "The Ecclesiology of the Constitution on the Church, *Lumen Gentium*," published in *L'Osservatore Romano* on 19 September 2001; available at www.ewtn.com/library/curia/cdfeccl.htm.

3. *Gravissimum Educationis*, n. 10; *Optatam Totius*, n. 15; cf. Sacred Congregation for Catholic Education, *Ratio Fundamentalis Institutionis Sacerdotalis* (1970), AAS 62, p. 367, par. 71 and esp. p. 370, par. 79; John Paul II, *Sapientia Christiana* (1979), nn. 71, 79, and 80; *Codex Iuris Canonici* (1983), can. 252 §3; *Fides et Ratio* (1998), nn. 43 and 61.

the Eucharist how to be faithful stewards of a Council that so often sends us to them for light and warmth?

Master in the School of the Liturgy

Through the liturgy, Christ the Head of the Church principally accomplishes three things: he teaches, he rules, and he sanctifies his people. He teaches us through Scripture and the sacred symbols with which liturgical worship is suffused. He rules us by being himself present as High Priest and Bread of Life, establishing his kingship in our souls and, through us, in the world. He sanctifies us by pouring out his grace through the seven sacraments, offering us means by which we can be transformed step by step from mere servants into intimate friends.

With regard to teaching in particular, it should be noted that in this our state of pilgrimage, the culmination of sacred doctrine, or theology enlivened by charity, consists in the contemplative ascent to God through the study of sacred scripture. Therefore *all* other speculative disciplines are ordered to the knowledge of the divine truths, the mysteries, revealed in scripture. This is manifestly Aquinas's understanding of theology, as it is that of the Church Fathers. The liturgy is the privileged setting for scripture, not only by proclaiming the readings and the Gospel, but by containing the very essence of revelation in the sacrifice of Christ himself. The very language of the liturgy is, in all its dimensions, a continual exegesis of scripture. The symbols of the liturgy are the "mystagogy," in the Patristic sense, that lead one into the precincts of divine truth. They are the guide for man's senses and intellect. We cannot attain divine realities unless there is a condescension parallel to that of the Incarnation. The liturgy (re)presents the mysteries to the eyes of the soul, it gives the context in which the meaning of the Word emerges. In order to "read" divine things well, one must be educated in how to "read" the liturgy and the truths it contains—a skill in large part built up through well-prepared sermons at Mass and ongoing catechesis outside the Mass. We should desire to plumb the profound depths of the liturgy because it is the gateway to our Lord's very mystery, the most perfect way he left us for drawing near to him in this life of pilgrimage. The liturgy of the Mass is the microcosm of the entire Christian life, as it is of the natural life of man, whose social and political nature is expressed and fostered in public ritual worship; it is an earthen vessel that holds the oil of spiritual gladness.

The culmination of liberal arts is philosophy; the culmination of philosophy is metaphysics. Metaphysics, in turn, rises above its most extravagant expectations when called to serve as humble handmaiden to the science of theology, which is brought into being by God's revelation of his own inner life through the Incarnation of his Son. If these divine realities are most of all manifested and made present to us in the sacred liturgy, it follows that the ultimate purpose of *all* educational efforts, as of all art, architecture, community life, the whole life of man, is the adoration of God in the Holy Sacrifice of the Mass. Indeed, all things whatsoever in a Christian commonwealth are for the sake of worshipping the Holy Trinity through, with, and in the God-Man Jesus Christ, bringing about man's divinization or *theosis*, his participation in God's blessed life. This is what we read in Vatican II's Decree on Christian Education, *Gravissimum Educationis*:

> A Christian education does not merely strive for the maturing of a human person as just now described [in terms of psychological and social maturity], but has as its principal purpose this goal: that the baptized, while they are gradually introduced to the knowledge of the mystery of salvation, become ever more aware of the gift of Faith they have received, and that they learn in addition how to worship God the Father in spirit and truth (cf. Jn 4:23) especially in liturgical action, and be conformed in their personal lives according to the new man created in justice and holiness of truth (Eph 4:22–24); also that they develop into perfect manhood, to the mature measure of the fullness of Christ (cf. Eph 4:13) and strive for the growth of the Mystical Body; moreover, that aware of their calling, they learn not only how to bear witness to the hope that is in them (cf. 1 Pet 3:15) but also how to help in the Christian formation of the world that takes place when natural powers, viewed in the full consideration of man redeemed by Christ, contribute to the good of the whole society.[4]

---

4. *Gravissimum Educationis*, n. 2.

Teacher of the Spiritual Life

The foregoing points, though important, are rather general. Jesus in the Eucharist is our teacher not only with regard to the overall "shape" of Christian life, but also with regard to a right understanding and practice of the spiritual life—that marvel of sanctifying grace, the indwelling of the divine Persons in our soul. By urging us to receive his very flesh and blood, the eucharistic Lord rids us of the perennial temptation of spiritualism, for he is truly, as Benedict XVI so often emphasized, "Emmanuel, God *with us*." The Lord once said to St. Gertrude the Great in a vision: "Beware, for the future, how you desire so importunately to be separated from the body, merely for the sake of being delivered from the flesh, into which I pour so freely the gifts of my grace."[5] Yet by giving himself to us in an utterly hidden and mysterious manner, to be received in the darkness of faith, in the interior of the incorporeal mind which rules the world of matter, he disabuses us of the fallen temptation of materialism. We are all born materialists; that is our inheritance from Adam and Eve. We have to be educated to see and act upon the primacy of the spiritual realities that sustain and permeate the material world, the invisible that grounds the visible, the divine that creates and holds the world in being, the eternal that alone constitutes the horizon of our hearts. This is a primacy that must continually assert itself against sensuality's downward spiral, the allurements of pleasure or power, worldly distractions, the whole gamut of material rebellion.

Christ is patient and full of compassion, ready to wean us from goods that are not him or do not lead us to him; he is prepared to cause in us the good wounds of love, as St. John of the Cross would say, a self-giving love that will heal us of the bad wounds of selfishness. In this struggle with the fallen "I" we come face to face, again and again, with our frightful lack of humility, strength, trust, and all the other virtues, and so we are prone to falter out of weariness and, at times, a sort of disgust with ourselves or with the world as it is.

---

5. *The Life and Revelations of Saint Gertrude* (Westminster, MD: The Newman Press, 1949), 108.

Against this temptation to despair on account of our weakness and sins, not to mention those of the whole world, the Lord urges us to "take and eat" (Mt 26:26)—to eat his life-giving body "given *for you*" (Lk 22:19) and drink his purifying blood "poured out *for you*" (Mt 26:27). He urges us to trust in his boundless mercy for sinners, his desire to bear our infirmities (cf. Is 53:4), so that by a wonderful exchange we may receive from him the grace to accomplish our journey in faith—for he who eats and drinks Christ receives everlasting life (Jn 6:54).

Yet, even in this, our Lord strikes at the root of Pelagian pride, for we are utterly *dependent* on his body and blood, we cannot make progress unless *he* works within us: "Apart from me you can do nothing" (Jn 15:5). We cannot do good works or attain the truth unless the one Teacher (Jn 13:13), the one who alone is Good (Lk 18:19), dwells within us, and so we are humbled in our dependence on the visible-invisible sacraments with their play of light and darkness. We receive everlasting life only by *always* clinging to Christ in repentance, longing, and love. We must be changed from within by receiving the only One who can really and truly transform us. The sign, guarantee, and first fruits of this transformation are nothing other than the paschal victory of Jesus over death. The resurrection proclaims the never-ending vitality of the covenant between heaven and earth, it heralds the ultimate fruit for which we long, the vision of God by a creature made whole and holy. The Cross was not intended merely to overthrow the devil's inglorious kingdom, but to initiate with blood and water an undying sacred love between God and man. It is by God's help that we are forgiven and perfected; it is by his help that goodness triumphs on the battlefield of our soul. It could only be with God's help that the desire for the transcendent, the desire to make life holy and eternal, could be realized. And this is precisely what our Lord Jesus Christ accomplishes in his sacrifice on Calvary, making possible our sanctification and bestowing life everlasting upon us. We cannot merely imitate Christ from without, as though spiritual maturity were a question of "growing up," a kind of increasing independence from authority. On the contrary we must submit our hearts to the school of his Heart and become pupils more and more, not less and less. The Eucharist simultaneously wars against our false pride *and* our false humility; it strikes at the root of spiritualism no less than that of materialism.

Our Lord in the Eucharist embodies and exemplifies all contraries in their original unity, their intended harmony. He teaches us simultaneously a generous love for the universal Church and an unstinting dedication to the local or particular church. He gives himself as one Lord and Master, one pierced and glorified body, to his entire Mystical Body that is indefectibly *one* owing to his unity; but he thus gives himself in the eucharistic sacrifice and banquet offered on *this* altar around which *this* parish or chaplaincy is built. He is no abstraction toward which we grope, but utterly distinct, immediate, local—within and nevertheless beyond every local community that offers the same sacrifice. This is what binds us to each other and to the whole with an unbroken bond of charity, and gives each part a responsibility for, as well as a dependency on, the whole.[6] The one true Church, as Vatican II emphasized so forcefully, is not something abstract, cloudy, an ideal forever beyond the reach of divided Christians; she, the Bride of Christ, really and substantially exists in the Catholic Church under her God-appointed shepherds in union with the Vicar of Christ.[7] At the Mass, even as we partake of the one bread of life at one particular altar, we pray for this one universal Church into which, by God's mercy, we have been grafted, and in which the Eucharist remains the singular source of every good gift and every perfect gift that comes down to us from the Father of lights (Jas 1:17). For this reason, Cardinal Journet can write: "In the Christian economy of salvation, the Mystical Body, which is formed around the Eucharist, is itself the center of convergence of all the graces bestowed on the world.... Hence it is impossible to conceive of the salvation of the world without the Eucharist and the grace that flows from it."[8]

6. See *Communionis Notio* (1992) of the Congregation for the Doctrine of the Faith as well as Cardinal Ratzinger's *Called to Communion* and *God is Near Us: The Eucharist, the Heart of Life.*

7. See, in addition to *Communionis Notio,* two other documents of the same Congregation: *Dominus Iesus* (2000) and "Responses to Some Questions Regarding Certain Aspects of the Doctrine on the Church" (2007).

8. Charles Journet, *Theology of the Church,* trans. Victor Szczurek, O. Praem. (San Francisco: Ignatius Press, 2004), 183.

By the same token, the eucharistic Lord teaches us not to set up an opposition, but to seek and foster the deepest harmony, between the "vertical" and "horizontal" dimensions of our lives as Christians, the God-oriented and the neighbor-directed. As the Gospels pointedly show us, Jesus lives for his Father: he is, in his very being, "toward God" (Jn 1:1).[9] He says nothing but what he has heard and received from the Father (Jn 8:26, 38; Jn 15:15). He spends the night "in the prayer of God" (Lk 6:12).[10] His sole motivation is "zeal for God's house" and God's glory (Jn 2:17; 7:18). But this means, at the same time, a zeal for the salvation of God's *people,* since they are called to be living stones in his holy temple (1 Pet 2:5; 1 Cor 6:19), and, through grace, become his joy and crown (cf. Phil 4:1, Rev 21:2). His very being is *mission* for mankind: his being sent into the world, says St. Thomas, is nothing other than a prolongation in time of his eternal procession from the Father.[11] What he *does and suffers* for us men and for our salvation, to the sounds of both the feasting at Cana and the pounding of nails at Calvary, is the audible echo of who he *is* in the silence of eternity.[12] He freely laid down his human life, yielding himself up as a pure oblation to the Holy Trinity, a love-offering to the honor of God, the only worthy and acceptable sacrifice that atoned for all the sins of mankind. Jesus *lives* to make intercession for us sinners (Heb 7:25), so that we who were his enemies might become his friends (Jn 15:13; Rom 5:6–10).

Hence, the Eucharist, memorial of the Passion,[13] demonstrates at once the absolute primacy of God to whom alone the sacrifice of our entire being is due, and the urgency of mission "to seek and to save

---

9. St. John writes: the *Logos*, the Son and Word of God, is *pros ton Theon,* "toward God."

10. This is what the Greek says. Translations usually flatten it out to "prayer *to* God"—true, but not quite the point St. Luke is making. In these solitary nights when the disciples are sleeping, Jesus is awake, enveloped in the very element of his being, at home *as man* in the bosom of the Father which, *as Son,* he has never left.

11. Cf. *ST* I, q. 43, a. 2, ad 3; Journet, *Theology of the Church,* 66–69; cf. 21, n. 12.

12. I mean this analogously; there is no suffering in God, but there is the Son's total receptivity of his entire identity as Son, his divinity, from the Father.

13. Cf. St. Thomas, *Super Evangelium S. Ioannis lectura* 6, lec. 6, n. 964; *In IV Sententiarum,* d. 8, q. 1, a. 2, qa. 2; *ST* III, q. 66, a. 9, ad 5 and q. 73, a. 5, ad 2.

that which is lost" (Lk 19:10)—in a word, it calls to mind and pushes into actuality the defining purpose of our life: to love God with our whole heart, mind, soul, and strength, and to love our neighbors as ourself by leading them to that same love of God (cf. Lk 10:26). "There is no commandment greater than these" (Mk 12:31).

Fidelity to the Past is Fruitfulness in the Present

Much more could be said, of course, about the lessons that Jesus Christ teaches us every day in the Mass and in the Eucharist. In keeping with the theme of this chapter, however, there is one special lesson we can learn as we ponder anew the teaching of the last ecumenical council.

The very structure of each of the seven sacraments left to us by the Lord proclaims the past event (the once-for-all work of salvation he accomplished on the Cross), the present event (our sanctification here and now by the Spirit), and the future goal (eternal life in God).[14] This is true above all of the Eucharist, which was inaugurated on the eve of Christ's brutal death with the poignant words: "Do this in remembrance of me" (Lk 22:19)—eat my body, given up for you on the Cross, drink my blood, poured out for you in love. This sacrament is not a faded memory but a *living commemoration*, the mysterious making-present of the great once-for-all sacrifice. In this past event, because of the ever-living Christ who was its subject and remains High Priest forever, there is perfect and total availability in and for the present moment, and so also for all time to come: "God is not a God of the dead, but of the living" (cf. Mt 22:32). In the Eucharist we see perfect and total continuity between past, present, and future, the very origin, model, and goal of all fidelity to what has come, readiness for what is now, and hope and victory in what shall be. "He remains faithful, for he cannot deny himself" (2 Tim 2:13); "Jesus Christ is the same yesterday and today and forever" (Heb 13:8).

So, if we are called to be wholly "eucharisticized" in our minds and hearts, this means that we are called to be faithful in every way to all that Christ has given to his Church in the past, all that he is

14. Cf. *ST* q. 60, a. 3.

giving us right now, and all that he has in store for us until his second coming. The Eucharist itself teaches us the unbroken continuity of Tradition, for everything we say and do, in our Creed and in our worship, is "in commemoration of Him" through whose Spirit we receive the knowledge of truth (Jn 16:13; 2 Tim 1:14) and the power to love (Rom 5:5; Gal 5:22). The Eucharist announces, in the name of the Lord and of his Mystical Body: Remain faithful to your past, which is the spring of youth, if you expect to have life now, and life forever.[15] "I will go unto the altar of God, to God who gives joy to my youth" (Ps 42:4 Vulg.), as the priest recites at the beginning of the classical rite of Mass, as if to say: There, there at the altar, in the mystery of the sacrifice ever ancient and ever new, in fidelity to the commandment of love that Jesus gave us not only in words but in flesh and blood, is the secret of a joy and peace that the world cannot give, no matter how advanced it may seem to become, no matter how much power it seems to acquire over reality. Genuinely *human* (one might say, *humane*) progress is progress in virtue, toward the kingdom of heaven; true power is the power to love, to give oneself and forget oneself in service of others. All else is an abuse, a ruse, an inbreaking of the underworld.

And it is just here that we return to our point of departure, the Second Vatican Council. For in the minds of its chief protagonists, John XXIII and Paul VI, and in the minds of the Council Fathers, the Council had one sovereign purpose: to bring the riches of the Catholic faith, with all of its Tradition, more effectively into the world of today; to spread the fragrance of Christ—his grace and truth—far and wide for the salvation of souls.

For John XXIII, writing in 1961, the chief task facing the Church was "bringing the modern world into contact with the vivifying and perennial energies of the Gospel," and accordingly, the chief task of the upcoming Council would be "to give greater efficacy to her

---

15. This principle, in itself, constitutes a point of departure for a critique of the liturgical reform as it was carried out in the late sixties and early seventies. In that attempt at reform, as Ratzinger has argued, there was a clouding-over of tradition, an amnesia from which the Church has not fully recovered, especially in view of distortions in vernacular translations, Church architecture, and sacred music.

sound vitality and to promote the sanctification of her members, the diffusion of revealed truth, the consolidation of her institutions." In such a way, the Church "radiates new light, achieves new conquests, while remaining identical in herself, faithful to the divine image impressed on her countenance by her Spouse."[16] At his opening address to all the bishops on October 11, 1962, John XXIII said he called the Council in order that "this magisterium [of the Catholic Church], taking into account the errors, the requirements, and the opportunities of our time, might be presented in an exceptional form to all men throughout the world."[17] He went on to specify that the reason for adapting to the needs of the present (*aggiornamento*) was to "make men, families, and peoples really turn their minds to heavenly things," and stated openly: "The greatest concern of the Ecumenical Council is this: that the sacred deposit of Christian doctrine should be guarded and taught more efficaciously."[18] He continued:

> That this doctrine may influence the numerous fields of human activity, with reference to individuals, to families, and to social life, it is necessary first of all that the Church should never depart from the sacred patrimony of truth received from the Fathers. . . . That is, the twenty-first Ecumenical Council . . . wishes to transmit the doctrine, pure and integral, without any attenuation or distortion, which throughout twenty centuries, notwithstanding difficulties and contrasts, has become the common patrimony of men.

Finally, this pastorally sensitive and dynamic pope, not wishing to be misunderstood, made clear for the whole world why he convened a Council:

> The salient point of this Council is not, therefore, a discussion of one article or another of the fundamental doctrine of the Church

---

16. *Humanae Salutis,* Bull of Convocation of the Council (December 25, 1961), n. 2 and n. 6.

17. *Gaudet Mater Ecclesia*, Solemn Allocution at the Opening of the Council (October 11, 1962), first paragraph.

18. Right after this, he says the main preoccupation of Christian doctrine is with man's tending to heaven and using earthly goods with a view to attaining heaven. He says this not disapprovingly or with qualifications, but simply to emphasize a basic truth.

which has repeatedly been taught by the Fathers and by ancient and modern theologians, and which is presumed to be well known and familiar to all. For this a Council was not necessary. But from the renewed, serene, and tranquil adherence to all the teaching of the Church in its entirety and preciseness, as it still shines forth in the acts of the Council of Trent and the First Vatican Council, the Christian, catholic, and apostolic spirit of the whole world expects a step forward toward a doctrinal penetration and a formation of consciousness in faithful and perfect conformity to the authentic doctrine, which, however, should be studied and expounded through the methods of research and the literary forms of modern thought. The substance of the ancient doctrine of the deposit of faith is one thing, and the way in which it is presented is another.

In other words, while the doctrine is to remain the same, not deviating from Trent or Vatican I or the Fathers of the Church, and nothing of its prior formulations will be repudiated or compromised, a concerted effort will be made to increase its communicability and transparency, its resonance with modern man. We are looking not at a binary logic (*either* the past *or* the present) but at an apostolic effort to present anew to our contemporaries the sole deposit of faith and the many treasures the Church has received from divine largesse over the course of her pilgrimage. Put differently, the vital memory of the past, the saving mysteries entrusted to the Church, will be cherished all the more when they are brought to bear still more closely on the needs of the present, for the healing and elevation of the human race in time to come. As we have seen, this is a thoroughly "eucharistic" logic and aspiration, and as the Council documents were later to say more than once, such great goals can be achieved only by the cultivation of an intensive liturgical life whose soul is a burning love for the Eucharist.

The Meaning of "Reform" in the Church

Executing John XXIII's intentions for the Council in difficult years, Pope Paul VI enunciated the same message in his own style. There is no need to cite more than a few representative texts. In his inaugural encyclical *Ecclesiam Suam* of August 6, 1964, promulgated between the second and third sessions of the Council, he describes the *authentic* "spirit of Vatican II" in words reminiscent of his predecessor's:

> This time, [the resolve to "reform" the Church] is not to remove from the Church any specific heresies or general disorders, which, by the grace of God, do not exist within her today, but rather to infuse fresh spiritual vigor into the Mystical Body of Christ, insofar as it is a visible society, purifying it from the defects of many of its members and stimulating it to new virtue.[19]

Elsewhere in the encyclical the pope reflects on how the Church is assaulted by temptations to "disavow herself and take up the very latest and untried ways of life."[20] In this situation the helmsman of Peter's barque offers counsel:

> Now it seems to us that to check the oppressive and complex danger coming from many sides, a good and obvious remedy is for the Church to deepen her awareness of what she really is according to the mind of Christ, as preserved in Sacred Scripture and in Tradition, and interpreted and developed by the authentic tradition of the Church.[21]

The reform the Church needs, Paul VI continues,

> cannot concern either the essential conception of the Church or her basic structure . . . . There dwells in us the great inheritance of truth and morality characterizing the Catholic Church, which today possesses intact the living heritage of the original apostolic tradition. . . . Hence, if the term "reform" can be applied to this subject [viz., the Church], it is not to be understood in the sense of change, but of a stronger determination to preserve the characteristic features which Christ has impressed on the Church.[22]

The central theme of the Council—and fittingly, says the pope in this encyclical—is the Church herself, in her deepest mystery, in every aspect of her inner life and her outward mission "for the life

---

19. Encyclical Letter *Ecclesiam Suam*, n. 44.
20. *Ecclesiam Suam*, n. 26; he mentions modernism as a vivid example (nn. 48, 51).
21. *Ecclesiam Suam*, n. 26.
22. *Ecclesiam Suam*, nn. 46–47.

of the world" (cf. Jn 6:33; 6:51). "The Second Ecumenical Vatican Council is but a continuation and a complement of the First, precisely because of the task incumbent upon it to take up again for study and definition the doctrine dealing with the Church."[23] After this statement, the pope mentions with special honor two encyclicals that "offer us ample and clear teachings on the divine institution by which Christ continues his work of salvation in the world": *Satis Cognitum* (1896) of Pope Leo XIII and *Mystici Corporis* (1943) of Pope Pius XII.

It comes as no surprise, then, that the great Dogmatic Constitution on the Church, *Lumen Gentium*—promulgated three and a half months after Paul VI's encyclical[24]—is rich in citations from both of these timeless sources, not to mention *their* sources, scripture and tradition, nor that the Pastoral Constitution on the Church in the Modern World, *Gaudium et Spes*, looks with such intensity of gaze to the mystery of the Word-made-flesh and the kingdom of God he has planted in the midst of this world, as presented to us in the Gospels and the other inspired books. When we look with unprejudiced eyes, we find at the heart of the Council just what these two popes wished for and insisted on: a "renewed, serene, and tranquil" *ressourcement* and consolidation of all the treasures of faith, not skipping over any constitutive element—be it written or unwritten revelation, conciliar or papal authority, patristic, medieval, or modern theology at their best. The Council was and will continue to be, for all who inherit it, a collective spiritual exercise in remembering or recollecting (*Hoc facite in meam commemorationem...*), giving thanks and praise (*Gratias agamus Domino Deo nostro...*), and going out again on mission (*Ite missa est*). It was and it is thoroughly eucharistic. If we want the "key" to the Council and the guarantee of its ongoing relevance, we know where to find it, where John XXIII, Paul VI, John Paul II, and Benedict XVI knew to look

---

23. *Ecclesiam Suam*, n. 30; cf. John Paul II, *Dominum et Vivificantem*, n. 26. For a superb exposition of Vatican II's ecclesiology, see Journet's essay "The Mystery of the Church According to the Second Vatican Council," given as Appendix I in *Theology of the Church*, 369–428.

24. Namely, on November 21, 1964.

for it, where Pope Francis now urges us to go: in church, on the altar, at the Mass, in the Blessed Sacrament, in the supreme gift of communion, which is the foretaste of eternal life.

As mentioned earlier, the Blessed Sacrament teaches us to look beyond appearances at the hidden substance of things. This is true first of the appearances of bread and wine, which, after consecration, are the miraculously suspended veil beneath which is found, by divine power, the true substance of the Body and Blood of Jesus; but it is also true, by analogy, of the visible body of his Church on earth, which in appearance is often marred and wounded, torn by division, spotted by the sins of Christians, and yet in substance, in her inmost reality as the communion of saints, is the immaculate, holy, sinless Bride of Christ, the vessel of election, the home of all grace and truth in this world.[25] This is a lesson that we must recall, too, when thinking about the Second Vatican Council. In itself and in its legitimate ramifications, it is a "Council of the Holy Spirit," a privileged means through which the Church's heavenly Teacher and Shepherd has spoken to all his members in this world and in this age. But nothing created is so divinely good that it cannot be twisted by men, and the same has occurred with the Council, whose "letter" has been contradicted in the name of a supposed "spirit of Vatican II" taken as *carte blanche* to reinterpret every element of Catholic dogma and life. We know how false this is, false for so many reasons; we have heard some of them eloquently expressed by the pope who called the Council and the pope who brought it to a close. We can hear it above all if we read Benedict XVI's Christmas

---

25. As Journet explains (see *Theology of the Church*, 208–17), a frontier passes through the soul of each Christian: inasmuch as he is in a state of grace, he belongs to the Church; inasmuch as he is a sinner, he belongs to himself and to the world, so to speak, not to Christ. In other words, in the measure that one is a sinner, one is not a member of the Body of Christ, for then Christ himself would be a sinner and the source of sin, which is impossible. Thus, while the Church is never inwardly contaminated by sin, her mission, witness, and "image" in the world are obviously deeply affected and colored by the degree of fidelity of individual Christians. When Christians sin, they fail to live up to their own calling, and to that extent they fail to act *as* members of Christ, yet the world not surprisingly attributes *their* faults to the Church herself.

Address to the Roman Curia on December 22, 2005, where he elaborated the now famous contrast between a "hermeneutic of reform in continuity" and a "hermeneutic of rupture and discontinuity." In faithfulness to the Lord really present for us in the Eucharist, let us begin anew to learn from *this* ineffable gift how to distinguish the substantial from the specious, reality from appearance, fleeting fashion from timely truth. Let us learn to live in perfect fidelity to the unchanging Truth who does not leave us orphans (Jn 14:18), but in the power of his Spirit remains with us always, "even to the consummation of the world" (Mt 28:20).

14

A Threefold Amnesia:
Sacred Liturgy, Social Teaching,
and Saint Thomas

MANY YEARS AGO a thought dawned on me. At first it seemed fanciful, but as I weighed the evidence, it gained in plausibility. My question was: What, more than anything else, is the cause of the disorder and paralysis that reigns in the Catholic Church and in the life of her people today? My conclusion was that a threefold amnesia, to put it gently, had descended in the wake of the Council and gives a specific shape to the rebellion:

1. The attenuation or negation of traditional liturgy.
2. The downplaying of integral Catholic social teaching.
3. The dismissal of St. Thomas Aquinas as Common Teacher.

It is by no means self-evident that these three are connected, so the burden of proof is on me to illustrate how they are linked.

If my analysis proves correct, it will lead to an exact prescription for healing the disease. Amnesia is healed by entering back into the life one used to lead, so as to recover one's memory by vital experience. Or, to change metaphors, when starvation is the problem, there can be no substitute for food and drink. What I shall urge is that the food and drink we desperately need right now are the sacred liturgy in all its sacredness, the Church's social doctrine in all its breadth and boldness, and the teaching of the Angelic Doctor in all its expansiveness and depth. A true, heart-felt adherence to Tradition is expressed in reverence for the Fathers and Doctors of the Church as epitomized in St. Thomas, reverence for the liturgy they prayed and handed down to us, and reverence for the kind of Christian society they aspired to build. Take away any of these, and you take away the others.

Areas of Self-Destruction

Let me begin by pointing out three areas of simultaneous self-destruction.

First, the dismantling of the Latin liturgical heritage. The warnings in Pope Pius XII's encyclicals *Mediator Dei* (1947) and *Humani Generis* (1950)[1] were ignored; Pope John XXIII's noble paean to Latin culture and liturgy, *Veterum Sapientia* (1962), was, in general, ignored.[2] Subsequently Pope Paul VI allowed the Consilium to mutilate the Roman Rite and wreak havoc on the Church's immemorial liturgy, which had nourished all of her saints and theologians. This dealt a deep blow both to the means of sanctification for the faithful and to the wellspring of inspiration for theology. Is it surprising that, in the absence of a liturgy that has power to shape the mind and the imagination, we find ourselves confronted in the upper echelons of Catholic academia either with sterile pedantry or with wild and idiosyncratic systems of thought that a solid devotional life would have nipped in the bud?

---

1. *Mediator Dei* is filled with responses to errors just then beginning to thrive but now widespread, e.g., extensive use of the vernacular (n. 60), an "exaggerated and senseless antiquarianism" that would replace altars with tables, exclude black as a liturgical color, remove statues and other images, or disdain polyphony (nn. 61–64), a misunderstanding of the priesthood of the faithful (nn. 82–84), and so on. Yet even more evident than dissent from *Mediator Dei* has been the dissent from *Humani Generis*, with its teaching on the origins of the human race, the real distinction between nature and grace, and so on, as well as its clarification on the inherent authority of papal encyclicals when the pope intends, through them, to settle any disputed question (cf. n. 20).

2. Most people have never even heard of this Apostolic Constitution. It was promulgated on the eve of the Second Vatican Council in a ceremony of premeditated solemnity, its sole purpose being to reassert the centrality of the Latin language in the liturgical offices and educational system of the Catholic Church. The document mentions recent views in favor of decentralizing Latin, and rejects them unequivocally. Though much in the document is disciplinary in nature and hence subject to change, it nevertheless makes a *doctrinal argument* for the primacy of Latin, especially in worship and in theological instruction. The Constitution was, in any case, never abrogated, although its prescriptions are followed nearly nowhere.

At exactly the same time as this liturgical revolution was taking place, the full truth of our Lord's Kingship—clearly enunciated in Pius XI's *Quas Primas* (1925) and countless other documents and deeds of the Holy See—was being quietly pushed aside, as, for example, when several verses of the hymn *Te saeculorum Principem* were suppressed,[3] or when the Vatican pressed for the alteration of various national Constitutions and Concordats so as to make Catholicism no longer the official religion of these nations—in order, so it was said, to implement the teaching of *Dignitatis Humanae*.[4] Pope John Paul II wrote a letter to the French episcopacy stating that the separation of Church and State in France is not only *not* objectionable, it is part of Catholic social teaching itself! And this, in a letter commemorating the centenary of the 1905 Law of Separation, which St. Pius X judged to be founded upon "a thesis absolutely false, a most pernicious error."[5] Let us be frank, even if the Franks fail to be so: the sovereign Kingship of Christ over *both* individuals *and* nations, in the order of nature no less than that of grace, is denied almost everywhere since the Council, whether by being simply forgotten as one might forget about grandmother's rocking-chair in the attic, or by being repudiated as an extravagant relic from the benighted Middle Ages. Our Lord's Kingship is qualified and spiritualized to the point of irrelevance, as if Jesus Christ had not come to change radically our lives and our world.

Finally, in contempt of the instructions of John XXIII, Paul VI, and Vatican II itself, St. Thomas Aquinas was all but forgotten, or

---

3. See Michael Davies, *The Second Vatican Council and Religious Liberty* (Long Prairie, MN: Neumann Press, 1992), 243–51, esp. 246–48.

4. Of course, a certain separation *is* demanded by Leo XIII and all the earlier popes—namely, the Church and the State have their proper domains which cannot be merged. But the other side of the teaching was that the Church's domain and authority take precedence over the State's, and that the latter is obliged to help the former as much as circumstances allow. It would be one thing if it were admitted that the modern State is not in a position to fulfill this noble role. But it is quite another to say that the State has nothing to do with, and no debts toward, the Church. This is an independence that leads ultimately to the exaltation of secular sovereignty and the suppression of the Church's proper visibility and primacy.

5. Encyclical Letter *Vehementer Nos* (February 11, 1906), n. 3.

rather, he was tossed aside by schools whose faculties could not boast a feeble spark of the Angelic Doctor's wisdom, learning, and holiness. What is worse, the setting aside of his doctrine was *allowed.* In the postconciliar malaise, the Vatican made no serious effort to ensure that seminaries and other institutes of higher education actually *follow* the forceful commendations of Thomistic theology and philosophy established in decrees emanating from all the modern Popes and confirmed by the Council—this, in spite of what John Paul II had stated in 1980:

> The words of the Council are clear: the [conciliar] Fathers saw that it is fundamental for the adequate formation of the clergy and of Christian youth that it preserve a close link with the cultural heritage of the past, and in particular with the thought of St. Thomas; and that this, in the long run, is a necessary condition for the longed-for renewal of the Church.[6]

It has become fashionable to assert that all along the popes had no intention of exalting Thomistic doctrine but only of putting Thomas forward as an example of a holy theologian, a man who put God first in his life. Apart from the fact that this is obviously a false reading of what the popes actually said, it is seen to be false by its very superficiality. There are scores of saints who were holy theologians. The constant recommendation of St. Thomas is on a different plane altogether.

In sum, the earthly rulers of the Latin Church repudiated, or allowed to be repudiated, much that was most sacred, efficacious, and wise in the Church's life: the classical Roman Rite of the Mass, with its rich musical and ritual vesture; integral Catholic social teaching and the social structures that still embodied it in certain Catholic nations; the Church's premier theologian and his age-old wisdom. These three goods so fundamental to the life of the Church and the accomplishment of her mission of honoring Christ and preaching his Gospel—the goods of worship and sacrament,

---

6. "Perennial Philosophy of St. Thomas for the Youth of Our Times," *Angelicum* 57 (1980): 139.

of cultural conversion, and of human learning ordered to divine contemplation—were betrayed. The Church shook hands with triumphant liberal Protestantism, bowed down before the golden calf of democracy, and burned incense to the emperors of present-day academia.

This is what the princes of the Church *allowed*, regardless of what the Council *says*. The Council *says* that the liturgy is, in this world, the most exalted, most sacred, most mysterious encounter between God and man. What we have now, however, thanks to the new Missal and forty years of flaccid decentralization, is neither exalted nor sacred nor mysterious, but exactly the opposite. The Council *says:* Let the laity be as leaven in the dough, as the salt of the earth—the policy of the ancient Christians responsible for creating the Holy Roman Empire. What we got, thanks to the dialoguing of Roman Congregations and papal tolerance, is an "empowered laity" that distributes Holy Communion and votes for pro-abortion politicians. The Council *says:* Let seminarians be rigorously trained, taking St. Thomas Aquinas as their guide. What we generally see, if we are lucky to be in a diocese that still has vocations, are priests who do not even know the catechism and whose pastoral wisdom can be summed up: Do what feels right to you. And some are talking about a renewal, a second spring, in the Church? It would be as if the Jews enslaved in Babylon were busy chatting about the schedule for next week's temple sacrifices. There was a Jubilee Year in A.D. 2000, with three preparatory years dedicated to the mystery of the Trinity. How noble and well-planned. But we have a Church the vast majority of whose members could not begin to respond to the question "What *is* the Trinity?" without lapsing into crude Arianism, modalism, or a cartoon version of Gnosticism ("the Trinity is a loving family patterned after father, mother, child").

Links Many and Profound

We now have to look into the intrinsic *connections* among these three goods of liturgy, social doctrine, and Thomism, for the links are many and profound.

Theology demands a liturgical setting or context. That is, reflection on faith requires a life of prayerful faith, which is intellectually fed and affectively kindled by the mysteries of the liturgy.[7] Traditional liturgy has the light and heat it takes to enkindle ecstatic love. Thus, one may conclude that true theology—true both in the sense of doctrinally orthodox and in the sense of authentic, evangelical, nourishing—flourishes only in a fitting liturgical atmosphere. Thomistic wisdom and the traditional liturgy stand or fall together: the deeply affective wisdom one finds in the writings of a preconciliar theologian like Garrigou-Lagrange arises out of, and makes sense in relation to, the full-bodied, warm-blooded life of prayer that St. Thomas, Fr. Garrigou-Lagrange, and all holy men and women have lived, thanks to the inexhaustible treasury of beauty and wisdom preserved in and communicated by the Church's traditional liturgy, the Divine Office as well as the Mass.

While the expression "traditional liturgy" here quite naturally refers to the classical Roman liturgy itself, I think it is important not to exclude entirely the modern Roman rite when celebrated in a manner that is solemn, dignified, beautiful, and reverent.[8] A community that celebrated the new *Ordo Missae* in Latin, *ad orientem*, with Gregorian chant, incense, and suitable vestments, would, in spite of all the flaws in that missal, be a community in which genuine theology *could* flourish—and out of which political insight and the right kind of social activism would arise. There is nothing more intensely opposed to the liberal Western mentality than a rediscovery of, and a renewed love for, the sacred liturgy. It is not surprising to find a combination of social modernism[9] and liturgical modernism in the same persons, nor is it any surprise that Pope Benedict's motu proprio on the two "uses" of the Roman Rite has been so violently attacked by proponents of the "spirit of Vatican II."

But there is a further connection. Liturgy and theology are both public acts; they are therefore political acts. They do not exist in isolation but in the context of a society, a state, a culture. Take away

---

7. See David Berger, *Thomas Aquinas and the Liturgy,* trans. Christopher Grosz (Ypsilanti, MI: Sapientia Press, 2004).

8. A notable example comes to mind: the Ordinary Form Masses celebrated in conjunction with the Sacred Music Colloquium of the Church Music Association of America.

9. See Pius XI, Encyclical Letter *Quadragesimo Anno,* nn. 60–61.

their social swaddling clothes, their cultural manger, their political stable, and the baby is left naked, shivering, on the ground, exposed to the bitter elements of winter. A baby so exposed would die. In like manner, a liturgy exposed to the cold and dark secularism of modernity will first be invaded by it, becoming ever more cold and dark itself, and, dying a slow death, will succumb to it in the end. A world without well-constituted governments and rulers seeking the common good is a world that *instinctively,* in a thousand subtle and open ways, undermines the liturgy, or rather, the liturgical way of life, and with it, the science of sacred doctrine as well as the contemplative tasting and suffering of the Divine that shape and guide this theology. Destroy the Catholic state and culture, and you destroy the liturgical atmosphere of life. In doing so, you marginalize and paralyze the liturgy's own powers; you effectively destroy the most significant context in which there can flourish a theology that is deeply rooted in *living tradition,* full of mystical piety opening out on the transcendent mystery of God. Foremost in St. Thomas and his school will you find a consistent and profound tendency toward the full integration of these elements of tradition, science, and piety, along with an expectation that they must be translated into, or embodied as, the reality indicated by the term "Christendom."

Theology pursued as a discipline has a scientific character, if we understand "science" as the ancients and medievals did: the knowledge of objectively knowable principles and of the conclusions that follow from them, in their proper order and dependency.[10] This arduous discipline is the reflection, in the domain of the mind, of well-constituted civil society, which is the most manifest and formative order that men encounter, an ordering of citizens in view of their *princeps* (ruler). The *polis* or political community is, *in its essence,* the image of the Church, not her natural antagonist; it is only so far as man is fallen that the *polis* foolishly wages war against the Church. Tradition is the domain of the liturgy so far as it images the *heart* of the Church: fidelity, reverence, gratitude, loving insight

---

10. Science, in this ancient sense of the word, is deductive in method and proceeds from principles grasped either through experience or received from a higher science; it is not science as a set of hypotheses tested through focused experiments.

into her own past. But tradition can survive only in a traditional society, a society that reveres its own heritage. The state and the culture are the secular guardians of sacred tradition and of the natural virtues on which the institutional life of the Church is, at least in part, based. If theology may be defined as a traditional science rooted in liturgical experience and ordered to a wisdom full of piety, then the state and its culture may be defined as that specific framework of natural conditions and virtues within which this science and its inward form, the sacred liturgy, can flourish. One might counter this statement with the observation that the Faith itself, when lived with sufficient intensity, *creates* a Catholic culture and society and eventually a Catholic state.[11] However, when the Faith is weakly lived and ambivalently expressed, it will be reshaped into the servile image of the culture, society, and state it dwells in, until it merges with them for all intents and purposes.

The interconnection of sacred liturgy, Thomistic theology, and Catholic social order is not only *not* accidental, it is *essential*. The three *rise and fall together*—not always at the same time or in the same ways, but broadly speaking, and sooner or later, their profound connection makes itself evident in their mutual flourishing or mutual decadence. It is not surprising that in the High Middle Ages, liturgy, theology, and political culture, in spite of flaws that can never be entirely avoided by sinners, reached unimaginable heights of perfection—one need only think of the Cathedral of Chartres, the Corpus Christi processions, the mystery plays and morality plays, the *Summa theologiae*, the kingship of Saint Louis IX—nor is it surprising that in modern times liturgy, theology, and political culture have each fallen into unprecedented banality, bankruptcy, and blasphemy.

In all the Catholic schools with which I have been associated, I have noticed a striking fact: a person who does not hold onto all three of these things faithfully and integrally cannot, in the end, manage to hold onto even one. When someone tries to be faithful to St. Thomas but rejects or neglects the social teaching (everything

11. For an exposition of this truth, see my "Conversion of Culture," *Homiletic & Pastoral Review* 107.9 (June 2007): 26–31, 46–47.

that is summed up in the phrase "the Kingship of Christ") and/or the traditional liturgy, his Thomism is either truncated to begin with, or will eventually become corrupted. This can be seen in the many American adherents of St. Thomas who want to be faithful to their master, but who, by embracing political liberalism, end up simply abandoning *his* vision of social reality and, more worrisomely, the Church's *integral* social teaching. A kind of canker has been introduced, though it may take time to issue in some definitely obnoxious opinion. Similarly, a person who wants to be "traditional" but spurns or sleights St. Thomas will not be able to avoid contaminating and perhaps undermining traditional philosophy and theology; and once those foundations are gone, everything is gone—including the social incarnation of Christ in Christian culture and society.

The Corpus Christi Procession

The connection runs deeper still, if we examine the centermost point in each of the three. Let us begin with the most evident. As the Magisterium has repeatedly emphasized, the Holy Eucharist is the "source and summit" of the Church's very life[12]; it is the *raison d'être* of her sacred liturgy, the sovereign mystery to be celebrated, commemorated, worshiped, received. Since our Lord's sacrifice on the Cross is the Alpha and Omega of the Christian economy, the Eucharistic sacrifice is the focal point of cosmic reality, in relation to which every intellectual creature stands. Every angel and every man stands in some relationship, whether of salvation or of condemnation, to the "bread of angels," Jesus Christ in his flesh and blood. For this reason, the sign and measure of the health of the liturgy is nothing other than the vigor and intensity of the people's devotion to the mystery of Jesus Christ really, truly, substantially present in the Sacrament of the Altar, a devotion that will make itself evident in a longing for communion, a love for adoration, a ready recourse to Confession in order to receive Communion worthily, and a plethora

---

12. The famous phrase comes from *Lumen Gentium* 11, but it echoes themes as ancient as the writings of the apostolic age.

of vocations to the priesthood and religious life, which are the most explicitly "Eucharistic" ways of life.

Already, however, our second theme comes into sight: St. Thomas Aquinas, the Doctor of the Eucharist *par excellence*. Has there ever been a great theologian of whose life and work it could *not* be said that this Sacrament, containing the very Person of Jesus Christ, was the source and summit? And of the great theologians (whose number is not immense), has not the Angelic Doctor exemplified this truth in the most admirable ways? He was and he remains, in the words of John Paul II, the "supreme theologian and impassioned singer of the Eucharistic Christ."[13] The mystery for which this Dominican master of theology provided a dogmatic analysis that surpasses in subtlety the metaphysics of Aristotle was the very same mystery before which he humbled himself daily in fervent adoration and to which he dedicated mystic verses whose tranquil beauty has warmed the hearts of Christians for centuries. No wonder the golden reliquary that holds his mortal remains beneath an altar in Toulouse depicts the saint standing alert and energetic, holding in one hand the flaming sword of the Word of God, and in the other hand a radiant monstrance proclaiming the Real Presence. The one leads to the other, and both to eternal life. Without the bread of the word and the bread of life, there is no life and no truth, no upward ascent to God at odds with fallen nature's downward spiral.

All the goods we rely upon during our earthly pilgrimage: peace, good will, joy, the social virtues and graces that glue communities together—these weaken and disappear when their supernatural principle, charity, is cut off. And where do we encounter most intimately the charity of God? Where do we feast on this divine gift? In the *sacramentum caritatis*, as St. Thomas calls it: the sacrament that shows forth, embodies, communicates, and confirms the love of men for God and for each other. Without the Eucharist, then, we are utterly lost. We are lost as individuals, as families, as societies

---

13. "*summus theologus simulque Christi eucharistici fervidus cantor*" (Encyclical Letter *Ecclesia de Eucharistia*, n. 62). Note that this phrase was inaccurately rendered in the official English version.

and nations.[14] Conversely, if men wish to be free men once more and not slaves, if families are destined to flourish and healthy societies spring into being, it will happen only when they are found gathered around the altar, on bended knee before the King of Kings. Even in our dark days there are communities like this, composed of faithful laity and clergy, often obscure and poor, but demonstrating in quiet ways the irrepressible vitality of the Gospel. *This* is where the future of the Church lies.

Let us consider more closely the salvation, the healing, of society. To the question "What are the fundamental principles of Catholic social teaching?" many compelling answers can be given, for it is a rich area of doctrine. I think, nonetheless, that two of the great principles of this body of teaching as it has developed in the past 150 years are surely the common good and the dignity of the human person. In the twentieth century, there has been a tendency to view these two concepts as opposites conjoined in irreconcilable tension: the person, as person, has a kind of limitless worth, which makes him subordinate to no one; yet the community, as such, deserves the person's attentive service, indeed it may ask of him his very life. But to think along these lines betrays a superficial conception of both principles. In reality, the human person derives his great dignity from his capacity to be ordered to (and even more, from his *actual* ordering to) God, the infinite good; and God, precisely as this inexhaustible good, is the extrinsic common good of the entire universe, who is rightly loved when he is loved as infinitely communicable.[15] In other words, what is most personal and worthy about the person is what is deepest in him, namely the goodness he receives as a gift, impelling him to communion with its Giver; and

---

14. Toward the end of his pontificate this was increasingly the message of Leo XIII. It is clear in his 1902 encyclical on the Eucharist, *Mirae Caritatis,* but also in *Tametsi Futura* (1900), *Annum Sacrum* (1899), and the retrospective apostolic letter *Annum Ingressi Sumus* (1902).

15. See Charles De Koninck's classic work *The Primacy of the Common Good,* in *The Writings of Charles De Koninck: Volume Two,* trans. Ralph McInerny (Notre Dame, IN: University of Notre Dame Press, 2009), 65–164; St. Thomas, *De caritate,* article 2.

the good that is most of all common, and worthy of our absolute self-abandonment, is not any earthly, created good, but God alone, who made us and all things.

Now, what is the connection between these seemingly abstract principles and the "daily bread" of the Eucharist? There is complete overlap. As St. Thomas teaches, the common good of the entire universe is found in Christ,[16] and the whole Christ is found in the Eucharist. The Eucharist is, therefore, the common good of all mankind, of all races and societies and nations. A people or a nation that does not actively order itself to Eucharistic worship, in all that this involves, both remotely and proximately—preserving orthodox faith and high morals, cultivating reverent worship, supporting sound education, producing good art and architecture, and so forth—is a nation with a deficient and dying common good, a nation splintering into factions, splintering further into envious, libidinous egos.[17] There is a cure for this mess; it has worked many times in the past, and will work again as many times as it is tried. That cure is the medicine of immortality, the holy Eucharist. Once again, is it any coincidence that the theologian who offers us the fullest and soundest treatment of the common good—divine, cosmic, political—is none other than St. Thomas Aquinas, "supreme theologian and impassioned singer of the Eucharistic Christ"?

In my life, the most poignant symbol of the flowing together of the three treasures we are speaking of has been the public Corpus Christi procession in which I participated several times during the years I lived in rural Austria, where, by the mercy of God, many traditional practices still survive.

On this most splendid day, the pastor, clad in gold vestments, walking beneath an embroidered canopy, leads a public procession along the main street, within sight and hearing of the whole town, accompanied by the local marching band, acolytes carrying bells and incense, little girls scattering flower petals, and townspeople dressed in their traditional outfits. The civic leaders march in sec-

---

16. See *Super I ad Cor.*, cap. 12, lec. 3.

17. I have in mind here Augustine's notion of the *libido dominandi*, the power for control and manipulation that is at the root of social sins.

ond place (their *due* place), followed by the rest of the children, Christ's favorites, their families, and indeed everyone who has a heart to participate. No one is excluded; all are welcome, because it is an occasion for joy and feasting. The priest gives fourfold Benediction with the Blessed Sacrament at four stations festooned with freshly-cut branches from the surrounding forests, to bless the people and the place in all directions of the compass. This is a political act, not a private devotion; it symbolizes a city ordered to, and nourished by, the Word-made-flesh, the Savior's body and blood, which he delivered up in love for us, *to make us one with him and with each other.* But it is also a liturgical act—it springs from the Mass, where the host has been consecrated; it returns to the Mass, in the tabernacle at the high altar, where the monstrance is finally set to rest after hours of veneration. Even in a country succumbing to the lure of secularization, the Body of Christ still receives this treatment: all businesses and offices closed, the entire town processing on the street, intercity traffic forced to pause, the gilt monstrance held high in clouds of incense.

Listen carefully ... listen to the beautiful hymns of the day's Mass and Office, hear the prayers of the day. Who wrote them? None other than Saint Thomas. Polity, liturgical piety, and the prince of theologians, converge at the still point.

A Christian Ecosystem

From whatever angle one looks, the connections are there, and run deep; an inquisitive person sooner or later begins to ask why this should be so. Whether or not my reflections can lead to an adequate answer, the first step is just to see that they *do* belong together with a kind of necessity, forming, if I may hazard the analogy, a Christian ecosystem. Each thrives in the presence of the other; each suffers in the absence of the others. There is real danger of mass extinction if we are not careful to preserve the fundamental components of the supernatural environment. To shift metaphors, in this decisive age of the Church, when her enemies are more numerous and their stratagems more subtle than ever, we are not lacking weapons for battle, nor means of superior intelligence; and ultimately, in some mysterious way, the victory is won, because Christ has died and risen. This much is certain: the Lord will not fail *us* (cf. 2 Tim 2:11–13). The question is: Will we fail *him*? (cf. Lk 18:8). That is the question all of us must ask ourselves as we try to do our part for the renewal of Catholic life in our day.

What, then, is to be done? Is there any hope? Is there any "plan" that could bring about a true religious renaissance, a true springtime? There is only one safe path: to honor and to love the ever-living tradition of the Church; to stop pretending that we can invent a new tradition to replace the perennial one, the holy and beautiful tradition that is our Lord's wedding gift to his Bride on earth. Pope John Paul II apologized for all the crimes of sinners who dishonored the Church by their sins; he even went so far as to apologize for the crimes committed by the Crusaders and by Catholics during the period of the Inquisition. Is it not high time, then, to apologize to God with profound humility for all the crimes that popes, cardinals, bishops, priests, and laity have committed against the sacred tradition of the Church?

To the question "what is to be done," the lover of Catholic tradition has an answer that is clear and reliable, with the added advantage that our shepherds can begin to implement it right away, provided they have the courage—namely, to heal the wounds exactly where the blows have fallen. The resurrection of the Church must consist of, or at least necessarily involve:

1. The restoration of traditional liturgy.
2. The proclamation of Catholic social teaching in its fullness.
3. The reestablishment of St. Thomas as Common Doctor.

Should one be tempted to say: "Easier said than done, now that we have had nearly fifty years of corruption," the right answer is: "We have vowed in baptism to be faithful to Christ no matter what, and so we must take up our cross and fight the good fight, to the very end." St. Thérèse of Lisieux once said that discouragement, too, is pride. What she meant is that discouragement indicates a lack of faith, a lack of trustful surrender to divine Providence. At such times, we are really saying "I know best what should happen, and it is not happening. I am angry about that." The crux is confidence in God, abandonment to his will. God "knows what He is about," as

Cardinal Newman said.[18] God has a purpose for permitting the corruption, the chaos. He alone can bring forth good from evil. We do not know his purposes, but we know that he is wise, merciful, and just. "And we know that to them that love God, all things work together unto good, to such as, according to his purpose, are called to be saints" (Rom 8:28).

Moreover, it is not clear that these three goals are, in reality, so unattainable. Any bishop with vision and perseverance can reintroduce the study of St. Thomas among his seminarians, educate his clergy and people in Catholic social doctrine, and restore the sacredness of the liturgy in manifold ways, both negative (e.g., abolishing female altar servers, curtailing extraordinary ministers of holy communion) and positive (e.g., mandating the chanting of the Mass propers in Latin or English, or encouraging the use of incense, noble vestments, the pipe organ, and *ad orientem* worship). Indeed, under the pontificate of Benedict XVI, we saw numerous bishops do one or more of these things, often with tremendous vigor and catechetical fervor, and always with tangible fruits of authentic renewal.

And, taking the ultimate perspective—the one we need to have in mind if we wish to stay sane in this valley of tears—we cannot forget that God promises us, after the wearying pilgrimage of this life, after we have wandered long in the valley of the shadow of death, he promises us a share in his joy: "If children, then heirs, heirs of God and fellow heirs with Christ, provided we suffer with him in order that we may also be glorified with him. I consider that the sufferings of this present time are not worth comparing with the glory that is to be revealed to us" (Rom 8:17–18). "He who eats my flesh and drinks my blood has eternal life, and I will raise him up at the last day" (Jn 6:54). "Enter into the joy of your master" (Mt 25:21).

Fortunately, the heavenly liturgy never changes; one need not fear the promulgation of yet another *editio typica*, with new read-

---

18. From the *Meditations and Devotions*, "Meditations on Christian Doctrine," March 7, 1848. The whole passage, entitled "Hope in God," cannot be read too often. The text is available at www.newmanreader.org/works/meditations/meditations9.html.

ings and prayers. The heavenly city is eternally ruled by Christ the King, the Eternal High Priest. The wisdom that St. Thomas taught is, as he himself glimpsed at the end of his life, "straw" compared to the beatifying vision of God's glory. If the Church on earth should seem to fail for a time, if even her leaders falter, how can we truly be surprised—especially if we are nearing the end times? "When the Son of Man comes, will he find faith on earth?" (Lk 18:8). "The charity of many shall grow cold" (Mt 24:12). Let it not be said of us, when we are standing before the throne of Christ, that *our* charity grew cold because we preferred the darkness of pessimism to the burning furnace of his Heart.

We have some short years in which to know, love, and serve God. Let us strive to know him better with the help of St. Thomas and all the great saints; let us strive to love him better by entering more deeply into the sacred liturgy and receiving more devoutly the ineffable gift of Christ's Body and Blood; let us strive to serve him better as we live our lives in the world, guided by the integral social teaching of the Church. What matters here is not how much progress we make, but our perseverance in the way of truth. As Blessed Teresa of Calcutta said: "God doesn't call me to be successful, God calls me to be faithful."[19] If we do *this*, there cannot be a moment's doubt that we shall hear those longed-for words: "Enter into the joy of your master."

---

19. This has been quoted in many different ways, but the point is always the same. The world's standards of success are, not unexpectedly, worldly; God judges by another measure, that of the heart.

Summorum Pontificum
Seven Years Later: Where We Are and Where We Ought to Be

IN THE POST-*Summorum* world, the traditional liturgy of the Roman Rite can no longer be considered forbidden, dubious, marginal, or obsolete. It enjoys equal rights of citizenship with the Novus Ordo: two forms of the Roman Rite—one called Ordinary because most recently promulgated and more widely used, the other called Extraordinary, the *usus antiquior,* deserving respect for its venerable use—with each able to be freely celebrated by any priest of the Roman Rite, no special permission needed. One would think that, as a gesture of reconciliation at the heart of the Church, the two forms would be flourishing side by side, with Catholics everywhere privileged to experience both of them offered reverently and beautifully.

But this is still far from the reality, and, sadly, there are still far too many bishops and priests who oppose the traditional Mass, tether it with burdensome conditions, or resort to power politics to ensure that its supporters are duly warned and penalized for their rash embrace of our Catholic heritage.

As we pass the milestone of the seventh anniversary of *Summorum Pontificum,* it will be both edifying and sobering to consider the meaning Joseph Ratzinger himself attached to opposition to the traditional Mass. What does it *mean* when someone opposes this Mass, or those who celebrate it, or those who cherish it as a form of prayer dear to them?

In the book-length interview *Salt of the Earth,* published in German in 1996, Ratzinger said:

> I am of the opinion, to be sure, that the old rite should be granted much more generously to all those who desire it. It's impossible to

see what could be dangerous or unacceptable about that. A community is calling its very being into question when it suddenly declares that what until now was its holiest and highest possession is strictly forbidden, and when it makes the longing for it seem downright indecent. Can it be trusted any more about anything else? Won't it proscribe tomorrow what it prescribes today?[1]

Ten years prior to *Summorum*, he was placing his finger on the crux of the matter. If the liturgy that was the Church's holiest and highest possession for centuries, the object of reverence and honor, the means of sanctification for countless Catholics, is suddenly forbidden, and if the desire to worship as our forefathers did is treated as wrong, what does that say about the Church herself, about her past, her tradition, her very saints? Truly, her credibility vanishes entirely, her proclamations become arbitrary diktats. Was there something fatally flawed, all this time, with our central act of worship? Were all the popes of the past who lovingly cultivated this liturgy mistaken, were all the missionaries who brought it around the globe misguided? Could they say, in the words of Gatherer, son of Vomiter, "I have not learned wisdom, and have not known the science of saints"?[2]

In *God and the World*, another of those splendidly insightful and doctrinally robust interviews which now, in retrospect, make for such wistful reading, Ratzinger returned to the point:

> For fostering a true consciousness in liturgical matters, it is also important that the proscription against the form of liturgy in valid use up to 1970 should be lifted. Anyone who nowadays advocates the continuing existence of this liturgy or takes part in it is treated like a leper; all tolerance ends here. There has never been anything like this in history; in doing this we are despising and proscribing the Church's whole past. How can one trust her present if things are that way? I must say, quite openly, that I don't understand why so many of my episcopal brethren have to a great extent submitted to this rule of intolerance, which for no apparent

---

1. Joseph Ratzinger, *Salt of the Earth: The Church at the End of the Millennium*, trans. Adrian Walker (San Francisco: Ignatius Press, 1997), 176–77.

2. Cf. Proverbs 30:1, 3 (Douay-Rheims).

reason is opposed to making the necessary inner reconciliations within the Church.[3]

Here we have language strikingly akin to what we will find five years later in Pope Benedict's Letter to the Bishops that accompanied *Summorum Pontificum*. Once again, we find the telltale insistence on possessing the right attitude towards the undying and life-giving heritage of the Church. The liturgical rites that arise from apostolic seeds in the Church's sojourn through history are the fruits of Him who is the Lord and Giver of Life, and they cannot, in themselves, either die or bring death—nor can they be legitimately prohibited.

This would explain why Pope Benedict XVI, in *Summorum Pontificum*, says that the traditional Latin Mass "*must* be given due honor for its venerable and ancient usage"[4] and, in the Letter to the Bishops, adds:

> What earlier generations held as sacred remains sacred and great for us too, and it cannot be all of a sudden entirely forbidden or even considered harmful. It behooves all of us to preserve the riches which have developed in the Church's faith and prayer, and to give them their proper place.

The giving of due honor, which translates into the actual celebration of the classical Roman liturgy, is not an optional matter, and this is why we should politely refuse to allow ourselves or our fellow Catholics to be categorized as people with certain "preferences": "Oh, you prefer the old and I prefer the new." No, it goes beyond preferences to the very structure of the Catholic Faith: those things that are venerable and ancient *must* be given due honor; what earlier generations held as sacred *must* be sacred—and great!—for us, too; it is incumbent on us to preserve these riches and to make sure that they occupy their proper place in the life of the Church today.

Again, a sign that we are reading Pope Benedict correctly is that the clarifying instruction *Universae Ecclesiae* goes out of its way to

---

3. Idem, *God and the World: A Conversation with Peter Seewald,* trans. Henry Taylor (San Francisco: Ignatius Press, 2002), 416.

4. Emphasis added.

emphasize these points. In fact, section 8 of this document is strik-ing in its uncompromising simplicity, its total lack of hedging qual-ifications or loopholes:

> The Motu Proprio *Summorum Pontificum* constitutes an impor-tant expression of the Magisterium of the Roman Pontiff and of his *munus* of regulating and ordering the Church's Sacred Liturgy. The Motu Proprio manifests his solicitude as Vicar of Christ and Supreme Pastor of the Universal Church, and has the aim of: (a) offering to all the faithful the Roman Liturgy in the *Usus Antiquior,* considered as a precious treasure to be preserved; (b) effectively guaranteeing and ensuring the use of the *forma extraordinaria* for all who ask for it, given that the use of the 1962 Roman Liturgy is a faculty generously granted for the good of the faithful and there-fore is to be interpreted in a sense favorable to the faithful who are its principal addressees; (c) promoting reconciliation at the heart of the Church.

With these points established, we can readily see why any move to obstruct or diminish the presence of the *usus antiquior* in the Church today would only cause great harm and long-term damage.

First, it would be an act and a symptom of disobedience, which is never blessed by God and always punished by Him. More specifi-cally, it would constitute disobedience to Pope Benedict XVI's legal provisions in *Summorum Pontificum* (and their clarifications in *Universae Ecclesiae*), as well as to Pope John Paul II's well-known statement that "respect must everywhere be shown for the feelings of all those who are attached to the Latin liturgical tradition, by a wide and generous application of the directives already issued some time ago by the Apostolic See for the use of the Roman Missal according to the typical edition of 1962." As has been demonstrated above, it is not enough to refrain from bad-mouthing the tradi-tional sacramental rites; they must be known and loved, re-intro-duced and promoted, studied in seminaries, offered generously to the faithful as a precious treasure.

Second, and more profoundly, divine worship goes to the heart of a person's spiritual life, that which is most intimate and cherished. Any refusal to share the treasures of the Church, any heavy-handed restrictions on what is already available (or should be available), can only provoke anger, disappointment, and mistrust, hurting the Church's unity, which is a fragile good of enormous value. Certain bishops, priests, and laymen may have no great love for the Extraordinary Form themselves, but they ought to recognize and respect the sizeable minority of Catholics who *do,* and appreciate that depriving them of it, or begrudging it to them, is pretty nearly the most offensive thing that could be done—rather like slapping a man's wife, mother, or grandmother. To be blunt, those who sincerely want peace and mutual understanding had better act generously or they may end up with another ecclesiastical Cold War on their hands. Who wants that?

It does not require special perspicacity to see that a significant and growing number of Catholics are flocking to parishes and chapels where the traditional Mass is being celebrated, and with their (on average) very large families and strong commitment to homeschooling, the future belongs to them. In 1988 there were about 20 weekly Sunday traditional Latin Masses; today there are over 500. There is no reason to fight this movement, and every reason to support it.

In spite of the anxieties of some who find it difficult to give peace and mutual coexistence a chance, the Extraordinary Form is not a problem for the Church, and, as Pope Benedict XVI helps us to see, never *could* be a problem in and of itself. Instead, one may encounter unfortunate traditionalist attitudes that alienate or provoke— and, to be quite fair, this cuts both ways, since the promoters of the Novus Ordo frequently exhibit offensive attitudes of their own, such as a peculiar fusion of theoretical liberalism and practical totalitarianism. The thing to do is not jealously to limit and control the *usus antiquior* as if it were a dangerous addictive substance, an approach that only fuels those unfortunate attitudes, but to teach and model a right attitude, receiving with open arms, with humility and childlike simplicity, all that the Church herself gives, so that it becomes something normal and natural, not something forbidden, controversial, or divisive.

* * *

Every Latin Rite member of the Catholic Church should therefore perform an examination of conscience, taking an inventory of attitudes, policies, and practices.

Bishops: Have you seen to it that the Extraordinary Form—which "must be given due honor for its venerable and ancient usage"—is widely available in your diocese, since "it behooves all of us to preserve the riches which have developed in the Church's faith and prayer, and to give them their proper place"? Have you seen to it that training sessions are made available for priests and seminarians, so that they may benefit from this profound school of prayer, the nourishment of countless saints, stretching back to the first millennium of the Church?

Priests: Have you taken advantage of the opportunities for learning the *usus antiquior*? Have you responded generously when the faithful ask for the sacraments in the traditional rites? Have you proactively taken steps to *offer* it to the faithful even when they do not request it, confident that the Holy Spirit can and will use this magnificent treasure of the Church to enrich the lives of many believers?

Religious: Have you requested that the classical Roman liturgy (or your own order's traditional liturgy, if such a distinctive form exists) be celebrated occasionally or even frequently within your community? Have you pointed out that its rediscovery has been for others, and can be for everyone, a potent source of renewal in charism, youth evangelization, and vocations?

Laity: Have you supported your diocese, your bishop, your pastor, your clergy, in a friendly and generous manner, so that they may more readily accede to legitimate desires for the *usus antiquior*? Do you pray for them when they are resistant, dismissive, irritated, or even spiteful? Have you repeatedly asked for the traditional Mass and sacraments, humbly but confidently? Have you been ready and willing to help defray the expenses associated with instruction in this rite and the celebration of it? Do you try to find ways to spread knowledge and love of the Extraordinary Form among the youth?

Everyone: Have we *fully and consistently* embraced the legislation of Pope Benedict XVI's motu proprio and the truly pastoral wisdom of his accompanying letter to all the bishops?

Things vary from diocese to diocese, of course, but, speaking generally, the answer to this last question cannot yet be in the affirmative. In spite of manifest desire among many groups of the faithful, made up of people of different age groups and backgrounds, the traditional Latin Mass has not joined the Ordinary Form as a regular occurrence (say, Sundays and Holy Days) in most parishes and chapels throughout the world, surely a sign that Pope Benedict's desire to effect a deep reconciliation in the Church and to inject into the Ordinary Form a new spirit of fidelity to tradition has been largely unheeded.

The situation as it stands points to a longstanding problem in the Church. For close to 50 years, those who loved (or who have come to love) the traditional Latin Mass have been treated like second-class citizens, if not lepers. This is not my own exaggerated perception; Joseph Ratzinger himself saw it this way, and said so more than once.

To judge from praxis, no Catholic is allowed to be without the Ordinary Form; but when it comes to the Extraordinary Form, it can be ignored, excluded, cancelled, discontinued, and decreased—regardless of the spiritual lives of those Catholics who attend it or desire it. Imagine the outcry if a pastor of a mainstream parish said to his people: "I'm going on vacation the next two weeks, and in my absence a priest from the Fraternity of Saint Peter will come and celebrate the Tridentine Mass for all of you. Sorry, there won't be any Novus Ordo Masses for those two weeks."

Why, then, does the same thing frequently happen in the other direction? Is it because trained clergy are not readily available? Yes, that's a challenge. But it is more honest to admit that there is a double standard at work—one that exists *in spite of* the law of the Church established in the motu proprio. The attitude would best be described thus: "If you are a Catholic who attends the Ordinary Form, you must be guaranteed access to it (and never should you be forced to attend the Extraordinary Form); but if you are an Extraordinary Form-loving Catholic, be content with whatever people are willing to give you, and know that you'll frequently have no choice but to attend the Ordinary Form."

Most Catholics have not submitted their intellects and wills to the authoritative determination of Pope Benedict XVI, who established in *Summorum Pontificum* that the two forms of the Roman Rite are canonically *equal* and that requests for the traditional form of Mass should be granted, as long as those requesting it do not deny the validity of the new missal.[5] He did not specify how *often* the Mass should be made available because he logically assumed that supply would meet demand, as long as no one failed to be as generous as they ought to be. Put simply, if there is a desire for a weekly Mass, let a weekly Mass be provided as soon as may be. If there is a desire for a daily Mass, and a congregation large enough to make such a thing reasonable in the circumstances, then let a weekday Mass be provided.

In the pre-*Summorum* world, Pope John Paul II asked bishops to provide generously for the faithful attached to the Latin liturgical tradition. Nevertheless, such a provision was still understood as a kind of favor, an exception, a special case. This model was decisively put aside by *Summorum Pontificum*, which regularized the Extraordinary Form as a treasure for all Catholics, to be provided directly by priests. It still happens far too often, however, that provision of the Extraordinary Form is treated as a favor or privilege rather than a just response to a legitimate request, a duty that corresponds to a genuine right on the part of the faithful.

Is it any wonder there is such a heightened sensitivity, even irritability, among the more traditionally-minded Catholics? If you are not so minded, try placing yourself in their shoes and see how it would feel if the thing that most of all enkindled and illuminated your life of faith—the thing that enkindled and illuminated the Church for 1,500 years—was rarely or irregularly given to you,

5. Indeed, one wonders if most of the Catholic laity are even aware of the existence of, much less the noble intentions behind, the motu proprio *Summorum Pontificum*—an ignorance that points, of course, to culpable negligence on the part of their bishops and priests. It is an urgent responsibility of pastors and laity who *are* aware of the motu proprio to do their utmost in spreading knowledge of it and working patiently for its implementation.

treated as harmful or dangerous, while you yourself were viewed as if you belonged to a fringe group or sect.

Pope Benedict XVI knew that there was only one way to get beyond this decades-old impasse: deregulate, destigmatize, depressurize the whole thing with a transparent and magnanimous welcoming of all that the Faith itself allows. *That* is what a full and consistent implementation of *Summorum Pontificum* would look like—and when each parish and chaplaincy has accomplished it, we will then be able to say, without the slightest qualm of conscience, that we are altogether faithful to the Magisterium and totally committed to the service of Christ and His Church.

Let us give the final word to Pope Benedict, from his Letter to the Bishops of July 7, 2007:

> I think of a sentence in the Second Letter to the Corinthians, where Paul writes: "Our mouth is open to you, Corinthians; our heart is wide. You are not restricted by us, but you are restricted in your own affections. In return . . . widen your hearts also!" (2 Cor 6:11-13). Paul was certainly speaking in another context, but his exhortation can and must touch us too, precisely on this subject. Let us generously open our hearts and make room for everything that the faith itself allows.

Bibliography

Works cited in this book (with the exception of magisterial documents) are found below, together with additional highly recommended reading.

Aillet, Marc. *The Old Mass and the New: Explaining the Motu Proprio Summorum Pontificum of Pope Benedict XVI*. San Francisco: Ignatius Press, 2010.

A Benedictine monk [Dom Gérard Calvet]. *Discovering the Mass*. Translated by Jean Pierre Pilon. London: The Saint Austin Press, 1999.

———. *The Sacred Liturgy*. London: The Saint Austin Press, 1999.

Benson, Robert Hugh. *The King's Achievement*. Edited by Francis X. Connolly. New York: P. J. Kenedy & Sons, 1957.

Berger, David. *Thomas Aquinas and the Liturgy*. Translated by Christopher Grosz. Ypsilanti: Sapientia Press, 2004.

Bugnini, Annibale. *The Reform of the Liturgy, 1948–1975*. Translated by Matthew J. O'Connell. Collegeville: The Liturgical Press, 1990.

Burke, Raymond Leo. "*Ius Divinum* and the Sacred Liturgy." In *Benedict XVI and the Roman Missal*. Edited by Janet E. Rutherford and James O'Brien, 21–39. Dublin: Four Courts, 2013.

———. "Sacred Liturgy and Asceticism: Respect for the *Ius Divinum*." *Antiphon* 17 (2013): 3–30.

———. "The Theo-Centric Character of Catholic Liturgy." *The Thomist* 75 (2011): 347–64.

Butler, Sara. *The Catholic Priesthood and Women: A Guide to the Teaching of the Church*. Chicago: Liturgy Training Publications, 2007.

Bux, Nicola. *Benedict XVI's Reform: The Liturgy between Innovation and Tradition*. Translated by Joseph Trabbic. San Francisco: Ignatius Press, 2012.

Cekada, Anthony. *Work of Human Hands: A Theological Critique of the Mass of Paul VI*. West Chester: Philothea Press, 2010.

Chaignon, Peter. *The Sacrifice of the Mass Worthily Celebrated*. Translated by Louis de Goesbriand. New York: Benziger Brothers, 1951.

Charmot, François. *The Mass, Source of Sanctity*. Translated by M. Angeline Bouchard. Notre Dame: Fides Publishers, 1964.

Convert, Abbé H. *Eucharistic Meditations: Extracts from the Writings and Instructions of St. John Vianney.* Translated by Mary Benvenuta. Wheathampstead: Anthony Clarke Books, 1964.

Davies, Michael. *Cranmer's Godly Order: The Destruction of Catholicism Through Liturgical Change.* Fort Collins: Roman Catholic Books, 1995.

———. *Pope John's Council.* Kansas City: Angelus Press, 2007.

———. *Pope Paul's New Mass.* Kansas City: Angelus Press, 2009.

———. *The Second Vatican Council and Religious Liberty.* Long Prairie: Neumann Press, 1992.

de Chivré, Bernard-Marie. *The Mass of Saint Pius V: Spiritual and Theological Commentaries.* Translated by Ann Marie Temple. Winona: STAS Editions, 2007.

De Koninck, Charles. *The Primacy of the Common Good.* In *The Writings of Charles De Koninck: Volume Two.* Translated by Ralph McInerny. Notre Dame: University of Notre Dame Press, 2009.

Descartes, René. *Discourse on Method and Meditations on First Philosophy.* Translated by Donald A. Cress. Indianapolis: Hackett, 1998.

de Margerie, Bertrand. *La Trinité chrétienne dans l'histoire.* Paris: Éditions Beauchesne, 1975.

de Tocqueville, Alexis. *Democracy in America.* Translated by Harvey C. Mansfield and Delba Winthrop. Chicago: University of Chicago Press, 2000.

Dobszay, László. *The Restoration and Organic Development of the Roman Rite.* New York: T&T Clark, 2010.

Gambero, Luigi. *Mary and the Fathers of the Church: The Blessed Virgin in Patristic Thought.* Translated by Thomas Buffer. San Francisco: Ignatius Press, 1999.

Gertrude the Great. *The Life and Revelations of Saint Gertrude.* Westminster: The Newman Press, 1949.

Giampietro, Nicola. *The Development of the Liturgical Reform as Seen by Cardinal Ferdinando Antonelli from 1948 to 1970.* Fort Collins: Roman Catholic Books, 2009.

Goodman, Dena. *The Republic of Letters: A Cultural History of the French Enlightenment.* Ithaca: Cornell University Press, 1996.

Guardini, Romano. *The Lord.* Translated by Elinor Castendyk Briefs. Chicago: Regnery, 1954.

Hauke, Manfred. *Women in the Priesthood?: A Systematic Analysis in the Light of the Order of Creation and Redemption.* Translated by David Kipp. San Francisco: Ignatius Press, 1988.

Hitchcock, James. "The Voices of Silence in the Liturgy." *Communio* 5.4 (1978): 352–62.

Hopkins, Gerard Manley. *Poems of Gerard Manley Hopkins*. Edited by Robert Bridges. London: Humphrey Milford, 1918.

Hourlier, Jacques. *Reflections on the Spirituality of Gregorian Chant*. Translated by Gregory Casprini and Robert Edmonson. Orleans: Paraclete Press, 1995.

John Damascene. *Three Treatises on the Divine Images*. Translated by Andrew Louth. Crestwood: St. Vladimir's Seminary Press, 2003.

Journet, Charles. *Theology of the Church*. Translated by Victor Szczurek. San Francisco: Ignatius Press, 2004.

Jungmann, Joseph. *The Mass of the Roman Rite*. Westminster: Christian Classics, 1986.

Kocik, Thomas. *The Reform of the Reform? A Liturgical Debate: Reform or Return*. San Francisco: Ignatius Press, 2003.

Kowalska, Maria Faustina. *Diary: Divine Mercy in My Soul*. Stockbridge: Marian Press, 2003.

Kwasniewski, Peter. "A Brief Introduction to Angels." *The Latin Mass* 16.2 (Spring 2007): 34–39.

———. "*Cantate Domino Canticum Novum*: Aspects of the Church's Liturgical Magisterium." *The Catholic Faith* 6.2 (March–April 2000): 14–23. Available at www.catholicculture.org/library/view.cfm?recnum=4440.

———. "Contemporary Music in Church?" *Homiletic & Pastoral Review* 107.1 (October 2006): 8–15. Available at www.catholicculture.org/culture/library/view.cfm?recnum=7192.

———. "Conversion of Culture." *Homiletic & Pastoral Review* 107.9 (June 2007): 26–31.

———. "Doing and Speaking in the Person of Christ: Eucharistic Form in the Anaphora of Addai and Mari." *Nova et Vetera* 4 (2006): 313–79.

———. "Extraordinary Ministers of the Eucharist." *The Catholic Faith* 6.6 (November-December 2000): 34–42. Available at http://www.ewtn.com/library/Liturgy/EXTRMIN.HTM.

———. "Golden Straw: St. Thomas and the Ecstatic Practice of Theology." *Nova et Vetera* 2 (2004): 61–89.

———. "John Paul II on Sacred Music." *Sacred Music* 133.2 (Summer 2006): 4–22. Available at www.musicasacra.com/publications/sacredmusic/pdf/sm133-2.pdf.

Laise, Juan Rodolfo. *Communion in the Hand: Documents and History*. Boonville: Preserving Christian Publications, 2011.

Lang, Uwe Michael. *Turning Towards the Lord*. San Francisco: Ignatius Press, 2004.

———. *The Voice of the Church at Prayer: Reflections on Liturgy and Language*. San Francisco: Ignatius Press, 2012.

Levering, Matthew, and Michael Dauphinais, eds. *Rediscovering Aquinas and the Sacraments*. Chicago: Liturgy Training Publications, 2009.

Mahrt, William Peter. *The Musical Shape of the Liturgy*. Richmond: Church Music Association of America, 2012.

Maritain, Jacques. *The Dream of Descartes*. Translated by Mabelle L. Andison. New York: The Philosophical Library, 1944.

———. *Three Reformers: Luther, Descartes, Rousseau*. New York: Apollo Editions, 1970.

Martindale, C.C. *The Words of the Missal*. New York: Macmillan, 1932.

Meconi, David Vincent. "Silence Proceeding." *Logos* 5.2 (Spring 2002): 59–75.

Monti, James. *A Sense of the Sacred: Roman Catholic Worship in the Middle Ages*. San Francisco: Ignatius Press, 2012.

Mosebach, Martin. *The Heresy of Formlessness: The Roman Liturgy and Its Enemy*. Translated by Graham Harrison. San Francisco: Ignatius Press, 2006.

Newman, John Henry. *Prayers, Verses, and Devotions*. San Francisco: Ignatius Press, 1989. The meditation "Hope in God" is also available at www.newmanreader.org/works/meditations/meditations9.html.

Nichols, Aidan. *Looking at the Liturgy: A Critical View of Its Contemporary Form*. San Francisco: Ignatius Press, 1996.

Pieper, Josef. *Enthusiasm and Divine Madness: On the Platonic Dialogue "Phaedrus."* Translated by Richard Winston and Clara Winston. South Bend: St. Augustine's Press, 2000.

———. *The Silence of St. Thomas*. Translated by John Murray and Daniel O'Connor. New York: Pantheon Books, 1957.

Pierik, Marie. *The Spirit of Gregorian Chant* (1939). Richmond: Church Music Association of America, 2007.

Pristas, Lauren. *Collects of the Roman Missal: A Comparative Study of the Sundays in Proper Seasons Before and After the Second Vatican Council*. New York: T&T Clark, 2013.

———. "Theological Principles that Guided the Redaction of the Roman Missal (1970)." *The Thomist* 67 (2003): 157–95.

Pseudo-Dionysius. *The Complete Works*. Translated by Colm Luibheid. Mahwah: Paulist Press, 1987.

Rahner, Hugo. *Our Lady and the Church*. Translated by Sebastian Bullough. Bethesda: Zaccheus Press, 2005.

Bibliography

Ratzinger, Joseph. "The Ecclesiology of the Constitution on the Church, *Lumen Gentium*." *L'Osservatore Romano*, 19 September 2001. Available at www.ewtn.com/library/curia/cdfeccl.htm.

————.*God and the World: A Conversation with Peter Seewald*. Translated by Henry Taylor. San Francisco: Ignatius Press, 2002.

————. *Salt of the Earth: The Church at the End of the Millennium*. Translated by Adrian Walker. San Francisco: Ignatius Press, 1997.

————. *Theology of the Liturgy: The Sacramental Foundation of Christian Existence*. Volume XI of *Collected Works*. [Includes *The Spirit of the Liturgy*.] Edited by Michael J. Miller. San Francisco: Ignatius Press, 2014.

Reid, Alcuin, ed. *A Bitter Trial: Evelyn Waugh and John Carmel Cardinal Heenan on the Liturgical Changes*. Expanded edition. San Francisco: Ignatius Press, 2011.

————, ed. *Looking Again at the Question of the Liturgy with Cardinal Ratzinger*. Farnborough: Saint Michael's Abbey Press, 2003.

————. *The Organic Development of the Liturgy*. Second edition. San Francisco: Ignatius Press, 2005.

Ripperger, Chad. *Topics on Tradition*. N.p.: Sensus Traditionis Press, 2013.

Robinson, Jonathan. *The Mass and Modernity: Walking to Heaven Backward*. San Francisco: Ignatius Press, 2005.

Rosmini-Serbati, Antonio. *The Philosophy of Right*. Volume IV. Translated by Denis Cleary and Terence Watson. Durham: Rosmini House Publications, 1995.

Saward, John. "Towards an Apophatic Anthropology." *Irish Theological Quarterly* 41 (1974): 222–34.

Schmitt, Francis P. *Church Music Transgressed: Reflections on "Reform."* New York: Seabury Press, 1977.

Schneider, Athanasius. *Dominus Est—It is the Lord: Reflections of a Bishop of Central Asia on Holy Communion*. Translated by Nicholas L. Gregoris. Pine Beach: Newman House Press, 2008.

————. "The Extraordinary Form and the New Evangelization." Available at www.paixliturgique.org.uk/aff_lettre.asp?LET_N_ID=863; also published in *The Latin Mass* 21.2 (Summer 2012): 6–10.

Terry, Richard R. *Catholic Church Music* (1907). Richmond: Church Music Association of America, 2007.

Thomas Aquinas. *The Sermon-Conferences of St. Thomas Aquinas on the Apostles' Creed*. Translated by Nicholas Ayo. Notre Dame: University of Notre Dame Press, 1988.

Totah, Mary David. *The Spirit of Solesmes*. Selections from the writings of Dom Prosper Guéranger, Abbess Cécile Bruyère, and Dom Paul Delatte. Petersham: St. Bede's Publications, 1997.

Tucker, Jeffrey. *Sing Like a Catholic*. Richmond: Church Music Association of America, 2009.

Wiles, Maurice F. *Archetypal Heresy: Arianism through the Centuries*. Oxford: Clarendon Press; New York: Oxford University Press, 1996.

Zundel, Maurice. *The Splendour of the Liturgy*. New York: Sheed & Ward, 1939.

CPSIA information can be obtained at www.ICGtesting.com
Printed in the USA
LVOW11s0328221114

415071LV00007B/630/P